sensitivity training
&
group encounter
an introduction

sensitivity training & group encounter

an introduction

Edited by Robert W. Siroka, Ph.D.,
Ellen K. Siroka, M.A.,
and Gilbert A. Schloss, Ph.D.

GROSSET & DUNLAP
A NATIONAL GENERAL COMPANY
New York

LIBRARY OF CONGRESS CATALOG CARD NUMBER: 70-145737
ISBN: 0-448-04099-9 (TRADE EDITION)
ISBN: 0-448-00254-x (UNIVERSAL LIBRARY EDITION)

PUBLISHED SIMULTANEOUSLY IN CANADA
UNIVERSAL LIBRARY EDITION, 1971

1972 PRINTING

PRINTED IN THE UNITED STATES OF AMERICA

Contents

Foreword

We believe in the potential value of individuals meeting in groups to help one another realize themselves. We have compiled this anthology because we are both excited by the possibilities of enriching human life through group interaction processes, and disturbed by the lack of clarity, standards, and goals in the field of sensitivity training and group encounter. As group leaders and participants we are aware of the potential for both growth and destruction, as well as of the confusions and contradictions evident in the field. Participants in successful sensitivity groups have come away with increased understanding of themselves and others. Participants in irresponsible groups, however, have been left with lowered self-esteem and the painful experience of personal exposure, without receiving any assistance in integrating that exposure in a productive way.

One of the major confusions we see is the distinction between sensitivity training and group psychotherapy. Our original plan for this book was to present sensitivity training in its own right, relating it as little as possible to psychotherapy. In practice we found this very hard to do, for two reasons. Much of the best work has been written by trained psychotherapists who are concerned with new approaches to group psychotherapy. Second, the distinctions between sensitivity training, group encounter, and group psychotherapy are blurred, perhaps because all are involved in some manner with complex human behavior and intense emotion.

As a result we have attempted, where possible, to draw distinctions between different kinds of sensitivity and group encounter methods, and to place them in a conceptual framework. We begin the book with a brief history and discussion of the development of the sensitivity training movement. Our second section contains articles on T-groups from the points of view of both participant and trainer. This is followed by a section on "attack approaches." We use this term to dispel the misconception that all encounter groups use an attack approach. The attack approach is the most parodied of the encounter styles and the one most readily abused by quasi-professionals. Part Four is concerned with psychodrama, the most highly developed of the sensitivity approaches. The articles in this section supply theoretical background, describe dramatic techniques, and answer criticisms leveled against some aspects of psychodrama. In Part Five our focus is on the marathon, where duration in time plays a significant role in the group process. The articles discuss the ground rules and basic structure of the marathon.

The final selections in "Buyer Beware" also form the conclusion of the book. These articles are primarily concerned with differentiation among the valuable, the dangerous, and the absurd in sensitivity training and encounter. Each contains favorable comments about sensitivity experiences, but voices grave misgivings, and offers suggestions for improving the field.

As consultants to growth centers, schools, and community agencies, we are constantly asked for materials which present a balanced view of the field. We have endeavored to provide such a balance, with the hope that it will serve as a basic resource for both trainers and participants.

The editors wish to acknowledge the work of members of the Institute for Sociotherapy, a non-residential therapeutic community, out of whose coordinated group effort this book emerged. We wish specifically to thank Nancy Arum for her help in coordinating the book, Jean Peterson for her valuable editorial assistance, Stephen Wilson, Joan Weinstock, Robert Dublirer and Suzanne Morfit for their editorial aid, and Katharine Froschauer and Elinor Goldstein for their assistance. Particular thanks go to Barbara Stein, Amy Schaffer and Josephine Bustos for lending us their organizational skills.

Part One
Overview

Some Contemporary Origins of the Personal Growth Group_____

GILBERT A. SCHLOSS, PH.D., ROBERT W. SIROKA, PH.D.,
ELLEN K. SIROKA, M.A.

Although sensitivity training is clearly a current phenomenon, its historical roots reach as far back as 1914, to the early work of J. L. Moreno. Moreno, as the creator of psychodrama, can be considered the forerunner of the Group Encounter movement.

He spoke then of encounter in much the same way as it is experienced in groups throughout the world today.[1] It is a confrontation, a meeting of two individuals who try to see the world for a moment through the other's eyes, and to relate in the most meaningful sense through mutual understanding. In psychodrama, one individual is representative of the group in an exploration of his life, undertaken with the help of a director and group members. He does this, in large part, by changing places with the significant others in his world and seeing them and himself through different eyes. Like other forms of sensitivity training, psychodrama uses verbal and nonverbal techniques to explore and develop the emotional interaction of the individual and the group. Almost all sensitivity trainers, perhaps without being aware of their origins, use techniques as part of their basic repertoire that were developed in psychodrama. This is understandable since many of the most important names in sensitivity training were at one time students or observers of Moreno. This list includes Kurt Lewin, Ronald Lippitt, and Leland Bradford, some of the original founders of the National Training Laboratories.[2] Kurt Lewin is usually credited with starting the first T-group (training group) in 1946, at a summer workshop in human relations in New Britain, Con-

---

[1] J. L. Moreno, *Einladung zu Einer Begegnung* (Vienna: Anzengruber Verlag, 1914), as cited in J. L. Moreno, "The Viennese Origins of the Encounter Movement, Paving the Way for Existentialism, Group Psychotherapy and Psychodrama," *Group Psychotherapy*, XXII (March–June, 1969), 14.
[2] J. L. Moreno, "The Viennese Origins . . . ," pp. 10–13.

necticut.[3] The T-group became the basic form for sensitivity training, as practiced in the late forties and fifties by the National Training Laboratories.

The N.T.L. first made current the term "sensitivity training." Until this time "human relations" was the name given to the training of leaders to meet the human needs of modern technological society. "Personal growth" groups were then unknown. Because academicians had developed most of the group interaction theories, training sessions followed traditional academic lines. There were lectures, seminars, and discussions of problems in the field. The interpersonal relationships among members of the workshops themselves were not considered part of the training process.

The T-group started informally, almost accidentally. Lewin originally scheduled it as a casual discussion by group leaders of events occurring in the afternoon workshop. Some group members also attended. This led to direct confrontations, as leaders and participants disagreed in their perceptions of what had occurred in the workshop sessions. The argument moved on to more personal and immediate ground, to what was happening in the "here and now." The group attempted to develop new structures for handling problems as they arose. Out of this developed a new approach to training, an unstructured group centered on the study of its own dynamics. The focus of the group was on the way members interacted in the process of organizing themselves into a group. Next summer, in 1947, a training laboratory using this T-group model was set up at Bethel, Maine.

The training laboratory approach provided for a small group of people to spend anywhere from two to three weeks together, removed from the personal and professional activities of their everyday lives. The tendency to retreat from the training experience into old established patterns was thereby reduced. The participants were immersed in the workshop community and spent most of their waking time together.

N.T.L. was the center of sensitivity training in the forties and fifties. Its work with the laboratory method and the T-group constituted the major developments in sensitivity training at that time. By the mid-fifties, however, a significant shift in emphasis was apparent at the N.T.L. Broadly speaking, the social psychological approach was replaced by a clinical psychological one. The study of organizational and community structures was de-emphasized as was the acquisition of behavioral skills. Groups focused more on the interpersonal events between trainer and individuals in the group.[4]

[3]Kenneth D. Benne, "History of the T-Group in the Laboratory Setting," *T-Group Theory and Laboratory Method*, eds. Leland P. Bradford, Jack R. Gibb, and Kenneth D. Benne (New York: John Wiley & Sons, 1964), pp. 80–136.
[4]*Ibid.*, pp. 130–36.

In the late fifties, a distinct dichotomy crystallized between those trainers working with organizational skills, and those emphasizing personal growth. Industrial and business firms, always significant patrons of sensitivity training, were not receptive when their managers returned more concerned with personal development, than with effective organization and production. Trainers wishing to continue working with industry once again focused training on vocational and organizational skill-learning, rather than on personal exploration. Trainers more concerned with self-awareness felt that whatever skills emerged from the group were secondary to emotional and sensual experiences. They attracted to their workshops primarily functional, productive, and often creative individuals, who were looking for a more meaningful and emotionally enriched life.

Those two aspects of sensitivity training appear also in the sixties. The organizational approach which follows traditional human relations lines, continues to center around the needs of personnel in industry. In addition to training executives it now diversifies to include middle management, supervisory and production personnel, and the hard-core unemployed.

The growing number of people interested in sensitivity experiences as a means toward personal growth gave impetus to creation of over a hundred independent growth centers in the past five or six years. These Human Growth centers, of which the Esalen Institute is probably the most widely known, offer weekend or ongoing workshops in various modes of sensitivity training. Some of these workshops have thematic titles, such as "The Courage to Be," "Beyond the Frontiers of Perception," and "Your True Self." Others present a particular form such as "Gestalt," "Bio-Energetics," or "Psychodrama." A third type uses a generic name, such as "Encounter," or "Marathon." These groups, oriented toward personal growth, form the spearhead of what is known today as the Human Potential Movement. We cannot fully appreciate the tremendous impact of these sensitivity groups on today's world, without some examination of their social and philosophical origins and associations. Indeed, if we are to help this movement continue to effect change, we must understand its connection with our changing world.

Since the early development of sensitivity training, many of man's values and goals have changed, and also the means of achieving them. After World War II many were weary of the long range and the large scale. The time was ripe for cultivating one's own garden, for individual prosperity, for the "other directed man" whose personal goals were the material goods he had never known as a child of the depression.[5] He

---

[5]The terms, "other directed" and "inner directed," if not coined, were made popular by David Riesman, with Nathan Glazer and Reuel Denney, *The Lonely Crowd*. (New Haven: Yale University Press, 1950).

tended to live by appearance, image, and role, careful not to expose himself, not to offend. He was the "organization man" working for family rather than himself, with a future laid out for him by society.[6]

At the other extreme was existential man, inner directed, seeking to define himself through his acts.[7] Existential man was removed from meaningful group involvement; he was responsible, but primarily to himself. He was alone and looking inward because outside he saw an absurd universe. On this world he could impose at best an arbitrary and unstable order. The individual was meaningful, but, paradoxically, impotent. What could one man achieve against world forces? A meaningful act was meaningful only to the doer, as expression rather than communication.

In the forties and fifties the organization man joined groups, for prestige, status, and company, or as good business practice. Through his groups he achieved some sense of community. He became part of an existing group over whose values and aims he usually had limited control, so that he had little personal power. His role was to fit himself into the pre-existing order. On the other hand, existential man was suspicious of groups. To him they were a conservative force, representing compromise.

Despite their apparent differences, both approaches were impotent as far as effecting social change was concerned. Because the middle-class organization man had to modify himself in order to belong, he was in no position to effect modification. Existential man was socially impotent because he remained alone. Thus, throughout the fifties, the group *per se* represented a relatively conservative force.

Over the last decade we see radical change. Young people revolt. Angry at the meaninglessness and emptiness they see around them, rich in education and material security, yet bewildered by their loneliness and isolation, they demand change. Rejecting the delayed gratification values of their parents they seek immediate satisfactions, and turn their backs on those emphasizing future and security. Their search is to feel, to touch, to experience, to come together. They look to the group to find themselves.

For some the group was an informal commune where people live as long as they stay, providing as much food and money as their means allow. When they leave, others take over. For others the desire for community results in more formal experiments, like setting up farms or small industries. There seems to be an attempt to find the good life in a simple rural setting, free from fear and the confining tensions and

---

[6]This term was made popular by William H. Whyte, Jr., *The Organization Man* (New York: Simon and Schuster, 1956).

[7]We refer here to Sartre's formulations, since his particular approach was probably the most popular and widely discussed during the fifties. For a detailed treatment of his position as discussed in this work, see Jean-Paul Sartre, *Being and Nothingness* (London: Methuen and Co., Ltd., 1957).

pressures of a hypocritical society. Perhaps this is not so different from what their parents were searching for when they moved from the cities to the suburbs. But communal living requires a life-style commitment. And what of those who want to experience a sense of community without such extensive commitment, without withdrawing from the world of today? Can intimacy and community be recreated in today's mechanized and alienated society?

Growing numbers of people are attracted to the personal growth group, which offers warmth and a ready-made temporary family. This is evidence that "community" can be experienced without uprooting oneself and opting for the communal life-style. In the personal growth group, individuals are together with at least one leader, sometimes two. They are confronted with a situation requiring more awareness of their feelings and of how they communicate with others. They share in others' experiences, learning that they all have areas of similarity. This makes it easier to face unpleasant, hostile, or aggressive feelings, which are difficult for most to express. The leader encourages the expression of the very feelings considered socially questionable or even taboo.

A member of a personal growth group can gain some measure of acceptance and camaraderie, perhaps even intimacy, with little falseness or facade. The values of responsible sensitivity training and group encounter are honesty and presentation of the authentic self. An individual desiring a personal growth experience may consider himself less emotionally, physically or sensually spontaneous than he would like. He may be lonely, and find it difficult to communicate honestly with another. In a workshop he may be helped, or help another, to experience a sensation — such as a sight, a taste, a smell, or a texture. He may learn to play a children's game unselfconsciously, because everyone else in the group is playing. In the group he may quickly move into close relations with others, showing aspects of himself he would ordinarily be reluctant to reveal. The group member benefits from the fact that the leader here acts as a permissive parent or guide, allowing, in fact encouraging, the group members to share feelings with each other. The group exerts pressure to help the member achieve a more honest expression of himself.

The personal growth workshop is more a group than an individual experience. During a workshop the member identifies, not only with individual members of the group, but with the group itself. The values expressed in the group become its tribal values, norms to which members respond or against which they react. Initially these values are introduced by the leader or a group member. They are then modified through group interaction until they become an expression of the whole group. The group forms an entity but it is not isolated from the world. It does not reject the world but incorporates aspects of its technology for its own purposes. It does not allow itself to be assimilated or fragmented.

The group focuses on the multi-sensual rather than just the visual. The sense of sequence is often replaced by a sense of simultaneous inter-action with no fixed beginning, middle or end. One must find meaning through the way he orients himself within his present environment. The result is a sense of being part of a flow, of immersion in the environment, rather than being an outside observer.

These aspects of sensitivity training resemble avant-garde develop-ments in the fine arts. Musical works which use common objects in place of instruments and noises made by movements of the performer, re-semble the focus on interaction in the sensitivity group as the subject for its exploration.[8] Alexander Calder's sculpture suggests a world in con-stant flux, yet kept within a fixed bound, a formal limit. He and other contemporaries use mixed media, multi-sensual approaches. Sculpture is combined with painting, and dance with music, in an attempt to create an environment rather than an object.[9] In this approach there is no viewer, but an active and interacting participant who is an essential part of the work itself.

Personal growth groups are described by participants as "real," "powerful," and "meaningful." They have received much general public attention, largely because this type of sensitivity training and group encounter seems to offer much that is sought after in our times. In these groups interpersonal relations are stressed on an emotional rather than intellectual level. Techniques which help the participant become more sensitized to himself and his environment offer the equivalent of a "turned on" feeling without drugs. As a result a true sense of intimacy can be created among group members, a sense of community.

As might be expected, however, personal growth oriented groups also reflect many of the disturbing elements of our age. There is a frantic search for easy answers, for fruits without toil. People search for intimacy without being willing to do the work necessary for a meaningful relation-ship. The inconsistencies of today's world are very evident in this new Human Potential Movement. There exists an appalling lack of training

---

[8]In traditional musical compositions, the noises made by a performer while he is playing his instrument, or the noises of an audience are, of course, considered incidental to the music itself. John Cage, however, makes these noises an essential part of his composition and writes in directions for making movements to achieve the noises. In "4'33"" (1952) Cage presented nothing but silence, the noises made by the audience itself being the entire composition. Other experimental compositions include "Rosart Mix" (1965) and "Variations V" (1965). For further discussion of Cage's work, see Richard Kostelanetz, *The Theatre of Mixed Means* (New York: The Dial Press, Inc., 1968), pp. 50–64.

[9]For example, Robert Rauschenberg created "combines," three dimensional paintings which stand away from the wall. In "Oracle" (1965) he created a five part sculpture, every piece containing a loudspeaker. His "Map Room I" (1965) combines elements from painting as well as theatre and dance. Claes Oldenburg's "The Store" (1961) creates pieces of sculpture painted to approximate materials found in a store. These works represent an attempt to approach the arts in a new, more intimate and more integrated way, by using traditional material — painting, sculpture, dance — in unusual combinations. Familiar objects are reintroduced to the viewer, giving him a new perspective. For a discussion and conversations with both artists, see Kostelanetz, *op. cit.*

and professionalism among group leaders. The same type of group may be offered both by highly qualified group psychotherapists, as well as by individuals untrained and inexperienced. We see, too, pervading the entire field of sensitivity training, a lack of clarity concerning important issues similar to that from which America suffers today. Goals of the group and the leader are not clearly defined, and in many cases the result differs from the original aim. A person may find in a workshop an intense but fragmented experience, which leaves him unprotected and without the understanding necessary to evaluate his experience in a meaningful way. When these groups have unclear goals, unprofessional standards, or untrained leaders, they should be avoided.

Perhaps in the sixties and seventies the individual and the family are no longer completely appropriate as the model to evaluate social networks. A more applicable framework might be Marshall McLuhan's concept of a new technological tribalism which makes the modern world a global village, and where the written word is replaced with multi-media approaches.[10] We are confronting a world less and less concerned with the "before and after," and immersing itself through the group in the "now."

References

BRADFORD, LELAND P., JACK R. GIBB, and KENNETH D. BENNE (eds.). *T-Group Theory and Laboratory Method.* New York: John Wiley & Sons, Inc., 1964.

KOSTELANETZ, RICHARD. *The Theatre of Mixed Means.* New York: The Dial Press, Inc., 1968.

MAY, ROLLO (ed.). *Existential Psychology.* New York: Random House, Inc., 1961.

McLUHAN, MARSHALL. *Understanding Media: The Extensions of Man.* New York: The New American Library, Inc., 1966.

——— and QUENTIN FIORE. *The Medium Is the Massage.* New York: Bantam Books, Inc., 1967.

——— and ———. *War and Peace in the Global Village.* New York: McGraw-Hill Book Company, 1968.

MORENO, J. L. "The Viennese Origins of the Encounter Movement, Paving the Way for Existentialism, Group Psychotherapy and Psychodrama," *Group Psychotherapy,* XXII (March–June, 1969), 7–16.

RIESMAN, DAVID, with NATHAN GLAZER and REUEL DENNEY. *The Lonely Crowd.* New Haven: Yale University Press, 1950.

RUITENBEEK, HENDRIK M. (ed.). *Psychoanalysis and Existential Philosophy.* New York: E. P. Dutton & Co., Inc., 1962.

[10]McLuhan himself uses a kind of multi-media montage of words and pictures. The words do not narrate a story, nor do the pictures illustrate what the words communicate. Each contributes equally to the effect, which is a mosaic of insights, rather than a series of pieces of information. See Marshall McLuhan and Quentin Fiore, *War and Peace in the Global Village* (New York: McGraw Hill Book Company, 1968), and *The Medium Is the Massage* (New York: Bantam Books, Inc., 1967). For a more conventional presentation of his ideas, see Marshall McLuhan, *Understanding Media: The Extensions of Man* (New York: The New American Library, Inc., 1966).

SARTRE, JEAN-PAUL. *Being and Nothingness*. London: Methuen and Co., Ltd., 1957.

SCHECHNER, RICHARD. *Public Domain: Essays on the Theatre*. Indianapolis: The Bobbs-Merrill Company, Inc., 1969.

WHYTE, WILLIAM H., JR. *The Organization Man*. New York: Simon and Schuster, 1956.

The Process of the Basic Encounter Group

CARL R. ROGERS

Carl R. Rogers, "Process of the Basic Encounter Group," chapter 28, pp. 261–276. From *Challenges of Humanistic Psychology* by James F. T. Bugental. Copyright © 1967 by McGraw-Hill, Inc. Used with permission of McGraw-Hill Book Company and the author.

I would like to share with you some of my thinking and puzzlement regarding a potent new cultural development — the intensive group experience.[1] It has, in my judgment, significant implications for our society. It has come very suddenly over our cultural horizon, since in anything like its present form it is less than two decades old.

I should like briefly to describe the many different forms and different labels under which the intensive group experience has become a part of our modern life. It has involved different kinds of individuals, and it has spawned various theories to account for its effects.

As to labels, the intensive group experience has at times been called the *T-group* or *lab group*, "T" standing for training laboratory in group dynamics. It has been termed *sensitivity training* in human relationships. The experience has sometimes been called a *basic encounter group* or a

---

[1] In the preparation of this paper I am deeply indebted to two people, experienced in work with groups, for their help: Jacques Hochmann, M.D., psychiatrist of Lyon, France, who has been working at WBSI on a U.S.P.H.S. International Post-doctoral Fellowship, and Ann Dreyfuss, M.A., my research assistant. I am grateful for their ideas, for their patient analysis of recorded group sessions, and for the opportunity to interact with two original and inquiring minds.

workshop — a workshop in human relationships, in leadership, in counseling, in education, in research, in psychotherapy. In dealing with one particular type of person — the drug addict — it has been called a *synanon*.

The intensive group experience has functioned in various settings. It has operated in industries, in universities, in church groups, and in resort settings which provide a retreat from everyday life. It has functioned in various educational institutions and in penitentiaries.

An astonishing range of individuals have been involved in these intensive group experiences. There have been groups for presidents of large corporations. There have been groups for delinquent and predelinquent adolescents. There have been groups composed of college students and faculty members, of counselors and psychotherapists, of school dropouts, of married couples, of confirmed drug addicts, of criminals serving sentences, of nurses preparing for hospital service, and of educators, principals, and teachers.

The geographical spread attained by this rapidly expanding movement has reached in this country from Bethel, Maine (starting point of the National Training Laboratory movement), to Idyllwild, California. To my personal knowledge, such groups also exist in France, England, Holland, Japan, and Australia.

In their outward pattern these group experiences also show a great deal of diversity. There are T-groups and workshops which have extended over three to four weeks, meeting six to eight hours each day. There are some that have lasted only 2½ days, crowding twenty or more hours of group sessions into this time. A recent innovation is the "marathon" weekend, which begins on Friday afternoon and ends on Sunday evening, with only a few hours out for sleep and snacks.

As to the conceptual underpinnings of this whole movement, one may almost select the theoretical flavor he prefers. Lewinian and client-centered theories have been most prominent, but gestalt therapy and various brands of psychoanalysis have all played contributing parts. The experience within the group may focus on specific training in human relations skills. It may be closely similar to group therapy, with much exploration of past experience and the dynamics of personal development. It may focus on creative expression through painting or expressive movement. It may be focused primarily upon a basic encounter and relationship between individuals.

Simply to describe the diversity which exists in this field raises very properly the question of why these various developments should be considered to belong together. Are there any threads of commonality which pervade all these widely divergent activities? To me it seems that they do belong together and can all be classed as focusing on the intensive group experience. They all have certain similar external characteristics. The group in almost every case is small (from eight to eighteen members), is relatively unstructured, and chooses its own goals and personal directions. The group experience usually, though not always, includes some cognitive input, some content material which is presented to the group. In almost all instances the leader's responsibility is primarily the facilitation of the expression of both feelings and thoughts on the part of the group members. Both in the leader and in the group members there is some focus on the process and the dynamics of the immediate personal interaction. These are, I think, some of the identifying characteristics which are rather easily recognized.

There are also certain practical hypotheses which tend to be held in common by all these groups. My own summary of these would be as follows: In an intensive group, with much freedom and little structure, the individual will gradually feel safe enough to drop some of his defenses and facades; he will relate more directly on a feeling basis (come into a basic encounter) with other members of the group; he will come to understand himself and his relationship to others more accurately; he will change in his personal attitudes and behavior; and he will subsequently relate more effectively to others in his everyday life situation. There are other hypotheses related more to the group than to the individual. One is that in this situation of minimal structure, the group will move from confusions, fractionation, and discontinuity to a climate of greater trust and coherence. These are some of the characteristics and hypotheses which, in my judgment, bind together this enormous cluster of activities which I wish to talk about as constituting the intensive group experience.

As for myself, I have been gradually moving into this field for the last twenty years. In experimenting with what I call *student-centered teaching*, involving the free expression of personal feelings, I came to recognize not only the cognitive learnings but also some of the personal changes which occurred. In brief intensive training courses for counselors for the Veterans Administration in 1946, during the postwar period, I and my staff focused more directly on providing an intensive group experience because of its impact in producing significant learning. In 1950, I served as leader of an intensive, full-time, one-week workshop, a postdoctoral training seminar in psychotherapy for the American Psychological Association. The impact of those six days was so great that for more than a dozen years afterward, I kept hearing from members of the group about the meaning it had had for them. Since that time I have been involved in more than forty ventures of what I would like to term — using the label most congenial to me — *basic encounter groups*. Most of these have involved for many of the members experiences of great intensity and considerable personal change. With two individuals, however, in these many groups, the experience contributed, I believe, to a psychotic break. A few other individuals have found the experience more unhelpful than helpful. So I have come to have a profound respect for the constructive potency of such group experiences and also a real concern over the fact that sometimes and in some ways this experience may do damage to individuals.

The Group Process

It is a matter of great interest to me to try to understand what appear to be common elements in the group process as I have come dimly to sense these. I am using this opportunity to think about this problem, not because I feel I have any final theory to give, but because I would like to formulate, as clearly as I am able, the elements which I can perceive at the present time. In doing so I am drawing upon my own experience, upon the experiences of others with whom I have worked, upon the written material in this field, upon the written reactions of many individuals who have participated in such groups, and to some extent upon the recordings of such group sessions, which we are only beginning to tap and analyze. I am sure that (though I have tried to draw on the experience of others) any formulation I make at the present time is unduly influenced by my own experience in groups and thus is lacking in the generality I wish it might have.

As I consider the terribly complex interactions which arise during twenty, forty, sixty, or more hours of intensive sessions, I believe that I see some threads which weave in and out of the pattern. Some of these trends or tendencies are likely to appear early and some later in the group sessions, but there is no clear-cut sequence in which one ends and another begins. The interaction is best thought of, I believe, as a varied tapestry, differing from group to group, yet with certain kinds of trends evident in most of these intensive encounters and with certain patterns tending to precede and others to follow. Here are some of the process patterns which I see developing, briefly described in simple terms, illustrated from tape recordings and personal reports, and presented in roughly sequential order. I am not aiming at a high-level theory of group process but rather at a naturalistic observation out of which, I hope, true theory can be built.[2]

Milling Around   As the leader or facilitator makes clear at the outset that this is a group with unusual freedom, that it is not one for which he will take directional responsibility, there tends to develop a period of initial confusion, awkward silence, polite surface interaction, "cocktail-

---

[2]Jack and Lorraine Gibb have long been working on an analysis of trust development as the essential theory of group process. Others who have contributed significantly to the theory of group process are Chris Argyris, Kenneth Benne, Warren Bennis, Dorwin Cartwright, Matthew Miles, and Robert Blake. Samples of the thinking of all these and others may be found in three recent books: Bradford, Gibb, & Benne (1964); Bennis, Benne, & Chin (1961); and Bennis, Schein, Berlew, & Steele (1964). Thus, there are many promising leads for theory construction involving a considerable degree of abstraction. This chapter has a more elementary aim — a naturalistic descriptive account of the process.

party talk," frustration, and great lack of continuity. The individuals come face-to-face with the fact that "there is no structure here except what we provide. We do not know our purposes; we do not even know one another, and we are committed to remain together over a considerable period of time." In this situation, confusion and frustration are natural. Particularly striking to the observer is the lack of continuity between personal expressions. Individual A will present some proposal or concern, clearly looking for a response from the group. Individual B has obviously been waiting for his turn and starts off on some completely different tangent as though he had never heard A. One member makes a simple suggestion such as, "I think we should introduce ourselves," and this may lead to several hours of highly involved discussion in which the underlying issues appear to be, "Who is the leader?" "Who is responsible for us?" "Who is a member of the group?" "What is the purpose of the group?"

Resistance to Personal Expression or Exploration   During the milling period, some individuals are likely to reveal some rather personal attitudes. This tends to foster a very ambivalent reaction among other members of the group. One member, writing of his experience, says:

> There is a self which I present to the world and another one which I know more intimately. With others I try to appear able, knowing, unruffled, problem-free. To substantiate this image I will act in a way which at the time or later seems false or artificial or "not the real me." Or I will keep to myself thoughts which if expressed would reveal an imperfect me.
> My inner self, by contrast with the image I present to the world, is characterized by many doubts. The worth I attach to this inner self is subject to much fluctuation and is very dependent on how others are reacting to me. At times this private self can feel worthless.

It is the public self which members tend to reveal to one another, and only gradually, fearfully, and ambivalently do they take steps to reveal something of their inner world.

Early in one intensive workshop, the members were asked to write anonymously a statement of some feeling or feelings which they had which they were not willing to tell in the group. One man wrote:

> I don't relate easily to people. I have an almost impenetrable facade. Nothing gets in to hurt me, but nothing gets out. I have repressed so many emotions that I am close to emotional sterility. This situation doesn't make me happy, but I don't know what to do about it.

This individual is clearly living inside a private dungeon, but he does not even dare, except in this disguised fashion, to send out a call for help.

In a recent workshop when one man started to express the concern he felt about an impasse he was experiencing with his wife, another member stopped him, saying essentially:

Are you sure you want to go on with this, or are you being seduced by the group into going further than you want to go? How do you know the group can be trusted? How will you feel about it when you go home and tell your wife what you have revealed, or when you decide to keep it from her? It just isn't safe to go further.

It seemed quite clear that in his warning, this second member was also expressing his own fear of revealing *him*self and *his* lack of trust in the group.

Description of Past Feelings In spite of ambivalence about the trustworthiness of the group and the risk of exposing oneself, expression of feelings does begin to assume a larger proportion of the discussion. The executive tells how frustrated he feels by certain situations in his industry, or the housewife relates problems she has experienced with her children. A tape-recorded exchange involving a Roman Catholic nun occurs early in a one-week workshop, when the discussion has turned to a rather intellectualized consideration of anger:

BILL: What happens when you get mad, Sister, or don't you?

SISTER: Yes, I do — yes I do. And I find when I get mad, I, I almost get, well, the kind of person that antagonizes me is the person who seems so unfeeling toward people — now I take our dean as a person in point because she is a very aggressive woman and has certain ideas about what the various rules in a college should be; and this woman can just send me into high "G"; in an angry mood. *I mean this*. But then I find, I . . .

FACIL.:[3] But what, what do you do?

SISTER: I find that when I'm in a situation like this, that I strike out in a very sharp, uh, *tone*, or else I just refuse to respond — "All right, this happens to be her way" — I don't think I've ever gone into a tantrum.

JOE: You just withdraw — no use to fight it.

FACIL.: You say you use a sharp tone. To *her*, or to other people you're dealing with?

SISTER: Oh, no. To *her*.

This is a typical example of a *description* of feelings which are obviously current in her in a sense but which she is placing in the past and which she describes as being outside the group in time and place. It is an example of feelings existing "there and then."

Expression of Negative Feelings Curiously enough, the first expression of genuinely significant "here-and-now" feeling is apt to come out in negative attitudes toward other group members or toward the group leader. In one group in which members introduced themselves at some length, one woman refused, saying that she preferred to be known for what she was in the group and not in terms of her status outside. Very shortly after this, one of the men in the group attacked her vigorously

---

[3]The term "facilitator" will be used throughout this paper, although sometimes he is referred to as "leader" or "trainer."

and angrily for this stand, accusing her of failing to cooperate, of keeping herself aloof from the group, and so forth. It was the first *personal current feeling* which had been brought into the open in the group.

Frequently the leader is attacked for his failure to give proper guidance to the group. One vivid example of this comes from a recorded account of an early session with a group of delinquents, where one member shouts at the leader (Gordon, 1955, p. 214):

> You will be licked if you don't control us right at the start. You have to keep order here because you are older than us. That's what a teacher is supposed to do. If he doesn't do it we will cause a lot of trouble and won't get anything done. [Then, referring to two boys in the group who were scuffling, he continues.] Throw 'em out, throw 'em out! You've just *got* to make us behave!

An adult expresses his disgust at the people who talk too much, but points his irritation at the leader (Gordon, 1955, p. 210):

> It is just that I don't understand why someone doesn't shut them up. I would have taken Gerald and shoved him out the window. I'm an authoritarian. I would have told him he was talking too much and he had to leave the room. I think the group discussion ought to be led by a person who simply will not recognize these people after they have interrupted about eight times.

Why are negatively toned expressions the first current feelings to be expressed? Some speculative answers might be the following: This is one of the best ways to test the freedom and trustworthiness of the group. "Is it really a place where I can be and express myself positively and negatively? Is this really a safe place, or will I be punished?" Another quite different reason is that deeply positive feelings are much more difficult and dangerous to express than negative ones. "If I say, 'I love you,' I am vulnerable and open to the most awful rejection. If I say, 'I hate you,' I am at best liable to attack, against which I can defend." Whatever the reasons, such negatively toned feelings tend to be the first here-and-now material to appear.

Expression and Exploration of Personally Meaningful Material   It may seem puzzling that following such negative experiences as the initial confusion, the resistance to personal expression, the focus on outside events, and the voicing of critical or angry feelings, the event most likely to occur next is for an individual to reveal himself to the group in a significant way. The reason for this no doubt is that the individual member has come to realize that this is in part *his group*. He can help to make of it what he wishes. He has also experienced the fact that negative feelings have been expressed and have usually been accepted or as-similated without any catastrophic results. He realizes there is freedom here, albeit a risky freedom. A climate of trust (Gibb, 1964, Ch. 10) is beginning to develop. So he begins to take the chance and the gamble of letting the group know some deeper facet of himself. One man tells of the trap in which he finds himself, feeling that communication between himself and his wife is hopeless. A priest tells of the anger which he has bottled up because of unreasonable treatment by one of his superiors. What should he have done? What might he do now? A scientist at the head of a large research department finds the courage to speak of his painful isolation, to tell the group that he has never had a single friend in his life. By the time he finishes telling of his situation, he is letting loose some of the tears of sorrow for himself which I am sure he has held in for many years. A psychiatrist tells of the guilt he feels because of the suicide of one of his patients. A woman of forty tells of her absolute inability to free herself from the grip of her controlling mother. A process which one workshop member has called a "journey to the center of self," often a very painful process, has begun.

Such exploration is not always an easy process, nor is the whole group always receptive to such self-revelation. In a group of institutionalized adolescents, all of whom had been in difficulty of one sort or another, one boy revealed an important fact about himself and immediately received both acceptance and sharp nonacceptance from members of the group:

GEORGE: This is the thing. I've got too many problems at home — uhm, I think some of you know why I'm here, what I was charged with.
MARY: I don't.
FACIL.: Do you want to tell us?
GEORGE: Well, uh, it's sort of embarrassing.
CAROL: Come on, it won't be so bad.
GEORGE: Well, I raped my sister. That's the only problem I have at home, and I've overcome that, I think. (*Rather long pause.*)
FREDA: Oooh, that's *weird!*
MARY: People have problems, Freda, I mean ya know . . .
FREDA: Yeah, I know, but *yeOUW!!!*
FACIL. (*to Freda*): You know about these problems, but they still are weird to you.
GEORGE: You see what I mean; it's embarrassing to talk about it.
MARY: Yeah, but it's O.K.
GEORGE: It *hurts* to talk about it, but I know I've got to so I won't be guilt-ridden for the rest of my life.

Clearly Freda is completely shutting him out psychologically, while Mary in particular is showing a deep acceptance.

The Expression of Immediate Interpersonal Feelings in the Group Entering into the process sometimes earlier, sometimes later, is the explicit bringing into the open of the feelings experienced in the immediate moment by one member about another. These are sometimes positive and sometimes negative. Examples would be: "I feel threatened by your silence." "You remind me of my mother, with whom I had a tough time." "I took an instant dislike to you the first moment I saw you." "To me you're like a breath of fresh air in the group." "I like your warmth and your smile." "I dislike you more every time you speak up." Each of these attitudes can be, and usually is, explored in the increasing climate of trust.

The Development of a Healing Capacity in the Group One of the most fascinating aspects of any intensive group experience is the manner in which a number of the group members show a natural and spontaneous capacity for dealing in a helpful, facilitative, and therapeutic fashion with the pain and suffering of others. As one rather extreme example of this, I think of a man in charge of maintenance in a large plant who was one of the low-status members of an industrial executive group. As he informed us, he had not been "contaminated by education." In the initial phases the group tended to look down on him. As members delved more deeply into themselves and began to express their own attitudes more fully, this man came forth as, without doubt, the most sensitive member of the group. He knew intuitively how to be understanding and acceptant. He was alert to things which had not yet been expressed but which were just below the surface. When the rest of us were paying attention to a member who was speaking, he would frequently spot another individual who was suffering silently and in need of help. He had a deeply perceptive and facilitating attitude. This kind of ability shows up so commonly in groups that it has led me to feel that the ability to be healing or therapeutic is far more common in human life than we might suppose. Often it needs only the permission granted by a freely flowing group experience to become evident.

In a characteristic instance, the leader and several group members were trying to be of help to Joe, who was telling of the almost complete lack of communication between himself and his wife. In varied ways members endeavored to give help. John kept putting before Joe the feelings Joe's wife was almost certainly experiencing. The facilitator kept challenging Joe's facade of "carefulness." Marie tried to help him discover what he was feeling at the moment. Fred showed him the choice he had of alternative behaviors. All this was clearly done in a spirit of caring, as is even more evident in the recording itself. No miracles were achieved, but toward the end Joe did come to the realization that the only thing that might help would be to express his real feelings to his wife.

Self-acceptance and the Beginning of Change Many people feel that self-acceptance must stand in the way of change. Actually, in these group experiences, as in psychotherapy, it is the *beginning* of change. Some examples of the kind of attitudes expressed would be these: "I *am* a dominating person who likes to control others. I do want to mold these individuals into the proper shape." Another person says, "I really have a hurt and overburdened little boy inside of me who feels very sorry for himself. I *am* that little boy, in addition to being a competent and responsible manager."

I think of one governmental executive in a group in which I participated, a man with high responsibility and excellent technical training as an engineer. At the first meeting of the group he impressed me, and I think others, as being cold, aloof, somewhat bitter, resentful, and cynical. When he spoke of how he ran his office it appeared that he administered it "by the book," without any warmth or human feeling entering in. In one of the early sessions, when he spoke of his wife, a group member asked him, "Do you love your wife?" He paused for a long time, and the questioner said, "OK, that's answer enough." The executive said, "No. Wait a minute. The reason I didn't respond was that I was wondering if I ever loved anyone. I don't think I *ever* really *loved* anyone." It seemed quite dramatically clear to those of us in the group that he had come to accept himself as an unloving person.

A few days later he listened with great intensity as one member of the group expressed profound personal feelings of isolation, loneliness, and pain, revealing the extent to which he had been living behind a mask, a facade. The next morning the engineer said, "Last night I thought and thought about what Bill told us. I even wept quite a bit by myself. I can't remember how long it has been since I have cried, and I really *felt* something. I think perhaps what I felt was love."

It is not surprising that before the week was over, he had thought through new ways of handling his growing son, on whom he had been placing extremely rigorous demands. He had also begun genuinely to appreciate the love which his wife had extended to him and which he now felt he could in some measure reciprocate.

In another group one man kept a diary of his reactions. Here is his account of an experience in which he came really to accept his almost abject desire for love, a self-acceptance which marked the beginning of a very significant experience of change. He says (Hall, 1965):

> During the break between the third and fourth sessions, I felt very droopy and tired. I had it in mind to take a nap, but instead I was almost compulsively going around to people starting a conversation. I had a begging kind of a feeling, like a very cowed little puppy hoping that he'll be patted but half afraid he'll be kicked. Finally, back in my room I lay down and began to know that I was sad. Several times I found myself wishing my roommate would come in and talk to me. Or, whenever someone walked by the door, I would come to attention inside, the way a dog pricks up his ears; and I would feel an immediate wish for that person to come in and talk to me. I realized my raw wish to receive kindness.

Another recorded excerpt, from an adolescent group, shows a combination of self-acceptance and self-exploration. Art had been talking about his "shell," and here he is beginning to work with the problem of accepting himself, and also the facade he ordinarily exhibits:

ART: I'm so darn used to living with the shell; it doesn't even bother me. I don't even know the real me. I think I've uh, well, I've pushed the shell more away here. When I'm out of my shell — only twice — once just a few minutes ago — I'm really me, I guess. But then I just sort of pull in the [latch] cord after me when I'm in my shell, and that's almost all the time. And I leave the [false] front standing outside when I'm back in the shell.

FACIL.: And nobody's back in there with you?

ART (*crying*): Nobody else is in there with me, just me. I just pull everything into the shell and roll the shell up and shove it in my pocket. I take the shell, and the real me, and put it in my pocket where it's safe. I guess that's really the way I do it — I go into my shell and turn off the real world. And here: that's what I want to do here in this group, ya know, come out of my shell and actually throw it away.

LOIS: You're making progress already. At least you can talk about it.

FACIL.: Yeah. The thing that's going to be hardest is to stay out of the shell.

ART (*still crying*): Well, yeah, if I can keep talking about it, I can come out and stay out, but I'm gonna have to, ya know, protect me. It hurts; it's actually hurting to talk about it.

Still another person reporting shortly after his workshop experience said, "I came away from the workshop feeling much more deeply that 'It is all right to be me with all my strengths and weaknesses.' My wife has told me that I appear to be more authentic, more real, more genuine."

This feeling of greater realness and authenticity is a very common experience. It would appear that the individual is learning to accept and to *be* himself, and this is laying the foundation for change. He is closer to his own feelings, and hence they are no longer so rigidly organized and are more open to change.

The Cracking of Facades   As the sessions continue, so many things tend to occur together that it is difficult to know which to describe first. It should again be stressed that these different threads and stages interweave and overlap. One of these threads is the increasing impatience with defenses. As time goes on, the group finds it unbearable that any member should live behind a mask or a front. The polite words, the intellectual understanding of one another and of relationships, the smooth coin of tact and cover-up — amply satisfactory for interactions outside — are just not good enough. The expression of self by some members of the group has made it very clear that a deeper and more basic encounter is *possible*, and the group appears to strive, intuitively and unconsciously, toward this goal. Gently at times, almost savagely at others, the group *demands* that the individual be himself, that his current feelings not be hidden, that he remove the mask of ordinary social intercourse. In one group there was a highly intelligent and quite academic man who had been rather perceptive in his understanding of others but who had not revealed himself at all. The attitude of the group was finally expressed sharply by one member when he said, "Come out from behind that lectern, Doc. Stop giving us speeches. Take off your dark glasses. We want to know *you*."

In Synanon, the fascinating group so successfully involved in making persons out of drug addicts, this ripping away of facades is often very drastic. An excerpt from one of the "synanons," or group sessions, makes this clear (Casriel, 1963, p. 81):

JOE (*speaking to Gina*): I wonder when you're going to stop sounding so good in synanons. Every synanon that I'm in with you, someone asks you a question, and you've got a beautiful book written. All made out about what went down and how you were wrong and how you realized you were wrong and all that kind of bullshit. When are you going to stop doing that? How do you feel about Art?

GINA: I have nothing against Art.

WILL: You're a nut. Art hasn't got any damn sense. He's been in there, yelling at you and Moe, and you've got everything so cool.

GINA: No, I feel he's very insecure in a lot of ways but that has nothing to do with me. . . .

JOE: You act like you're so goddamn understanding.

GINA: I was *told* to act as if I understand.

JOE: Well, you're in a synanon now. You're not supposed to be acting like you're such a goddamn healthy person. Are you so well?

GINA: No.

JOE: Well why the hell don't you quit acting as if you were.

If I am indicating that the group at times is quite violent in tearing down a facade or a defense, this would be accurate. On the other hand, it can also be sensitive and gentle. The man who was accused of hiding behind a lectern was deeply hurt by this attack, and over the lunch hour looked very troubled, as though he might break into tears at any moment. When the group reconvened, the members sensed this and treated him very gently, enabling him to tell us his own tragic personal story, which accounted for his aloofness and his intellectual and academic approach to life.

The Individual Receives Feedback In the process of this freely expressive interaction, the individual rapidly acquires a great deal of data as to how he appears to others. The "hail-fellow-well-met" discovers that others resent his exaggerated friendliness. The executive who weighs his words carefully and speaks with heavy precision may find that others regard him as stuffy. A woman who shows a somewhat excessive desire to be of help to others is told in no uncertain terms that some group members do not want her for a mother. All this can be decidedly upsetting, but as long as these various bits of information are fed back in the context of caring which is developing in the group, they seem highly constructive.

Feedback can at times be very warm and positive, as the following recorded excerpt indicates:

> LEO (*very softly and gently*): I've been struck with this ever since she talked about her waking in the night, that she has a very delicate sensitivity. (*Turning to Mary and speaking almost caressingly.*) And somehow I perceive — even looking at you or in your eyes — a very — almost like a gentle touch and from this gentle touch you can tell many — things — you sense in — this manner.
>
> FRED: Leo, when you said that, that she has this kind of delicate sensitivity, I just felt, *Lord yes!* Look at her eyes.
>
> LEO: M-hm.

A much more extended instance of negative and positive feedback, triggering a significant new experience of self-understanding and encounter with the group, is taken from the diary of the young man mentioned before. He had been telling the group that he had no feeling for them, and felt they had no feeling for him (Hall, 1965):

> Then, a girl lost patience with me and said she didn't feel she could give any more. She said I looked like a bottomless well, and she wondered how many times I had to be told that I *was* cared for. By this time I was feeling panicky, and I was saying to myself, "My God, can it be true that I can't be satisfied and that I'm somehow compelled to pester people for attention until I drive them away!"
>
> At this point while I was really worried, a nun in the group spoke up. She said that I had not alienated her with some negative things I had said to her. She said she liked me, and she couldn't understand why I couldn't see that. She said she felt concerned for me and wanted to help me. With that, something began to really dawn on me, and I voiced it somewhat like the following. "You mean you are all sitting there, feeling for me what I say I want you to feel, and that somewhere down inside me I'm stopping it from touching me?" I relaxed appreciably and began really to wonder why I had shut their caring out so much. I couldn't find the answer, and one woman said: "It looks like you are trying to stay continuously as deep in your feelings as you were this afternoon. It would make sense to me for you to draw back and assimilate it. Maybe if you don't push so hard, you can rest awhile and then move back into your feelings more naturally."
>
> Her making the last suggestion really took effect. I saw the sense in it, and almost immediately I settled back very relaxed with something of a feeling of a bright, warm day dawning inside me. In addition to taking the pressure off of myself, however, I was for the first time really warmed by the friendly feelings which I felt they had for me. It is difficult to say why I felt liked only just then, but, as opposed to the earlier sessions, I really *believed* they cared for me. I never have fully understood why I stood their affection off for so long, but at that point I almost abruptly began to trust that they did care. The measure of the effectiveness of this change lies in what I said next. I said, "Well, that really takes care of me. I'm really ready to listen to someone else now." I *meant* that, too.

Confrontation There are times when the term "feedback" is far too mild to describe the interactions which take place, when it is better said that one individual *confronts* another, directly "leveling" with him. Such confrontations can be positive, but frequently they are decidedly negative, as the following example will make abundantly clear. In one of the last sessions of a group, Alice had made some quite vulgar and contemptuous remarks to John, who was entering religious work. The next morning, Norma, who had been a very quiet person in the group, took the floor:

NORMA (*loud sigh*): Well, I don't have *any* respect for you, Alice. *None!* (*Pause.*) There's about a hundred things going through my mind I want to say to you, and by God I hope I get through 'em all! First of all, if you wanted us to respect you, then why couldn't you respect *John's* feelings last night? Why have you been on him today? Hmm? Last night — couldn't you — couldn't you accept — *couldn't you* comprehend in any way at all that — that *he felt* his unworthiness in the service of God? Couldn't you accept this, or did you have to dig into it today to find something *else there?* And his respect for womanhood — he *loves* women — yes, he does, because he's a real person, but you — you're not a real woman — to me — and thank God, you're not my mother!!!! I want to come over and beat the hell out of you!!! I want to slap you across the mouth so hard and — oh, and you're so, you're many years above me — and I respect age, and I respect people who are older than me, *but I don't respect you, Alice. At all!* And I was so *hurt* and *confused* because you were making someone else feel *hurt* and *confused.* . . .

It may relieve the reader to know that these two women came to accept each other, not completely, but much more understandingly, before the end of the session. But this *was* a confrontation!

The Helping Relationship outside the Group Sessions   No account of the group process would, in my experience, be adequate if it did not make mention of the many ways in which group members are of assistance to one another. Not infrequently, one member of a group will spend hours listening and talking to another member who is undergoing a painful new perception of himself. Sometimes it is merely the offering of help which is therapeutic. I think of one man who was going through a very depressed period after having told us of the many tragedies in his life. He seemed quite clearly, from his remarks, to be contemplating suicide. I jotted down my room number (we were staying at a hotel) and told him to put it in his pocket and to call me anytime of day or night if he felt that it would help. He never called, but six months after the workshop was over he wrote to me telling me how much that act had meant to him and that he still had the slip of paper to remind him of it.

Let me give an example of the healing effect of the attitudes of group members both outside and inside the group meetings. This is taken from a letter written by a workshop member to the group one month after the group sessions. He speaks of the difficulties and depressing circumstances he has encountered during that month and adds:

I have come to the conclusion that my experiences with you have profoundly affected me. I am truly grateful. This is different than personal therapy. None of you *had* to care about me. None of you had to seek me out and let me know of things you thought would help me. None of you had to let me know I was of help to you. Yet you did, and as a result it has far more meaning than anything I have so far experienced. When I feel the need to hold back and not live spontaneously, for whatever reasons, I remember that twelve persons, just like those before me now, said to let go and be congruent, to be myself, and, of all unbelievable things, they even loved me more for it. This has given me the *courage* to come out of myself many times since then. Often it seems my very doing of this helps the others to experience similar freedom.

The Basic Encounter   Running through some of the trends I have just been describing is the fact that individuals come into much closer and more direct contact with one another than is customary in ordinary life. This appears to be one of the most central, intense, and change-producing aspects of such a group experience. To illustrate what I mean, I would like to draw an example from a recent workshop group. A man tells, through his tears, of the very tragic loss of his child, a grief which he is experiencing *fully*, for the first time, not holding back his feelings in any way. Another says to him, also with tears in his eyes, "I've never felt so close to another human being. I've never before felt a real physical hurt in me from the pain of another. I feel *completely* with you." This is a basic encounter.

Such I-Thou relationships (to use Buber's term) occur with some frequency in these group sessions and nearly always bring a moistness to the eyes of the participants.

One member, trying to sort out his experiences immediately after a workshop, speaks of the "commitment to relationship" which often developed on the part of two individuals, not necessarily individuals who had liked each other initially. He goes on to say:

> The incredible fact experienced over and over by members of the group was that when a negative feeling was fully expressed to another, the relationship grew and the negative feeling was replaced by a deep acceptance for the other. . . . Thus real change seemed to occur when feelings were experienced and expressed in the context of the relationship. "I can't *stand* the way you talk!" turned into a real understanding and affection for you the *way* you talk.

This statement seems to capture some of the more complex meanings of the term "basic encounter."

The Expression of Positive Feelings and Closeness   As indicated in the last section, an inevitable part of the group process seems to be that when feelings are expressed and can be accepted in a relationship, a great deal of closeness and positive feelings result. Thus as the sessions proceed, there is an increasing feeling of warmth and group spirit and trust built, not out of positive attitudes only, but out of a realness which includes both positive and negative feeling. One member tried to capture this in writing very shortly after the workshop by saying that if he were trying to sum it up, ". . . it would have to do with what I call confirmation — a kind of confirmation of myself, of the uniqueness and universal qualities of men, a confirmation that when we can be human together something positive can emerge."

A particularly poignant expression of these positive attitudes was shown in the group where Norma confronted Alice with her bitterly angry feelings. Joan, the facilitator, was deeply upset and began to weep. The positive and healing attitudes of the group, for their own *leader*, are an unusual example of the closeness and personal quality of the relationships.

> JOAN (*crying*): I somehow feel that it's so *damned* easy for me to — to put myself *inside* of another person and I just guess I can feel that — for John and Alice and for you, Norma.
> ALICE: And it's *you* that's hurt.
> JOAN: Maybe I am taking some of that hurt. I guess I am. (*crying*.)
> ALICE: That's a wonderful gift. I wish I had it.
> JOAN: You have a lot of it.
> PETER: In a way you bear the — I guess in a special way, because you're the — facilitator, ah, you've probably borne, ah, an extra heavy burden for all of us — and the burden that you, perhaps, you bear the heaviest is — we ask you — we ask one another; we grope to try to accept one another as we are, and — for each of us in various ways I guess we reach things and we say, *please* accept me. . . .

Some may be very critical of a "leader" so involved and so sensitive that she weeps at the tensions in the group which she has taken into herself. For me, it is simply another evidence that when people are real with each other, they have an astonishing ability to heal a person with a real and understanding love, whether that person is "participant" or "leader."

Behavior Changes in the Group   It would seem from observation that many changes in behavior occur in the group itself. Gestures change. The tone of voice changes, becoming sometimes stronger, sometimes softer, usually more spontaneous, less artificial, more feelingful. Individuals show an astonishing amount of thoughtfulness and helpfulness toward one another.

Our major concern, however, is with the behavior changes which occur following the group experience. It is this which constitutes the most significant question and on which we need much more study and research. One person gives a catalog of the changes which he sees in himself which may seem too "pat" but which is echoed in many other statements:

> I am more open, spontaneous. I express myself more freely. I am more sympathetic, empathic, and tolerant. I am more confident. I am more religious in my own way. My relations with my family, friends, and co-

workers are more honest, and I express my likes and dislikes and true feelings more openly. I admit ignorance more readily. I am more cheerful. I want to help others more.

Another says:

Since the workshop there has been a new relationship with my parents. It has been trying and hard. However, I have found a greater freedom in talking with them, especially my father. Steps have been made toward being closer to my mother than I have ever been in the last five years.

Another says:

It helped clarify my feelings about my work, gave me more enthusiasm for it, and made me more honest and cheerful with my co-workers and also more open when I was hostile. It made my relationship with my wife more open, deeper. We felt freer to talk about anything, and we felt confident that anything we talked about we could work through.

Sometimes the changes which are described are very subtle. "The primary change is the more positive view of my ability to allow myself to *hear*, and to become involved with someone else's 'silent scream.' "

At the risk of making the outcomes sound too good, I will add one more statement written shortly after a workshop by a mother. She says:

The immediate impact on my children was of interest to both me and my husband. I feel that having been so accepted and loved by a group of strangers was so supportive that when I returned home my love for the people closest to me was much more spontaneous. Also, the practice I had in accepting and loving others during the workshop was evident in my relationships with my close friends.

Disadvantages and Risks

Thus far one might think that every aspect of the group process was positive. As far as the evidence at hand indicates, it appears that it nearly always is a positive process for a majority of the participants. There are, nevertheless, failures which result. Let me try to describe briefly some of the negative aspects of the group process as they sometimes occur.

The most obvious deficiency of the intensive group experience is that frequently the behavior changes, if any, which occur, are not lasting. This is often recognized by the participants. One says, "I wish I had the ability to hold permanently the 'openness' I left the conference with." Another says, "I experienced a lot of acceptance, warmth, and love at the workshop. I find it hard to carry the ability to share this in the same way with people outside the workshop. I find it easier to slip back into my old unemotional role than to do the work necessary to open relationships."

Sometimes group members experience this phenomenon of "relapse" quite philosophically:

The group experience is not a way of life but a reference point. My images of our group, even though I am unsure of some of their meanings, give me a comforting and useful perspective on my normal routine. They are like a mountain which I have climbed and enjoyed and to which I hope occasionally to return.

Some Data on Outcomes   What is the extent of this "slippage"? In the past year, I have administered follow-up questionnaires to 481 individuals who have been in groups I have organized or conducted. The information has been obtained from two to twelve months following the group experience, but the greatest number were followed up after a three- to six-month period.[4] Of these individuals, two (i.e., less than one-half of 1 percent) felt it had changed their behavior in ways they did not like. Fourteen percent felt the experience had made no perceptible change in their behavior. Another fourteen percent felt that it had changed their behavior but that this change had disappeared or left only a small residual positive effect. Fifty-seven percent felt it had made a continuing positive difference in their behavior, a few feeling that it had made some negative changes along with the positive.

A second potential risk involved in the intensive group experience and one which is often mentioned in public discussion is the risk that the individual may become deeply involved in revealing himself and then be left with problems which are not worked through. There have been a number of reports of people who have felt, following an intensive group experience, that they must go to a therapist to work through the feelings which were opened up in the intensive experience of the workshop and which were left unresolved. It is obvious that, without knowing more about each individual situation, it is difficult to say whether this was a negative outcome or a partially or entirely positive one. There are also very occasional accounts, and I can testify to two in my own experience, where an individual has had a psychotic episode during or immediately following an intensive group experience. On the other side of the picture is the fact that individuals have also lived through what were clearly psychotic episodes, and lived through them very constructively, in the context of a basic encounter group. My own tentative clinical judgment would be that the more positively the group process has been proceeding, the less likely it is that any individual would be psychologically damaged through membership in the group. It is obvious, however, that this is a serious issue and that much more needs to be known.

Some of the tension which exists in workshop members as a result of this potential for damage was very well described by one member when he said, "I feel the workshop had some very precious moments for me when I felt very close indeed to particular persons. It had some frighten-

---

[4]The 481 respondents constituted 82 percent of those to whom the questionnaire had been sent.

ing moments when its potency was very evident and I realized a particular person might be deeply hurt or greatly helped but I could not predict which."

Out of the 481 participants followed up by questionnaires, two felt that the overall impact of their intensive group experience was "mostly damaging." Six more said that it had been "more unhelpful than helpful." Twenty-one, or 4 percent, stated that it had been "mostly frustrating, annoying, or confusing." Three and one-half percent said that it had been neutral in its impact. Nineteen percent checked that it had been "more helpful than unhelpful," indicating some degree of ambivalence. But 30 percent saw it as "constructive in its results," and 45 percent checked it as a "deeply meaningful, positive experience."[5] Thus for three-fourths of the group, it was *very* helpful. These figures should help to set the problem in perspective. It is obviously a very serious matter if an intensive group experience is psychologically damaging to *anyone*. It seems clear, however, that such damage occurs only rarely, if we are to judge by the reaction of the participants.

Other Hazards of the Group Experience   There is another risk or deficiency in the basic encounter group. Until very recent years it has been unusual for a workshop to include both husband and wife. This can be a real problem if significant change has taken place in one spouse during or as a result of the workshop experience. One individual felt this risk clearly after attending a workshop. He said, "I think there is a great danger to a marriage when one spouse attends a group. It is too hard for the other spouse to compete with the group individually and collectively." One of the frequent aftereffects of the intensive group experience is that it brings out into the open for discussion marital tensions which have been kept under cover.

Another risk which has sometimes been a cause of real concern in mixed intensive workshops is that very positive, warm, and loving feelings can develop between members of the encounter group, as has been evident from some of the preceding examples. Inevitably some of these feelings have a sexual component, and this can be a matter of great concern to the participants and a profound threat to their spouses if these feelings are not worked through satisfactorily in the workshop. Also the close and loving feelings which develop may become a source of threat and marital difficulty when a wife, for example, has not been present, but projects many fears about the loss of her spouse — whether well founded or not — onto the workshop experience.

A man who had been in a mixed group of men and women executives wrote to me a year later and mentioned the strain in his marriage which

---

[5]These figures add up to more than 100 percent since quite a number of the respondents checked more than one answer.

resulted from his association with Marge, a member of his basic encounter group:

> There was a problem about Marge. There had occurred a very warm feeling on my part for Marge, and great compassion, for I felt she was *very* lonely. I believe the warmth was sincerely reciprocal. At any rate she wrote me a long affectionate letter, which I let my wife read. I was *proud* that Marge could feel that way about *me*, [Because he had felt very worthless.] But my wife was alarmed, because she read a love affair into the words — at least a *potential* threat. I stopped writing to Marge, because I felt rather clandestine after that.
>
> My wife has since participated in an "encounter group" herself, and she now understands. I have resumed writing to Marge.

Obviously, not all such episodes would have such a harmonious ending.

It is of interest in this connection that there has been increasing experimentation in recent years with "couples workshops" and with workshops for industrial executives and their spouses.

Still another negative potential growing out of these groups has become evident in recent years. Some individuals who have participated in previous encounter groups may exert a stultifying influence on new workshops which they attend. They sometimes exhibit what I think of as the "old pro" phenomenon. They feel they have learned the "rules of the game," and they subtly or openly try to impose these rules on newcomers. Thus, instead of promoting true expressiveness and spontaneity, they endeavor to substitute new rules for old — to make members feel guilty if they are not expressing feelings, are reluctant to voice criticism or hostility, are talking about situations outside the group relationship, or are fearful of revealing themselves. These old pros seem to be attempting to substitute a new tyranny in interpersonal relationships in the place of older, conventional restrictions. To me this is a perversion of the true group process. We need to ask ourselves how this travesty on spontaneity comes about.

Implications

I have tried to describe both the positive and the negative aspects of this burgeoning new cultural development. I would like now to touch on its implications for our society.

In the first place, it is a highly potent experience and hence clearly deserving of scientific study. As a phenomenon it has been both praised and criticized, but few people who have participated would doubt that *something* significant happens in these groups. People do not react in a neutral fashion toward the intensive group experience. They regard it as either strikingly worthwhile or deeply questionable. All would agree, however, that it is *potent*. This fact makes it of particular interest to the behavioral sciences since science is usually advanced by studying potent and dynamic phenomena. This is one of the reasons why I personally am devoting more and more of my time to this whole enterprise. I feel that we can learn much about the ways in which constructive personality change comes about as we study this group process more deeply.

In a different dimension, the intensive group experience appears to be one cultural attempt to meet the isolation of contemporary life. The person who has experienced an I-Thou relationship, who has entered into the basic encounter, is no longer an isolated individual. One workshop member stated this in a deeply expressive way:

> Workshops seem to be at least a partial answer to the loneliness of modern man and his search for new meanings for his life. In short, workshops seem very quickly to allow the individual to become that person he wants to be. The first few steps are taken there, in uncertainty, in fear, and in anxiety. We may or may not continue the journey. It is a gutsy way to live. You trade many, many loose ends for one big knot in the middle of your stomach. It sure as hell isn't easy, but it is a *life* at least — not a hollow imitation of life. It has fear as well as hope, sorrow as well as joy, but I daily offer it to more people in the hope that they will join me. . . . Out from a no-man's land of *fog* into the more violent atmosphere of extremes of thunder, hail, rain, and sunshine. It is worth the trip.

Another implication which is partially expressed in the foregoing statement is that it is an avenue to fulfillment. In a day when more income, a larger car, and a better washing machine seem scarcely to be satisfying the deepest needs of man, individuals are turning to the psychological world, groping for a greater degree of authenticity and fulfillment. One workshop member expressed this extremely vividly:

> [It] has revealed a completely new dimension of life and has opened an infinite number of possibilities for me in my relationship to myself and to everyone dear to me. I feel truly alive and so grateful and joyful and hopeful and healthy and giddy and sparkly. I feel as though my eyes and ears and heart and guts have been opened to see and hear and love and feel more deeply, more widely, more intensely — this glorious, mixed-up, fabulous existence of ours. My whole body and each of its systems seems freer and healthier. I want to feel hot and cold, tired and rested, soft and hard, energetic and lazy. With persons everywhere, but especially my family, I have found a new freedom to explore and communicate. I know the change in me automatically brings a change in them. A whole new exciting relationship has started for me with my husband and with each of my children — a freedom to speak and to hear them speak.

Though one may wish to discount the enthusiasm of this statement, it describes an enrichment of life for which many are seeking.

Rehumanizing Human Relationships   This whole development seems to have special significance in a culture which appears to be bent upon dehumanizing the individual and dehumanizing our human relationships. Here is an important force in the opposite direction, working toward making relationships more meaningful and more personal, in the family, in education, in government, in administrative agencies, in industry.

An intensive group experience has an even more general philosophical implication. It is one expression of the existential point of view which is making itself so pervasively evident in art and literature and modern life. The implicit goal of the group process seems to be to live life fully in the here and now of the relationship. The parallel with an existential point of view is clear cut. I believe this has been amply evident in the illustrative material.

There is one final issue which is raised by this whole phenomenon: What is our view of the optimal person? What is the goal of personality development? Different ages and different cultures have given different answers to this question. It seems evident from our review of the group process that in a climate of freedom, group members move toward becoming more spontaneous, flexible, closely related to their feelings, open to their experience, and closer and more expressively intimate in their interpersonal relationships. If we value this type of person and this type of behavior, then clearly the group process is a valuable process. If, on the other hand, we place a value on the individual who is effective in suppressing his feelings, who operates from a firm set of principles, who does not trust his own reactions and experience but relies on authority, and who remains aloof in his interpersonal relationships, then we would regard the group process, as I have tried to describe it, as a dangerous force. Clearly there is room for a difference of opinion on this value question, and not everyone in our culture would give the same answer.

Conclusion

I have tried to give a naturalistic, observational picture of one of the most significant modern social inventions, the so-called intensive group experience, or basic encounter group. I have tried to indicate some of the common elements of the process which occur in the climate of freedom that is present in such a group. I have pointed out some of the risks and shortcomings of the group experience. I have tried to indicate some of the reasons why it deserves serious consideration, not only from a personal point of view, but also from a scientific and philosophical point of view. I also hope I have made it clear that this is an area in which an enormous amount of deeply perceptive study and research is needed.

References

BENNIS, W. G., K. D. BENNE, and R. CHIN (eds.). *The Planning of Change.* New York: Holt, Rinehart and Winston, 1961.

BENNIS, W. G., E. H. SCHEIN, D. E. BERLEW, and F. I. STEELE (eds.). *Interpersonal Dynamics*. Homewood, Ill.: Dorsey, 1964.

BRADFORD, LELAND P., JACK R. GIBB, and KENNETH D. BENNE (eds.). *T-Group Theory and Laboratory Method*. New York: John Wiley & Sons, Inc., 1964.

CASRIEL, D. *So Fair a House*. Englewood Cliffs, N.J.: Prentice-Hall, 1963.

GIBB, J. R. "Climate for Trust Formation," *T-Group Theory and Laboratory Method*, eds. L. Bradford, J. R. Gibb, and K. D. Benne. New York: John Wiley & Sons, Inc., 1964.

GORDON, T. *Group-Centered Leadership*. Boston: Houghton Mifflin, 1955.

HALL, G. F. "A Participant's Experience in a Basic Encounter Group." Mimeographed, Western Behavioral Sciences Institute, 1965.

Part Two
T-Groups

Introduction

The T-group was designed to allow participants to be involved in the very group processes they were studying. It was first inaugurated by Kurt Lewin in the late forties, and formed the basic educational instrument of the National Training Laboratory. N.T.L. was set up by Lewin's associates in Bethel, Maine, shortly after his death in 1947. The laboratory is a one- to three-week residential training program which also includes conferences and lectures. In a T-group, eight to ten people meet in a room with no formal leader, no agenda, no textbooks, only a seemingly passive trainer. The trainer does not direct the group process; his primary function is to help the participants become aware of what is happening to them and to the group. Learning in a T-group takes place through the group's struggle to create a meaningful structure for itself out of a largely unstructured situation.

The three articles included here present accounts of particular T-group experiences from different perspectives. Spencer Klaw, a writer with no previous group exposure, attended a T-group for business executives as an interested observer. William Glueck writes as a businessman and a professor of management. Louis A. Gottschalk, psychiatrist and psychoanalyst, discusses his experience from this professional perspective.

Klaw's "Two Weeks in a T-Group" is a detailed account of the process of one T-group. He describes how individuals, frustrated because they were leaderless and lacked a fixed agenda, became a cohesive group with a sense of purpose. Much of the article concentrates on the feelings and reactions of individual members during the two-week lab.

Glueck, in "Reflections on a T-Group Experience," reports from the position of a participant rather than of an observer. He structures his discussion around what he considers the four major phases of the group's development: individual-centered, frustration and conflict, consolidation and harmony, and individual self-assessment. These provide a useful framework for understanding the T-group process.

Glueck had entered the T-group with many doubts and defenses, some of which remained with him to the end. His final evaluation is generally positive; he strongly believes in the usefulness of training. But he also stresses the importance of skilled and responsible group leadership and the need for careful screening of participants.

Gottschalk's "Psychoanalytic Notes on T-Groups at the Human Relations Laboratory, Bethel, Maine," is both an experiential and a theoretical treatment. He points out that T-groups are promoted as short-term, essentially non-stressful, educational experiences. However, he also notes that the T-group process is, in fact, very similar to that of a psychotherapy group. Gottschalk's position is that sensitivity training in general lacks a disciplined and uniform theoretical approach. He found the trainers in his group inconsistent in their ideas and haphazard in their actions. According to Gottschalk, trainers are often neither emotionally nor professionally equipped to handle responsibly the psychological dynamics arising in their groups. A leader is needed with sufficient professional training to enable him to separate his own anxieties and projections from the feelings and reactions of the participants. Gottschalk strongly emphasizes the need for research on T-group processes, responsible training of trainers, and careful selection of participants.

Two Weeks in a T-Group_____

SPENCER KLAW

Spencer Klaw, "Two Weeks in a T-Group," *Fortune*, LXIV (August, 1961), 114–117+. Reprinted from the August 1961 issue of *Fortune* magazine by special permission; © 1961 Time, Inc.

Thousands of American businessmen have undergone a strange educational ordeal in recent years. It has consisted of taking part, as trainees, in what is commonly called a human-relations laboratory. The distinguishing feature of such a laboratory is not the subject matter it teaches, since lectures on leadership and human relations have long been staples of management-development programs, but the remarkable pedagogical methods it employs. These include sequestering a group of trainees on a "cultural island" — which may be a resort hotel in the off season, for instance — and encouraging them to give one another what can amount to a fairly stiff psychological buffeting.

This buffeting takes place while the trainees sit around a table as members of a body called a T-Group. The T-Group (T stands simply for training) is an offshoot of the study of group dynamics, which in turn is an offshoot of social psychology, and it is by far the most important piece of educational apparatus used at a training laboratory. Its purpose is to let trainees study at first hand the psychological forces that operate in groups, and, further, to help them learn how their own behavior affects other people. Members of a T-Group are not only permitted, but urged, to discuss one another's behavior, and the feelings that may underlie that behavior, with a frankness not usually advisable in real life. In the jargon of the laboratory, this is known as giving and receiving "feedback." Recipients of a particularly bitter dose of feedback sometimes leave the room or even break into tears.

Although more and more people are going off each year to training laboratories, published accounts of what goes on in a T-Group have been few and, on the whole, not very illuminating. Nor are the comments of ex-trainees revealing as a rule. Most people who have been to a laboratory return to the cultural mainland with a conviction that the expedition they have made was worth while. But they are usually hard put to say exactly how or why — or, indeed, to convey any but the vaguest notion of what they have actually experienced.

The writer recently arranged to attend, as an observer, a laboratory planned specifically for business executives. It was conducted by the National Training Laboratories, a branch of the National Education Association, and far and away the leading organizer and sponsor of human-relations laboratories in the U.S. (See "A Short History of T-Grouping," p. 50.) The laboratory was held at Arden House, a ninety-six-room mansion built by the late Edward H. Harriman in 1909 and now owned by Columbia University. This cultural island is situated on a thickly wooded mountaintop about sixty miles north of New York City. N.T.L. has held a number of laboratory sessions there, all of them designed for men at the middle and upper-middle levels of corporate management and earning, say, $12,000 to $30,000 a year. Tuition at this particular laboratory session, which lasted for two weeks, was $500, and room and board was another $250 or so. Among the companies picking up the tab were Westinghouse, Esso, General Electric, International Telephone & Telegraph, Boeing, Maytag, Eli Lilly, Monsanto, Pillsbury, Union Carbide, Western Electric, and the Bessemer & Lake Erie Railroad. There were forty-seven trainees in all. The following is an account of how they spent their time at Arden House — and in particular of what went on at the daily meetings of one T-Group — together with some reflections on what, if anything, laboratories do for the people who attend them.

Who's Nervous?

The laboratory, or Management Work Conference as it was officially titled, began on a Sunday afternoon with a talk by Leland Bradford, N.T.L.'s director and one of the inventors of the T-Group. Bradford, a slight, owlish man in his middle fifties, welcomed the conferees, noted that sports clothes would be in order except at dinner, and introduced the other members of the laboratory staff. Then he described briefly what the conferees would be doing at Arden House. "This is a situation in which we are utilizing for our learning our own behavior," he said. "What we're saying is that here is a laboratory in human behavior, in which we are not only scientists but also our own subjects."

The conferees did not have to wait long before getting an opportunity, as members of a T-Group, to play this dual role. On arrival, each conferee had been assigned to an eleven- or twelve-man T-Group, which was scheduled to hold its first meeting on Sunday evening. (Thereafter, conferees would meet with their T-Groups every day, usually for two hours in the morning and again in the evening; the rest of their time would be taken up largely with lectures — on "Logical and Psychological Factors in Problem Solving," for example — and with training exercises whose nature was not specified on the mimeographed conference schedule.)

The writer had accepted an invitation to observe T-Group II, for whose training Bradford himself would be directly responsible. At the appointed hour of eight o'clock, its members, who seemed to range in age from the early thirties to the middle fifties, took seats around a huge rectangular table. Although they were all wearing name tags, Bradford suggested that they also write their first names or nicknames in large letters on big place cards that had been provided, and then stand these cards on the table in front of them. When this had been done, he said, in a tentative way, "I assume our purpose is to learn how groups behave by observing how we do as a member of this group." He added that neither he nor the group's associate trainer, Douglas Bunker, a young Harvard-trained psychologist who had taken a seat almost directly across the table from him, intended to act as a discussion leader. "Our idea would be simply that we observe our behavior in the here and now," Bradford said. Then he fell silent.

The silence lasted for more than a minute. It was broken by a thin, gray-haired man named Hank.* He said he didn't know about anybody

---

*Conferees' real names have not been used in this account.

else, but that he felt nervous. "You feel like a June bride," he said. "You know what's coming, but you don't know what to expect." A proposal was made that members introduce themselves, and several did so, describing in considerable detail their jobs as assistant controllers, chief engineers, manufacturing superintendents, and the like. Some members also told what they hoped to get out of Arden House. "I talk too much, and I don't listen enough, and it's something I hope to change in the next two weeks," one man said. Most of those who spoke said that, unlike Hank, they didn't feel in the least nervous.

These disclaimers were challenged by Bradford. When a systems engineer named Maurice announced that he had come to Arden House quite prepared to be "shot down in flames," Bradford said there had been a lot of this kind of imagery used, and that maybe people were more worried than they were willing to admit. Maurice insisted that he wasn't worried at all. Another member, Steve, who had identified himself as an industrial psychologist, objected tartly to "pseudo-Freudian interpretations," as he characterized Bradford's prior remark. Bunker, the associate trainer, said he shared Bradford's impression that other people at the table besides Hank were feeling nervous; he suggested that the group might usefully talk about the discrepancy that sometimes exists between what a person says he feels — for instance, that he is feeling comfortable and easy — and what other people think he is feeling. Bradford inquired: "Why did Maurice and Steve feel it necessary to prove how wrong I was?" Nobody answered the question.

The members of Group II seemed, not surprisingly, to find all this pretty baffling. But after the meeting, in a lecture to all four T-Groups, Bradford explained that bafflement and frustration are part of the learning process at a laboratory. The trainers in each T-Group, he pointed out, were refusing to be real "leaders" — that is, to specify agenda or procedures — and were thereby deliberately creating a kind of vacuum. He said he knew that confronting such a vacuum made many people nervous even though they might deny it — an observation that was confirmed by the loud laughter of the conferees. The important thing, Bradford concluded, was that in their efforts to fill the vacuums in their T-Groups, members would be exposing for examination their characteristic ways of doing and seeing things.

"Let's Put a Rudder on This Ship"

Later that evening Bradford remarked privately that some members of T-Groups invariably try to fill the vacuum he had spoken of by proposing that the group elect a leader and draw up an agenda and rules of procedure. In the case of T-Group II, the first proposal to this effect was made on Monday morning, at the group's second meeting. The most vocal proponent of organization was Maurice, the systems engineer, who suggested that the group "put a rudder on this ship" by electing a temporary chairman. He said the group could then decide in an orderly way what it really wanted to talk about. Several members agreed. But others opposed Maurice on the ground that, so long as the group didn't know what it wanted (or was supposed) to do, there was little point in organizing to do it.

At Monday evening's meeting Bradford suggested that, instead of arguing about rudders and agenda, it might be more useful for Group II to examine the frustrations members had been feeling while trying to cope with the lack of a group leader. That way, he said, "we might get at the core of our feelings." The suggestion was ignored, and the argument went on. The frustrations of the members, though as yet unexamined, were clearly mounting. A member who plumped tediously for an agenda headed by a discussion of staff-and-line relationships in industry was sharply accused by other members of trying to grind a personal ax, that is, of wanting simply to expound his own theories of management organization. A man named George, an executive of a small West Coast electronics firm, proposed that the group talk about jaguars. He said he was about to leave for Central America on a jaguar-hunting expedition, and that jaguars were *his* personal ax. "What do you want to do with the ax," Bradford asked, "chop us?" George said he just wanted to get it out on the grindstone and shine it up. "I want to learn something damned quick," he said angrily. "I'm tired of drifting."

Escapism in the Crystal Ball

On Tuesday, Maurice tried to stop the drifting by proposing the election of a committee that would be charged with drafting a set of group goals. Bradford indicated that he thought this was escapism. "What I see," he said, peering down at the table with his head between his hands, as though he were looking into a crystal ball, "is people trying to have something logical, rational, something not part of *me* to talk about — something to avoid the discomfort of discussing our feelings." A vote on appointing a goals committee was nevertheless taken, and carried. But the majority then found, somewhat to its surprise, that it had no stomach for imposing its will on the minority, and so no committee was appointed after all.

The question of organization, which had been the almost exclusive subject of discussion for two days, was finally settled on Wednesday. Another vote on the issue was called for, and this time half the members, apparently unwilling to vote either for or against Maurice's proposal, didn't vote at all. One of the abstainers, a bald, rough-voiced chemical engineer named Pete, said that although he had started out supporting Maurice, he had now changed his mind. He said that if some people in the group didn't want organization, then the others shouldn't try to ram it down their throats. He added that he suspected many people in the group felt this way.

Bradford nodded. "I think Pete has verbalized one of the most important statements yet," he said solemnly. "If the group is not going to drive anybody out, then we have concern about its members, and we can begin to help one another." Maurice said skeptically that he didn't see that the group, simply by refusing to organize, was in a better position to get down to *his* inner self. But the consensus seemed to be that the group would just have to get on as best it could without a chairman, an agenda, or rules of order.

Group II now had to find something other than its own organization to talk about, and as the week wore on the members began, as Bradford had been urging, to discuss their own behavior and their feelings about one another.

The first sustained discussion of this kind grew out of a competitive exercise in which the group was pitted against T-Group IV. For purposes of the exercise, each group was required to draft a statement of "the conditions needed in the T-Group for effectively helping one another change and improve skills in dealing with people." This job had to be done in a two-hour period on Thursday evening. Then, on Friday morning, a five-man panel of judges, made up of trainees and staff members, would decide which of the two statements was better.

The exercise was taken with great seriousness, for most of the conferees were by now deeply involved in the affairs of their T-Groups. In the dining room, in the bar, or walking in the woods around Arden House late in the afternoon, they talked less and less about the lives they had temporarily left behind, and more and more about the events taking place in their T-Group meetings. At the same time, strong group loyalties were developing. "I don't know where in hell we're going," a Kansas construction man remarked one evening, "but I know we've got the best goddam group up here."

Group II went about drafting its statement in a mood of grim determination, though with a good deal of procedural confusion. A subcommittee of two was chosen to do the actual writing, but a third man, Dick, an assistant controller of a midwestern steel company, added himself to the committee on his own initiative. A tall, red-faced man named Ted, the vice president for manufacturing of a New England textile firm, complained that the group was delegating entirely too much authority to the drafting committee. When his objection was brushed aside, he stood up and announced grumpily that he was sleepy and was going to bed. He was persuaded to sit down again, but he sulked for the rest of the evening.

Kindly Helpers and Critical Thinkers

On Friday morning the five-man panel of judges heard arguments by representatives of the two groups — Maurice spoke for Group II — and then each judge gave his verdict. What turned out to be the deciding vote was cast by a staff member, a young man named Barry Oshry, who teaches business administration at Boston University. Oshry said he preferred Group IV's statement, partly because its tone was a little warmer. At this pronouncement, the members of Group IV shouted and threw their arms in the air.

The members of Group II were, by contrast, gloomy and depressed. At a meeting later that morning they hashed over a number of possible explanations for their defeat. One member blamed it on Oshry's personality. Recalling a lecture earlier in the week, in which people had been categorized as Kindly Helpers, Strong Achievers, and Critical Thinkers, he said that Oshry was obviously a Kindly Helper, and that if the group had had the foresight to draft a more kindly paper it might have won.

When the group met again that evening, however, its members accepted a suggestion by Bradford that they stop looking for scapegoats, and look instead at the parts played by various people during the performance of the exercise. Maurice, the systems engineer, began by asking Dick why he had taken it on himself to join the drafting committee on Thursday night. Dick replied that he hadn't been sure the committee could get the job done in time without him. Furthermore, he said, the committee had been hand-picked by George, the jaguar hunter, and he hadn't liked that. (George was not present to comment on this remark; he had had to leave for home earlier in the day to deal with a business emergency.) "Two things disturbed me," Dick said. "One was that the selection of writers was done without my participation. The other was that I didn't think George was the kind of person to be selecting people for the group."

Bradford said he had noticed that Dick, a stocky, blond young man with a brusque way of talking, had invariably raised his voice when speaking to George. Maurice said he had noticed this too, and asked Dick if he had been competing with George for leadership. Dick acknowledged that maybe he had, but said it was mainly because "I want cooler heads — like mine — to be in on things."

Steve, the industrial psychologist who had objected to Bradford's pseudo-Freudianism, leaned forward and pointed a finger at Dick. "Let me drive in on Dick," he said. "Did you resent George's choices because you wanted that writing job yourself?" Dick agreed that this was more than possible. Steve asked if Dick had resented the selection of Maurice to argue the group's case before the judging panel. Dick said no, because he had had a hand in that selection himself. "In other words," Bradford asked, "manipulation is O.K. if you're one of those doing the manipulating?" Dick said angrily, "Well, you see a bunch of people sitting around the table like a bunch of asses, getting absolutely nowhere, and after a while it gets under your skin." He went on to say that he didn't think everybody in the group was an ass, but that there were at least two people — he named Hank, the man who had felt like a June bride on the first night, and an earnest young personnel man named Walker — whom he had pretty well written off. Bradford said, "If you write people off — damn it, this sounds preachy — how can you help them to change?" Dick didn't answer.

Who Kept Ted from Walking Out?

Thursday night's events were further analyzed when the group gathered on Saturday morning for its last meeting before the weekend. Someone suggested discussing why Ted, the New England textile man, had almost walked out on the group, and how he had been kept from doing so. Ted said ruefully that part of his trouble had been that he had begun the cocktail hour a little too early on Thursday. "The procedure the group was following didn't suit me," he said. "When I said so, I got shoved right down, and to tell the truth I wasn't in too good shape to get back up there again."

Jerry, a nervous, soft-voiced man employed by a chemical company as coordinator of its foreign operations, said he himself had spent much of his life struggling with a terrible temper. He said he had seen Ted getting angry, and had rushed around the table to persuade him not to leave. Jerry added that he had done this because he had a distinct impression that Ted hadn't really wanted to walk out. Ted said, "You were very perceptive, Jerry. I might have gotten right through the door, and I'd have been damn disappointed if no one had stopped me."

Jerry said he had had a lot of help from Pete, the chemical engineer. He said Pete had thrown a "key block" by ordering Ted in a rough, joking way to sit down, and that this had given him (Jerry) time to get around the table and go to work on Ted. Despite the compliment, Pete seemed troubled by his role in the affair. "You said I threw a key block, Jerry," he said. "And that's what I did — I clobbered Ted." Pete added that he guessed he was destined to be a thrower of rough blocks. Bradford disagreed, however. He pointed out that Pete had consistently rushed to the aid of people he thought were in trouble — for example, by suggesting at one point in Friday night's discussion that perhaps Dick, the impatient young controller, had had enough feedback — and that Pete was probably "the No. 1 fencemender in the group."

The Reluctant Mother Hen

Several members agreed, including Ted, who said Pete's role had been a surprise to him because on the first night he had tabbed Pete as a hard-boiled roughneck. Dick, sounding chastened after the going-over he had received the night before, said, "Pete, do you feel you have these fence-mending ideas, but that you carry them out like a bull in a china shop?" Pete nodded, and Dick went on to say, in a conciliatory manner, that while Pete might have a tendency to blurt things out, "when you do, you hit the nail on the head — what you say is honest and true."

A short time later Dick reverted to his earlier form. He commented harshly to Walker, the personnel man, that he wasn't the only one who had written Walker off — that most of the other people in the room apparently had too. There was an awkward silence, during which Walker smiled fixedly and rearranged some papers on the table in front of him. It was ended by Pete, who told a joke. When the laughter had died, Bradford congratulated him on having lowered the tension so deftly. Pete protested uneasily that he wasn't really such a nice guy as some people seemed to think. Bunker, the associate trainer, said, "Pete, you're not entirely happy, are you, about being the mother hen of this group?" Pete said he thought of himself not as a mother hen but as a real pusher. He smiled doubtfully, and said that he guessed he had better practice clucking over the weekend.

When Group II met again on Sunday night, its members were relaxed. Many of them had gone home for the weekend, or had visited New York, and they swapped anecdotes like passengers on a cruise ship after a day ashore. Several members went on to talk about how they felt after a week at Arden House. Dick said he had learned that "if you hammer too long and hard at the other fellow, he may simply throw more dirt on his earthworks." He said he had decided, moreover, to keep his mouth shut except when he had something constructive to say.

Harry, an airline executive with a somewhat emotional way of speaking, who had been hammered fairly hard by Dick during the previous week, said he was no longer mad at Dick, or at anyone else. He said he had undergone a profound transformation, and now felt wonderfully kindly toward everybody. "It's like having a number of drinks, a fine edge, and you're up there in the clouds," he said. This revelation was met with polite skepticism. "I don't think we're going to change the habits of a lifetime in two weeks," Pete said. He added, however, that he himself had changed to the extent of deciding that maybe he really was a mother hen, and that maybe this wasn't such a bad thing to be.

Why Is Steve Like Snoopy?

During the second week of the laboratory, discussions at Group II's meetings tended to be focused for long periods on the behavior of some one particular member. On Monday, for instance, most of the morning session was devoted to Steve, the industrial psychologist. He began the discussion himself by saying that some members of the group had told him privately that they felt they didn't really know him. "How come?" he asked. Several people suggested that Steve had, in effect, kept others from getting to know him by seeming to hold himself apart from and above the group. "Steve sits back there, smiling and smoking his cigar," Dick said. "Then he comes in and pounces like a cat pouncing on a mouse." Pete said the way Steve seemed to stay perched up in a tree reminded him of Snoopy, a dog in a comic strip called *Peanuts*, who sometimes pretends to be a buzzard.

Some members said they regarded Steve as a sort of "third trainer," as Dick put it. Steve said that he had made a bad slip by announcing, at the group's first meeting, that he had come to the laboratory mainly to appraise it in a professional way. Bradford suggested that perhaps this had not really been a slip. "Maybe you *want* it this way," he said. "You get respect, differentiation — but also, people see you as lurking, waiting to pounce on them."

Pete suggested that perhaps Steve now wanted "to come down out of that tree and get his hands dirty with the rest of us." Steve said he wasn't sure he knew how to do this, and in any case he wondered if he should try to change a role — that is, of guarded detachment — that he felt had served him well in his work. Pete observed that Pontius Pilate had tried to play it safe by washing his hands but hadn't succeeded. "There's risk in everything," he said earnestly, turning to Steve. "You can lose by *not* getting involved in a situation too." Steve smiled noncommittally and said nothing.

"Please, Dear Trainer, Please Don't Die . . ."

On Monday afternoon and evening the conferees took part in an exercise designed to show the superiority of "participative" management. The exercise began with a lecture on what Douglas McGregor, a professor at M.I.T., has designated as "Theory Y" — i.e., that people are more productive if they have a say in decisions affecting their work. After the lecture the conferees were split into two sections, one consisting of Groups II and IV, and the other of Groups I and III. Each of these supergroups was told to organize itself, along lines consistent with the tenets of Theory Y, into a factory for making greeting-card verses.

The exercise couldn't have worked out better from Bradford's point of view. The Group II-IV combination went all out for Theory Y. It elected no factory manager, had no straw bosses, and let everybody write the kind of greetings he liked best — that is, birthday greetings, Mother's Day greetings, or one of several specialty items also included in the specified "product mix," such as get-well verses for sick T-Group trainers. (One specimen of the last-named variety read: "Please, dear trainer, please don't die,/You haven't finished up with 'I.'") In the forty-five minutes allotted for production, an impressive total of nearly three hundred verses was turned out.

By contrast, the Group I-III combination overorganized itself. It had too many editors and production-control men, and too few writers. The latter complained that they were being kicked around, and threatened to strike. They were persuaded to stay on the job, but they turned up for their writing stint wearing lamp shades and carrying whiskey bottles. They said this getup was meant to suggest beatniks, and their point seemed to be that if the editors and other bosses were going to treat them like irresponsible beatniks, they might as well play the part. This did not make for efficient production of doggerel. When their forty-five minutes were up, they had produced fewer than half as many verses as had the Group II-IV writers, who later gathered in the bar (together with their permissive editors) to celebrate the victory they had won.

Dogmatism On Tape

Recordings had been made of all T-Group discussions, and on Tuesday evening Group II gathered to perform one of the standard rituals of T-Grouping: listening to itself on tape. But as it turned out, the group did less listening than talking.

The first passage played back included an argument about agenda and leadership, with Dick, the young man who had been worked over by the group the previous Friday, as one of the principal disputants. Dick listened intently to the playback, and when the machine had been switched off, Bradford asked if he didn't think he had sounded pretty dogmatic. "That's a loaded word," Dick said. "I had very positive views. I think I knew what I was talking about." He said he had felt it was silly not to have some sort of structure in the group, that he still felt that way, and that he wasn't going to change his mind just because eleven other people felt differently. "I don't think we're talking about leadership and structure," Bradford said. "I think we're talking about behavior — about a tendency to be more certain than it is usually possible to be in life."

Maurice, the systems engineer, said he objected strongly to any implication that criticizing other people's ideas was bad. "I submit that the Constitution of the United States was drafted in a critical atmosphere," he said. Bunker said that he and Bradford were not against criticism, "but it's a matter of increasing our range for two kinds of things, empathy and criticism." "If you're only critical, or only empathic," Bradford said, "you see only half a world." A member of the group named Don, a management consultant, referred to Dick's tendency to sound cocksure and said seriously, "Let me put it in a personal way, Dick. I've been accused of being opinionated, and often the less I know the more opinionated I am. Maybe in many situations people just can't make final judgments."

Bradford asked why the group was spending so much time on Dick. Three people gave the same reason. They said they were fond of Dick, that they thought part of his difficulty was just being young, and that they would like to help him learn not to be so rigid and dogmatic. Bunker asked Dick if he had been listening, and he said he had. But when he tried to summarize what had been said, it was clear that he hadn't heard any of the three say that they liked him. Bunker pointed this out, and Dick nodded and said quietly that it was no news to him that he had a hard time accepting affection and support. "Until you accept the fact that we care, and that you don't have to fight us, it's hard for us to help you," Bradford said as the meeting ended.

Brandy and *Alouette*

The laboratory was scheduled to come to a close on Friday, and as the day approached, the emotional climate at Group II's meetings grew warmer and more friendly. When the group met for the next-to-last time on Thursday its members drifted easily into a valedictory mood. The question was raised (but not answered) as to what the group could have done to help Steve climb down out of his tree. This led Dick to ask, in a puzzled way, how a "group" could help anyone, and whether a group really *existed* apart from its individual members. Pete said that so far as he was concerned T-Group II had a very real existence. "In this group we are safe to reveal ourselves," he said. "It has a special feeling for me — maybe sacred is too strong a word, but it's something like that."

The talk turned to ways in which people get accepted by a group. Don, the management consultant, recalled Dick's question about whether a group exists, and said, "Our acceptance of you, Dick, was furthered by the fact that you came out and asked an honest question. It was the first time you didn't have the answer to something." Bunker remarked that even though the group hadn't lured Steve down to the ground it had at least come to accept him more comfortably as a tree-sitter. When eleven o'clock came, and it was time for midmorning coffee, the group stayed seated at the table for several minutes, as though reluctant to break the spell.

On Thursday evening Arden House seemed like a ship nearing port. There were T-Group cocktail parties, and wine flowed copiously at dinner. Toasts — sometimes two at a time — were proposed to individual T-Groups and to their trainers. Just before dessert, the members of Group II paraded through the dining room calling loudly for the election of Leland Bradford as President of the United States. Later there was brandy and singing (a trainer, waving a fork, led the assembly in *Alouette*) and the day ended in cacophony and good fellowship. However, the dominant note that evening seemed different from that sounded at Group

II's meeting that morning — there was less sense of regret at imminent parting, more of relief at having survived a perilous ordeal.

Group II's last meeting on Friday morning had an anticlimactic air. Many members appeared already to have taken leave, psychologically, of Arden House, and at eleven o'clock there was no disposition to linger.

The laboratory ended, as it had begun, with a talk by Bradford. He recalled to the conferees that "we came here to engage in an adventure leading to our own growth." After the anxiety of the early days of a laboratory, he said, "we discover, sometimes for the first time in our lives, that we are with people we can trust. We learn to care about other people." He went on to suggest that the conferees could now act, with due modesty and caution, as "change agents." That is, he said, they could try to create "a climate of learning in the back-home situation" that would help others to learn some of the things they themselves had learned at Arden House. "I wish all of us a good trip — to wherever we're going," he concluded. The conferees applauded enthusiastically, and as they streamed from the lecture room, many stopped to shake hands with Bradford, who was standing, like a minister on the steps of his church, in the corridor outside.

Did Anybody Change?

The aim of laboratories, Bradford has written, is "to bring about change and improvement in the way the learner behaves back on the job." In support of their conviction that such change does in fact take place, Bradford and his associates in N.T.L. cite a follow-up study of thirty-four men and women who took part in a laboratory in the summer of 1958. Associates of these thirty-four people, most of whom were elementary-school principals, were asked to note any changes they had observed in their colleagues. Many reported that the people who had been to the laboratory had become more sensitive to others, more frank and direct in their dealings, and generally more tolerant.

But there is little else in the way of hard evidence that laboratories have any effect at all on how people behave. And even this one 1958 study has to be interpreted with caution: the people who said they saw changes in their associates may have been influenced by the knowledge that people who go off to training laboratories are *supposed* to come home more sensitive, more tolerant, etc.

For the time being, therefore, the case for laboratory training has to rest mainly on the testimony of people who have undergone it. Generally, they say that they have learned to be better listeners, or to be more aware of how they affect other people, or to be less bossy, or to be freer about expressing anger — or simply to feel less upset by anger, whether expressed by themselves or by other people. Many of them, indeed, say that the important thing is not that they behave differently since going to a laboratory, but that they *feel* different. "I am more comfortable with myself than before," a college instructor who went through a laboratory last year has written, "and believe that this comfort is having consequences for better relations with other people." Some graduates can't say what it is they have got out of a laboratory, but are enthusiastic anyway. "My boss said he got something out of this," a conferee remarked at lunch one day at Arden House. "He said he knew he's not so stupid he could stay anywhere two weeks without getting something out of it — but damned if he knew what it was."

There is, of course, a question as to whether laboratories foster groupiness at the expense of individuality. In the early years of N.T.L., laboratories were often staffed by the kind of true believers who preached that groups could always decide things better than individuals. At Arden House, however, there was little nonsense of this kind. To be sure, Bradford and some of his colleagues still seem overenthusiastic about the joys of the "participative society." But it is a fact that, for better or worse, many people do have to spend a lot of time working with groups. And it can be argued that someone who has been in a T-Group is likely to find his ability to resist group pressures strengthened rather than weakened. Furthermore, even though T-Grouping tends to emphasize such qualities as modesty, sensitivity, and group-mindedness, members of a T-Group may also gain some notion as to why many people are *not* sensitive and modest and group-minded — and thereby become more ready to listen to the arrogant boor who nevertheless happens to know what he's talking about.

In the end, what one makes of T-Groups and laboratories depends on a number of things: on how one feels about the propriety of intimate conversations staged, as it were, under institutional auspices and with a tape recorder running; on one's tolerance for talk about helping and caring and adventures in growth; and on the degree to which one shares the assumption, seemingly held by many people who serve as trainers at human-relations laboratories, that there is not much wrong with the human condition that a little social engineering cannot cure.

One last observation may be in order, though. "I was amazed," a young psychologist wrote last fall after taking part in a laboratory at Bethel, Maine, "at how each of us appeared hungry for authentic interpersonal relations. In the climate of Bethel an openness and freedom were possible which, I believe, few had experienced elsewhere." At Arden House, too, it was clear that many of the conferees were starved for a chance to talk seriously about their feelings for others, and others' feelings for them. Perhaps the most significant thing about laboratories is not what they teach, but, rather, what their popularity reveals about the decline of intimate talk in a country where guarded, if genial, impersonality is the accepted mode.

A Short History of T-Grouping

The unstructured training group, to give the T-Group its proper name — it is also known as a D (for diagnostic) Group and an ST (for sensitivity training) Group — was, appropriately, a group invention. Of the four social scientists who invented it, the best known was a German-born psychologist named Kurt Lewin. In the 1930's, Lewin and a graduate student of his named Ronald Lippitt stirred up a lot of interest with some experiments, conducted at the University of Iowa, indicating that democratically run work groups were not only pleasanter than groups run on authoritarian lines, but often more efficient too. Lewin was concerned with teaching people to lead groups (and to take part in them) more effectively, and just after the war he and some associates hit on the idea of using, as a training device, discussion groups that initially have no leaders and no agendas. Lewin died in 1947, but his colleagues were eager to try out this notion, and to do so they formed an organization called the National Training Laboratory in Group Development. It was sponsored by the National Education Association (and, for a time, by the Research Center for Group Dynamics, then located at M.I.T. but now affiliated with the University of Michigan). The new organization's director was, and still is, Leland P. Bradford, a social psychologist and a specialist in adult education, who was one of the inventors of the T-Group.

In 1947, Bradford and a faculty made up mostly of university professors organized the first of a series of so-called training laboratories. The laboratories were subsidized for some years by the Carnegie Corporation, and they were held each summer at Gould Academy, in Bethel, Maine. Each laboratory was attended by roughly a hundred "delegates," who were fed, for three weeks, a rich diet of T-Grouping, role playing, and lectures.

The atmosphere at Bethel during the late 1940's and early 1950's was pretty intoxicating. Delegates went home announcing, like converts to Moral ReArmament, that they had changed. They also seemed bent on changing other people, and often insisted on introducing their friends to the rites of role playing and leaderless meetings. These and other symptoms of cultism disturbed many people, including some who served as staff members at Bethel in the early days. Fritz Redl, a well-known psychoanalyst who was at Bethel in 1950, compared some aspects of what went on there to the popular water cures of central Europe. "This concept of 'cleansing through one bath,' which religious sects have in common with German *sprudel* spas, is seeping into our way of acting," he warned his colleagues in a memorandum. He added laconically: "Stop overplaying idea of total salvation for remainder of life through Bethel Bath."

Bradford and his associates in the National Training Laboratories, as it is now called, insist that they no longer give people emotional baths at

Bethel. Their claim is supported by the fact that latter-day Bethel graduates may say they have been helped, but seldom act as if they had been Saved.

Training laboratories have nevertheless been getting more and more popular not only with businessmen but with educators, social workers, and the like, who constituted N.T.L.'s main clientele in the early days. This summer N.T.L. is putting on a total of seven laboratories at Bethel, and it has held laboratories this past winter and spring in Barranquitas, Puerto Rico (for employees of the Puerto Rican government); at Green Lake, Wisconsin (for Protestant Church leaders); and at the Edgewater Beach Hotel in Chicago (for wives of members of the Young Presidents' Organization). Laboratories are also sponsored by a number of universities, among them Michigan, Utah, U.C.L.A., Texas, Temple, and Boston University.

It is just in the last four or five years that businessmen have become leading patrons of laboratories. Some companies have even set up laboratories of their own. Standard Oil (New Jersey), to name the outstanding example, has put more than a thousand managers and engineers at its Baton Rouge, Bayway, and Bayonne refineries through company laboratories staffed mainly by outside consultants. N.T.L. puts on some laboratories that are limited to "key executives" — that is, to presidents, vice presidents, general managers, and the like. One such laboratory is held each fall at N.T.L.'s conference center at Bethel. A brochure announcing this year's session notes discreetly that no one earning less than $25,000 a year need apply, and goes on to speak of "developing self-awareness, sensitivity . . . and understanding of group situations" while living in "a quietly elegant Colonial mansion with yawning fireplaces . . . especially charming at this time of year, with its vistas of fall's colorings blazing across the countryside."

Reflections on a T-Group Experience

WILLIAM F. GLUECK

William F. Glueck, "Reflections on a T-Group Experience," *Personnel Journal*, 47: 500–4, July, 1968. Reprinted with permission of publisher.

In the last few years, many corporations have been using sensitivity training (or T-group training) as part of their management development program. Spencer Klaw's "Two Weeks in a T-Group" in the August 1961 *Fortune*, is typical of some of the better descriptions of this training by observers present during the sessions. This article is a report by a participant of what happened to him and others in a T-group composed of middle-aged top managers of corporations and state government divisions. The purpose is to describe what went on in one such program so that personnel executives and top managers of American corporations can evaluate whether or not they should send their executives to such programs.

Sensitivity training varies in its objectives and methods. But most of it seems to set out to help the participant to gain self insight and understanding, improved understanding of others' feelings and attitudes, understanding of the behavior of groups, and the sharpening of interpersonal behavior skills.[1] For example, Greening says

> The purpose [of T-Group training] is to provide an existential setting in which participants can intensively review and possibly revise their basic views about man's nature, group behavior and roles and procedures necessary for accomplishing tasks with others.[2]

The training program in which I participated described its purpose as

> designed specifically to improve our understanding of ourselves and others, personal effectiveness and leadership qualities, to better understand individual responsibilities to ourselves and others, to improve communication and to take positive steps toward the alleviation of problems caused by misunderstanding and misinterpreting the motives of others. . . .

The program, which took place in an isolated lodge in the offseason, lasted six days. It included about nine hours per day of T-group sessions, each composed of nine persons, with recreation periods and general lectures and programs with all three T-groups together spaced in between. Thelen and Dickerman's[3] four-phase approach best describes the experience.

Phase 1: Individual Centered

For the first day, we focused on ourselves and others in the room as individuals. The trainers used exercises to shift our attention from our

---

[1]See, for example:

Warren G. Bennis, "Goals and Meta-Goals of Laboratory Training" in Warren Bennis *et al.* (eds.) *Interpersonal Dynamics* (Homewood, Illinois: The Dorsey Press, 1964), pp. 692–98.

Edgar Schein and Warren Bennis, *Personal and Organizational Change Through Group Methods* (New York: John Wiley & Sons, 1965), p. 37.

Robert Tannenbaum, Irving Wechsler, and Fred Massarik, *Leadership and Organization* (New York: McGraw-Hill Co., 1961), Chapter 9.

[2]Thomas Greening, "Sensitivity Training: Cult or Contribution?", *Personnel*, Vol. 41, p. 21. (See Part Six, "Buyer Beware," for this article. — Ed.)

[3]Herbert Thelen and Watson Dickerman, "The Growth of a Group," in Warren Bennis *et al.* (Eds.), *The Planning of Change* (New York: Holt, Rinehart, and Winston, 1962), pp. 340–47.

everyday life to this. In our first general session exercise, each T-group was told to form two teams. These groups had to prepare two exhibits for "The World's Fair of the Imagination: 1967," without using verbal communication. Each group was given a table of materials such as crepe paper, paste, ribbons, and balloons to use for this purpose.

At first, most of us laughed and were puzzled about the exercise. Then one member of our group drew a picture of a possible exhibit and we began to build it. Other groups seemed to be working individually and without a plan. One member of our group, Ben, did not enter into these activities, but watched us in bemused silence.

After time was up, each group explained its project, examined the other projects and retired to the T-group rooms.

This exercise served several purposes: it took us away from typical experiences (to "unfreeze" us and perhaps open us up to new experiences) and gave us an opportunity to observe each other. In the T-group room, the trainer (Sam) said: "I am here to help you if I can and I know the week will be useful." He sat back, lit his pipe, and waited. Nothing happened, so I suggested each of us describe his position, background, and himself. A group member (Frank) took about fifteen minutes to do this. As he was talking, Sam made his first intervention by abruptly asking (in the middle of Frank's sentence), "Is this the way we want to spend our time here?" Most of us said, "Yes," and Frank continued. Frank then said he had an inferiority complex. Sam scoffed and said, "Anyone who can talk this long about himself doesn't have that problem." Frank shortened his self-description and the rest of the self-descriptions got progressively shorter under this prodding. Then, Sam intervened again. He said, "Maybe we'd like to talk about the exercise earlier this evening. Did any of you have any comments on it?" Many of the group made comments like, "Well, it was like returning to kindergarten, etc." I said, "Ben did not participate." Typical of his response, Sam said, "How did you feel about that?" Several people said they didn't like it. Ben explained that he had not participated because the whole thing seemed silly to him. The group began asking him why he felt this way. Perhaps they did so because they had participated, even if some of them felt a bit silly.

Much of the next day was frustrating and boring. Several members of the group discussed auto safety, music, etc. Sam attempted to shift the discussion to the people in the group and away from these "extraneous" issues. I couldn't help but wonder: "Have I come 1200 miles for this?" In my frustration, I would occasionally make remarks similar to Sam's, asking such things as, "Is auto safety really important here?" Many of these were in question form. Sam began criticizing me for this. Initially, he was relatively mild. He would say, "Don't ask questions — make statements." Later, he almost shouted at me, "Quit acting like a high

school teacher. Be more of a college professor. Make statements —
don't ask questions."

That night, there was a group session. It involved listening to music in
the dark, and swaying to it to "experience our bodies." This time I did
not participate. It seemed ridiculous to take off my shoes and do this
and no one challenged me.

Phase 2: Frustration and Conflict Over Stereotypes

About this time, and at Sam's insistence, we began to describe what
kinds of people we thought we had in our T-group. I began to ask myself
which individuals I liked, which I didn't. The group tried to decide what
type of man the participant was by asking him about something he said
or stating an impression they had about him. The group would confront
him with one of his statements. This member would become defensive,
and the group would press him on it. He would then explain himself. Then
the group would reassure him of their interest in him by giving him
suggestions for improvement. For example, one participant (Johnny) was
perceived by the group to be shy. Then Sam began to push him. "The
trouble with you, Johnny, is that you have no 'guts.' " After elaborating
on this for a while, Sam told Johnny to express non-verbally his feeling
for others in the group. Johnny went around the group shaking hands.
He inadvertently did not shake Sam's hand. When this happened, Sam
said, "Hey, what about me — aren't I a part of this group?" Johnny came
back and jokingly motioned a kick toward Sam (as Sam had done in
good humor before). In another case, a participant (let us call him Hal)
was perceived as talkative. So Sam said, "Hal, you're just a frustrated
preacher. Stand up on that chair and preach us a one-minute sermon on
love." When this talk was over, there were one-minute sermons on several
other topics.

At least partially because of Sam's methods, several members left the
training center and returned to their jobs. Only six remained.

The experience I remember the best was my own. At some point in
Phase 1, I had expressed the opinion that I, as an academician, had less
formal power in society than the executives in the group. About this time,
one participant observed that I was probably one of the trainers. This I
denied, of course, but at that point realized that I had unintentionally
imitated some of Sam's criticism and methods. On the fifth day, I
realized that all the others in the group had been "analyzed." *Later*, I
realized that my turn was next. Unconsciously, I steered the conversation
to the Viet Nam War. After about an hour of this, Sam blew up. He
accused me of deliberately diverting the group. Several others observed
that I had been the loudest in protesting the "auto safety" talks and now
I had done the equivalent myself.

Sam then used an intervention technique. He asked us to line up (with no talking) in the order of the individual who contributed the most to least to the T-Group. I placed myself near the end of the line, for I realized I had not participated much and did not see myself as too influential. The group placed me last. Sam then asked us to sit down. He looked at me and said, "How did you feel about being last?" I said, "I'm not surprised." He said, "Is that all?" I said, "Yes." He said, "Did you like it?" I said, "No, but I expected it."

But really, secretly, I didn't expect to be *last*. As I sat there thinking, though, I realized that I had made few real contributions to the group per se. Sam then said "You who were so interested in power, you don't have any here. Don't try to kid me that you liked it." My defense was, "Well, as I observed before, academics have little power. The group lined up in order of most to least powerful roles in society."

"And you had nothing to do with it — *you* are, of course, not to blame" — Sam observed very sarcastically. "Oh, come off it, you're nothing but a high school teacher." He continued this abuse for a while. Then a member observed, "Of all the people in this room, I think you are the least likely to be elected to public office." [This was beginning to bother me. I had been elected to several offices in college with no problem. I began to say to myself, "This is a farce — they are not seeing me at all — they are criticizing the wrong guy."]

The emotion shifted now. I had had more interaction with two members (call them Ron and Don) than most. They began to say soothing things to me. Ron began to ask me about my background. I explained some aspects of my youth, and several critical decisions for me — a change in career and religion. During this discussion, I watched the other participants. They began nodding as I spoke and they seemed to be very interested. When I had finished, they began making remarks such as, "Well, now I can better understand how he acts," etc. Shortly after this we went to lunch. I then went to my room. My mind was whirling. My previous feelings that the experience was frustrating returned. These were reinforced now by the feeling that the abuse and boredom were not worth it, for they were attacking a personality that was not the "real" me.

Phase 3: Attempted Consolidation and Group Harmony

About the second half of the fifth day, the emphasis shifted. Group cohesion seemed to be developing. This came about partly in self-defense. Three of our group had left the program. Other T-Groups made remarks to us about "putting up with Sam's actions." The man who organized the program came into our T-Group and confronted Sam with several accusations: poor tactics, loss of members, etc. The group supported Sam against the "outsider."

A general session was used to express our newly formed shared values — "The Profession of Faith," I called it. Small groups were organized by dividing up the T-Groups. Then spokesmen from each were asked to tell the group session their feelings about the program. The statements became progressively stronger about how meaningful, important, wonderful, challenging, the program was.

One of the participants (who had just told me he had that day fired half his sales force, and was requiring lie-detector tests of his employees now and as a condition of future employment) stated that he had learned to trust people because of the program. My doubts of the program were growing. I felt like the little boy in "The King's New Clothes" Fable — Wasn't the king naked? Wasn't this program a bit unreal?

Yet, real emotions did get expressed. Several members of my group knew of my doubts and felt I might leave the group (as I was indeed contemplating). They were seriously concerned. One said, "You know, I began to understand my brother in listening to you. Please stay in the group. You are now making a real contribution." I went to Sam and told him that if this was intended to teach us sensitivity to others, he apparently was not sensitive to me regarding some of his methods. He was very apologetic and encouraged me to stay (as he had encouraged the others who subsequently left). His motives were mixed, I felt, but I liked the group's expression, so I stayed.

Phase 4: Individual Self-Assessment

The last phase involved self-reflection on strengths and weaknesses. Sam began to emphasize the positive side of our behavior from his vantage point. The last evening, the group encouraged him to give some suggestions and impressions of each member. It was an unique experience. Lying on the floor, looking up at the ceiling, and in an almost dark room, he told his "stories." In my case, he told a story of how he had driven to a wedding of a friend with the convertible top down (in mid-winter) and the night before his most important doctoral examinations. He stayed longer than he should have because the friend asked him to, drove back to the University arriving in the middle of the exams and passed with flying colors. He told me later that he felt I was trying too hard, trying to be too rational, working too hard. That with much less effort, and more time for fun and family, I would do as well or better and be a better human being.

Evaluation of Sensitivity Training

The best way to evaluate the program is to do so in light of its objectives. The objectives which this T-Group seemed to work towards were: a better understanding of the self and improved interpersonal skills. The objectives were to be attained by a more realistic understanding of how each of us was perceived by other group members. As I initially reflected on some of the criticism of Sam and the group, I rejected them as not applying to the "real" me. But later, it hit me. They had seen a side of me. As I looked at myself as honestly as I could, I realized that I had moods and days like the behavior they had seen. Perhaps, I liked to believe it wasn't the predominant mood, but only others could tell me that. And the fact was that when I was in those moods, in that behavior pattern, I would elicit similar responses from colleagues, friends, students. I had not received these criticisms in the past because few would feel free to discuss their responses with me. And even if they did, I might rationalize it away.

If they had not seen the predominant mood, this was my fault. My caution in showing myself had prevented them from assessing my total personality. It is irrelevant that the group might not have had the time to see all of that. Yet they can help those aspects they do see. And I, as a group member, could help the other group members. As corny as it may seem, and even with my predispositions to be careful, I developed a strong interest in and desire to help some members of the group.

Sensitivity training is an unique experience, coming closest to a religious retreat. But even in a retreat, it is a self-analysis or perhaps a dialogue with a counselor. I don't believe any other type of training can have the impact on a participant that T-group training can.

The negative feelings I have about the experience are related to the trainer. I did not like the language, the pyrotechniques and interventions he used. He took over the group and I think we could have done better with less interference from him. Perhaps we left a void for him to step into initially and did not take over later. So again, it may have been our fault. On balance, however, I'm convinced the training is very useful. It satisfied its objectives of better self-awareness, better understanding of the feelings of others, provided an opportunity for me to revise my attitudes and (hopefully) to attempt to modify my behavior towards others. To the extent that I do so, I will be more effective in my interpersonal relationships.

Who should participate in sensitivity training? After my experience, I believe that two conditions are critical:

1. The willingness or ability to expose one's personality to others;
2. The degrees of interpersonal effectiveness necessary for successful performance on the job.

I do not believe that people whose positions do not involve a great deal of interpersonal activity and/or someone who has difficulty in revealing himself will gain much from the experience. In fact, they may lose something in it: the personality "props" may be weakened, and in some cases no replacing strengtheners are given.

After all, the training is expensive in time and fees. The most likely executive for a T-Group I believe is one who is open about himself, knows relatively little about the importance of interpersonal relations on a job, and whose job requires interpersonal expertise.

Anyone interested in such training should contact such reliable sources as the American Management Association or the National Training Laboratories.

Psychoanalytic Notes on T-Groups at the Human Relations Laboratory, Bethel, Maine

LOUIS A. GOTTSCHALK

Louis A. Gottschalk, "Psychoanalytic Notes on T-Groups at the Human Relations Laboratory, Bethel, Maine," *Comprehensive Psychiatry*, 7: 472–87, December, 1966. Reprinted by permission of author, publisher and editor.

The insights derived from psychoanalytic practice and theory have been applied to the understanding of literature, art, music, group psychology, somatic disease, criminality, and to countless other phenomena. A youthful phenomenon has appeared on the national scene which seems to have great potential for influencing human attitudes and behavior. This is the training group or T-group which is an essential part of the Human Relations Laboratories sponsored by the National Education Association. A study of T-groups from the psychoanalytic point of view is warranted for a number of reasons. Like psychoanalysis, the T-group's function is to create insight into one's interpersonal relations. Secondly, the T-group has become in recent years increasingly highly regarded by management and labor groups in industry, by civic leaders, by social scientists, and by educators as a valid and effective means of teaching individuals both fundamental and subtle factors promoting and hindering human relationships. Thirdly, the T-group procedure is capable of evoking dramatic psychopathological reactions in individuals, as well as more favorable responses, all within a relatively short period of time — that is, one or two weeks. Lastly, the T-group procedure includes one or two features which simulate certain aspects of the psychoanalytic procedure itself; hence, this provides a possibility of exploring the potency and effect of such procedural features in a different context from that of psychoanalytic treatment.

The T-Group Situation — Early Phases

The Initial Procedure

The starting procedure in the T-group has been described much more fully elsewhere.[1,2,9] I will only sketch it here. The procedure is one which provides a minimum number of cues to the participants in the group on how to proceed. The T-group situation has been called, in fact, the "leaderless group." The group interaction may be initiated in a variety of ways by an individual called a "trainer." One example of how the group process may be launched is by a short statement from the trainer that name tags are on the table to identify who each member is, thereby suggesting that each group member select or write out an identifying name tag and place it in front of himself as the trainer has done. The trainer may introduce himself by his first name, thus encouraging everyone to be on a first name familiarity with each other. He might then say that he understands that everyone present has come to the laboratory to learn about groups and his functioning in groups, and that he hopes that observations of what happens will provide everyone with what he wants from the experience. Thereupon the trainer may lapse into expectant silence. The new T-group member is usually not advised that he will be expected to learn what he wants, not from formal lectures or readings, but from careful observation of the behavior of himself and others in attempting to lend a semblance of organization and order to a life situation which possesses all the ingredients for a group except a modus operandi and a definitive leader. The trainer functions, not to provide the operational guidelines, but to point out and help the group members become aware of what is happening.

Early Phases of the T-Group Situation

In their effort to supply structure where it is absent, group members vie with one another to propose a program of operation, an organization and rules of procedure. However, to do so each group member falls back on his personal experiences of how groups should function, and each participant attempts to set up the organization of the group in a way that fits his experience, inadvertently attempting to reproduce in the T-group his typical role and function in other groups. Other group members are at the same time attempting to fill in the leadership gap and to set up their concept of group organization. In this competition there is a vying for leadership. Individual approaches which are proposed that do not take into consideration the individuality of each group member but rather tend to force the other members into a mould, stemming from one's previous private experiences in other different groups, are met with opposition and challenge. The self-centered individual, the manipulator, the person who neglects to keep his fingers on the pulse of each individual in the group, the rebel for rebellion's sake, the peacemaker, the person who characteristically stays on the sidelines — all these personality types and others reveal themselves to the group. If they are attuned to the feedback available from other group members, they will be offered a reflection of themselves as they perform in their customary roles.

From my observations the reflection is usually distorted rather than clear and sharp, for the reflecting surface of these human mirrors is roughened and distorted by the perceiver's own opinions, values, and emotional conflicts.

The Extent of My Personal Experience with T-Groups

The Schedule of a Typical Human Relations Laboratory

My impressions of T-groups were obtained during attendance at a Human Relations Laboratory during the summer of 1964 at Bethel, Maine, and from discussions in 1965 and 1966 of my observations with T-group trainers on the faculty of the University of Cincinnati.

The overall schedule of a typical Human Relations Laboratory covers a period of 2 weeks. The schedule of the one I attended is described in Tables 1 and 2.

Table 1. — *Human Relations — Lab: First Week Schedule*

	Monday	Tuesday	Wednesday	Thursday	Friday
8:00	.... BREAKFAST				
8:45	T-Group	T-Group	T-Group	T-Group	T-Group
10:45	...... COFFEE			...... COFFEE	
11:00	Self-Confrontation		Observation	Research	Research
11:30	Self-Confrontation Session			Feedback	
12:00					
12:30	.... LUNCH				
1:30		Large Groups	T-Groups	Large Groups	
			Observation		
3:30		FREE		FREE	
6:30	.... DINNER				
7:30	T-Group	T-Group	FREE	T-Group	T-Group
9:30					

Table 2. — *Human Relations — Lab: Second Week Schedule*

Sunday	Monday	Tuesday	Wednesday	Thursday	Friday
8:00	.... BREAKFAST				
8:45	General session 9:15	T-Group	T-Group	T-Group	CLOSING
10:45	Small group	COFFEE		COFFEE	
11:00	experiment 11:30		Observation		SESSION
	Small group discussion	T-Group		Research	
12:00	.... LUNCH				
12:30	.... Large Groups				
1:30	.... FREE				
3:30	.... DINNER				
6:30					
7:30	T-Group	T-Group	FREE	T-Group	
9:30					

In the first week, as indicated in Table 1, each participant was involved in group activity. There were 8 hours of "large groups," which involved application of the T-group procedure to all eight T-groups (comprising about 100 individuals) in this Human Relations Laboratory. During the time period designated as T-group observation (5+ hours), the T-groups observed each other at work. During the "self-confrontation" sessions (two ½-hour periods), individuals reviewed privately their reactions and observations during the earlier T-group sessions and these self-confrontations were discussed within the T-groups for two ½-hour periods. The "research" periods (totalling 2 hours) involved filling out forms providing information useful in the assessment of attitudinal and emotional change during the course of the T-groups sessions.

In the second week (see Table 2) there were about 16–18 hours of small T-group activities and 8 hours of the large T-group activities. Again there was another period (about 3½ hours) of T-groups observing each other in action.

General Reactions Noted in the T-Groups, with Special Attention to Psychopathological Reactions

My impressions of the range and types of reactions to T-groups are based on participation in one small T-group (containing 13 people) and one large T-group (100 people), on the observation of two other T-groups, and on discussion with many participants in other T-groups at this Human Relations Laboratory Session. It is quite unlikely that what I have had the opportunity to observe provides a valid picture of the average incidence of participant reactions, but I am assuming that what I observed is an example of the range of reactions possible. I have been told, in fact, by people very active in group work of this sort that the incidence of psychopathological reactions I observed in T-groups was unusually high.

Let me first describe briefly some general observations with respect to reactions of participants in the T-group procedure. After doing so, I will attempt to account for these reactions. My principal observation is that the T-group sets up a powerful situation which is capable of evoking many kinds of dramatic reactions in individuals. Most of these reactions involve more than a mild exaggeration of the typical psychopathological traits of the participants.

For instance, in T-group #2, the group in which I participated, out of 11 participants (and two trainers) there occurred: one borderline acute psychotic withdrawal reaction; two severe emotional breakdowns with acute anxiety, crying and temporary departure from the group; one sadistic and exhibitionistic behavior pattern; two marked isolation and withdrawal reactions with lack of participation in the group (six obviously acute pathological emotional reactions).

In T-group #3, one of the groups I observed, of 10 participants (and one trainer) there occurred: one frank psychotic reaction; two severe depressive reactions with anxiety and withdrawal; two withdrawal reactions and nonparticipation (five obviously acute pathological emotional reactions).

In T-group #1, the other group I observed, composed of 11 participants and two trainers, there occurred the least untoward emotional reactions: two mild anxiety reactions and two mild to moderate depressive reactions.*

With the careful selection of participants now occurring (although the sponsoring National Education Association does no formal psychiatric screening), a procedure and situation which can evoke such pathological personality reactions of these types and intensities is indeed worth examining closer. The T-group is a situation which is promoted, not as a kind of therapy, but as an educational experience, which lasts only 2 weeks and which employs no psychotomimetic drugs and no obviously stressful features. Yet it becomes psychiatrically disrupting (possibly only acutely and transiently) to almost half of the participants in some groups. However, it undoubtedly promotes the self-esteem and sense of achievement of the other half of the participants in these groups, for they

---

*To check my diagnostic evaluations of the incidence of psychopathological reactions in group #1, I corresponded with one of the participants of this group who is a psychiatrist (Dr. Warden Rimel) to get his impression. He corroborated my general impression, adding that one of the participants who was depressed lost 11 pounds during the 2-week period and that he rarely slept over 2 or 3 hours per night during the first eight days, but that everyone was "quite well recovered" by the end of the workshop period. He suggested the diagnostic designation of "acute situational reactions characterized by anxiety and/or depression" to describe these responses in group #1.

report feeling as well and comfortable as they were or even better before the T-group experience. Such a phenomenon demands closer scrutiny, if only from the viewpoint of research in how to influence people to mental health and mental illness.

Factors Which May Account for High Reactability of the Participants in T-Groups

The Official Prelaboratory Public Relations Information

Most of the participants of the Human Relations Laboratories come to the scene with mixed but relatively high expectations of having a favorable and exciting learning experience. A number of factors account for this high readiness and anticipation.

1. Many participants have learned about "group dynamics" from other individuals who have attended the laboratories at Bethel or elsewhere. Enthusiastic participants appear to be the most voluble ones and those who have had disturbing or unpleasant experiences tend to keep their experiences to themselves to avoid being nonconformists. For instance, in the psychiatric literature the author has encountered principally commendatory and glowing reports which contain few, if any, adversely critical comments about the events and experiences occurring at these "group dynamics" laboratories.[3,7,10,11] Furthermore, enthusiastic participants who have been to Bethel are inclined to talk about their experiences to their colleagues in enthusiastic terms and to arouse hopes in interested listeners that they too will have similar gratifying experiences if they attend.* The unenthusiastic participants are not likely to publicize their reservations about T-groups, especially individuals who have been emotionally traumatized by the experience.

2. Even in instances where high-level management in industrial firms or government organizations have ordered or strongly recommended that certain key individuals in management or employee or public relations attend human relations laboratories, in effect giving these individuals little or no freedom of choice, they have been exhorted to attend by the citing of personal or other anecdotes relating how the laboratories exerted favorable influences. Frequently, such a corporation or organization assumes all the financial obligations of the training expenses (tuition, $225.; room and board, $150.; 2 weeks' absence from work, etc.), which implicitly signifies to most cost-conscious business administrators that

---

*Similar effects have been described elsewhere: for example, the "hello-goodbye" effect which refers to the tendency of persons seeking help to overestimate their difficulties early in a treatment (to justify their need for the procedure) and to underestimate their problems at the end of treatment (to indicate gratitude for the therapist's efforts).[4]

the sponsoring organization has solid expectations of a profitable experience and a beneficial behavioral change for the employee.

Several such participants spontaneously reported to the writer that they saw no organization-wise beneficial interpersonal behavioral changes or improvement in many of their business colleagues who had attended human relations laboratories, although sometimes such individuals reported they felt more comfortable in group activities.

3. The printed brochures and advertisements of the National Training Laboratories (N.T.L.) help set the stage of expectations for prospective participants in the Human Relations Laboratory. These brochures relate in a subdued, professionally authoritative tone, and in an appealing way, why participation (in group activities) is crucial to personal, community, and national life, what are reasons for nonparticipation, and what are some of the kinds of changes that seem to be needed to promote more widespread participation and a higher quality of participation. (See, for example, the *Human Relations Training News*, 1963–1964.) Other publications of the N.T.L. announce that the Human Relations Laboratory helps one discover oneself and find one's place in the group. Into this attractive package, acquirable in the short space of 2 weeks, is thrown the respectability and academic sanction that comes with the news that attendance at the laboratory can count for academic credit from the University of Maine (for a small additional charge).

All the publications of the N.T.L. come out under the sponsorship of the National Education Association and they uniformly have a serious, usually polished and articulate presentation. Furthermore, the liberal sprinkling of article and book advertisements on group activities and "sensitivity" training show the fine handiwork of skillful and perceptive public relations craftsmanship.

The Physical Setting

Imagine a concentrated learning experience taking place in a milieu where the weather is comfortable (summer temperature daily range 45–80 degrees), where some of this nation's most beautiful scenery abounds (Bethel, Maine; Lake Arrowhead, California; Cedar City, Utah), where population is sparse, and where there are no competing cultural distractions — except Nature's beauty and the companionship of fellow participants. There you have the Human Relations Laboratory. Actually, there is no appearance of contrivance by the N.T.L., but the setting of the prospective learning experience enhances the expectant attitude of pleasurable anticipation of everyone except the most misanthropic and pessimistic person. It is probably unlikely that any of the latter kinds of individuals attend a N.T.L. session, for such individuals would not be likely to be attracted to training in group dynamics.

Other Information Cues Impinging on the Participants from Outside the T-Group

It is quite possible to overlook or ignore potent extra-laboratory group cues shaping the participant's expectations and mental set operating within the human relations group to which he has been assigned. These cues originate outside the participant's Human Relations Laboratory group and reach him at intervals when his own T-group is not meeting. The potency of these cues is enhanced for every participant who is seeking some ideas for structure and for an agenda about what might and should occur within the time periods when the T-group is in session.

It was my impression that practically every participant in the T-groups fought strenuously for an organization, for leadership, and for a meaning in the T-group situation, which most of the time had no definitive leadership, explicit goal, or agreed-upon rules of procedure. Outside cues were sought from what previous participants (i.e., alumni) have reported, from abundant reading material in the large loose-leaf notebook provided each participant by the N.T.L. at the beginning of the Human Relations Session, and from the research team and research instruments attempting to evaluate the individual and social changes occurring in the T-groups.

Most participants in T-groups have heard, directly or indirectly before their first T-group experience, from other participants about the unstructured nature of the groups, and they have usually inquired about strategies used by others to organize the group's activities into some purposeful or goal-directed process. After they became involved in the T-group and the lack of structure began to make them feel anxious, they were likely to try anything within the repertoire provided by their own experience or hearsay. Soon they customarily introduced an idea or action which a helpful advisor had told them did the trick in his group. These strategies, though not in the least time-tested or proved, usually involved a formula which was supposed to induce group participation and involvement.

> For example, one member of a group, irritated by the slow steps her group was taking to become cohesive and organized, stood up and lectured to the other members what an ex-T-group participant had told her about how to get the group going. "Tell them what you do and what you are interested in and ask them to tell you about themselves," she repeated, as if these statements might be the magic she needed to guide the group to follow her organizing leadership. Though the other members, at the moment, ignored her exhortations because she emphasized her own interests and accomplishments rather than manifesting serious interest in the other members, the group did later get around to telling each other about themselves.
>
> Another T-group member made it a point to introduce questions such as, "How does a group come to make decisions?" or "How does a group decide who is to be a leader?" He admitted later that he was told by a T-group alumnus that these are major issues with which T-groups work.

I suggest that some of these phenomena are reminiscent of what occurs in the formalized but agenda-free atmosphere of the classical psycho-analytic situation. The psychoanalytic patient responds to the lack of direction and guidelines from the analyst with a selection (presumably while free-associating) of content that fits his stereotypes of what is expected of him. And these stereotypes are influenced by the firsthand revealed confidences of ex-analysands and portrayals of psychoanalysis in television, radio and theatre, and fiction. The point I am making is that, in unstructured situations, an individual tends to supply his concept of what is missing and, in so doing, first draws from all available recent sources, valid and invalid, to supply some order, meaning, organization, structure, and purpose.

The Trainer in the T-Group

The Position of the T-Group Trainer. An ethic is promulgated in the T-group — rarely, if ever, contradicted by any trainers I observed — that the group should be trusted and can be trusted. There is an implication moreover, no more than an implication certainly, that the trainers in a T-group have not only the sanction and blessing but the stamp of approval of the National Training Laboratories as wise, experienced teachers of group dynamics, counsellors, and emotionally well-adjusted individuals.

Unfortunately, just as the distortions of the group members enter into the group processes, the unresolved emotional conflicts, the private value judgements, etc., of the T-group trainers may obtrude themselves into the group process. These colorful contributions to the group activities need not in themselves be a cause for concern, for the music of groups in real life has its cacophony and dissonances. But a participant in the T-group has the idea, somehow, that the group-appointed trainer, as any other group-appointed leader, has some way of checking and correcting deep-seated neurotic conflicts or blind spots, or of refraining from not enforcing his own private value judgements or orientations, unless invited to do so, on the other group members. But there is apparently not yet a satisfactory system for such check-outs for trainers. Few have ever had a personal psychoanalysis, so that this avenue is not available for repeatedly exploring pathological countertransference reactions or other neurotically determined attitudes or behavior. Each trainer goes through several T-groups himself, but one has the misgiving that this procedure selects the more extraverted, self-confident, and socially proficient individuals, but guarantees nothing about the trainer's acumen with respect to recognizing and preventing the development of disrupting emotional breakdowns in T-group members nor his ability to examine critically and discover his role in permitting or even inciting such to occur.

This may sound like a strong indictment. It is not intended to be one, for I cannot say with confidence that the evidence is all in. It is, indeed, an expression of concern and a note of caution.

Theoretical orientation of the typical T-group trainer: Trainers for the National Training Laboratories have a variety of academic backgrounds, including major training in education, psychology, philosophy, and psychiatry. The number who are professional psychiatrists are few. During the Human Relations Laboratory which I attended, I noted only two of the trainers who were psychiatrists. Although I run the risk of inviting the criticism that I have a professional bias or condescension toward nonmedically trained confreres, a criticism that is quite invalid, the psychodynamic perceptiveness and comprehension of most of the trainers I had the opportunity to observe at work was wanting.* This was quite possibly due largely to lack of interest in psychoanalytically oriented theory of human behavior, and, indeed, most of the trainers had some other type of theoretical orientation to the individual and group phenomena being observed. The relative merit of different theoretical orientations to individual and group psychology is largely an empirical question that will require considerable time to resolve, and hence it is useless to debate such an issue here. But I am assuming that a psychoanalytic frame of reference has at least the assurance of directing an observer's attention to some significant and pertinent group events and behavioral and verbal sequences that may possibly be overlooked by observers without a psychoanalytic orientation.

The relevance of extra-T-group activities and contacts: The trainers appear to disregard or deal in a desultory fashion with the effect of extra T-group contacts with group members. Between T-group sessions, trainers may enjoy many different kinds of activities with T-group members. They may eat meals with, indulge in sports with, drink beer with T-group members. The strict rules of psychoanalysis against contacts outside therapeutic sessions of analyst with patient — the role of abstinence — are largely disregarded in Human Relations Laboratories, though there appears to be an arrangement set up to have trainers eat most of their meals separately from the T-group members.

On one occasion, one of the trainers explained to the group he and the other trainers would have to leave the T-group session promptly at 12:00 noon in order to attend a luncheon meeting of trainers. Other group members protested the trainers' trying to decide termination time for the group's activities without discussing the matter with the total group. After some discussion, someone proposed to drive the trainers to their luncheon appointment, which would enable them to remain with the group about 15 minutes after the noontime hour, so there could be some flexibility in the T-group

*All 15 trainers of the Human Relations Laboratory I attended participated in the large T-group (100 people) in which I was a member.

plans for an exact time to close their morning sessions. The group, on this day, did not close its morning session until 12:05, and the trainers were driven to their luncheon by one of the group members. At least two more times thereafter, the trainers asked to use this group member's car to attend a luncheon meeting, on one occasion borrowing the car and driving it to their destination. These good turns ingratiated this group member with the trainers and made it difficult for the trainers to be critically assertive of him in the T-group; immediately before these series of events they had been so, and not thereafter. Other T-group members did not witness these extra-group contacts or some of the others I personally had, and yet they were not brought into the group's verbal interchanges. I learned of many extra-group contacts of trainers with group members or of group members with group members, only a few of which were discussed and then only casually and briefly mentioned in the group interactions. The fact that there was very scant and haphazard processing of such extra-group encounters inside the group, so that all group members had the same data to survey and analyze and work with, probably added to the varying appraisals group members had about the meaning and nature of interpersonal events witnessed during the T-group sessions. People simply had access to differing data, as well as being inclined, quite often, to react to exactly the same human relation events in differing ways.

I do not think it is reasonable to advise that extra-T-group contacts of Human Relations Labs be avoided or minimized, as in the psychoanalytic procedure. The extra-group contacts, indeed, may be more useful and conducive to the significant changes thought to occur as a result of T-group attendance. But they certainly cannot be ignored as affecting the course of T-group events and increasing the variance of attitudes and behaviors noted within the T-group horizon. Conceivably there should be developed some way of recording these events and examining their influence on behavior within the T-group.

The typical viewpoint of trainers towards the expression of emotions: The trainers were observed to treasure, by precept and example, the expression within the group situation of positive or negative affects thought to be experienced by a group member. A recurring method trainers used to convey such attitudes was by making statements such as: "I feel you are angry with me" or "I feel you are afraid to be friendly with me." High priority was given to the facility to report such feelings or inferences.

Unfortunately, the appropriateness of such feelings — that is, whether they were commensurate to some precipitating circumstance — seemed to be largely ignored. Indeed, when one of the trainers repeatedly and incorrectly imputed certain strong feelings to one of the participants which he genuinely denied experiencing, the trainer insisted that he personally felt that the participant had such feelings. For a while the trainer argued that his perception of another person's emotions was tantamount to an accurate and objective appraisal of this emotion.

Typically, the trainers emphasized the importance of recognizing emotions by their comments that it was important for individuals to identify their own emotional reactions and that of others, that it was important to pay attention to nonverbal as well as verbal cues signifying the presence of emotions, and that it was useful to be aware of and label accurately subjective cues pertinent to emotional states and reactions. As mentioned previously, there were usually no attempts by the trainers to question the appropriateness or rationality of emotional reactions. On rare occasions comments were heard from the trainers questioning or actually disapproving certain provocative emotional displays of group members. The latter kinds of statements by the two trainers in group #2 did not appear until the last two laboratory sessions, and these comments came forth as a summary personality survey presented to any group member who formally invited the group and trainers to provide "feedback" with respect to how the person was seen and experienced in the group situation. Needless to say, some of these statements were as revealing of the personality of the observer as they were of the observed.

The conflicts among trainers over whether or not T-groups are engaged in psychotherapy: Some of the trainers were found to have naive stereotypes of psychotherapy, and if certain behaviors fitting this stereotype were avoided, the T-group activities did not count as psychotherapy. One of these stereotypes was that whenever a group member discussed past experiences he was trying to avoid discussing some aspect of his interpersonal relationship in the present situation (occasionally, but certainly not invariably, a valid interpretation) and/or he was trying to change the goal of the T-group experience to a psychotherapeutic goal. Presumably the latter conception was based on the idea that psychotherapists always try to trace back an individual's present-day attitudes and behaviors to past events, and, hence, when a group member spontaneously begins to discuss pre-T-group events of his life in detail he is trying to transform the T-group situation into a kind of psychotherapeutic procedure.

The trainers in my T-group explicitly stated that the goal of the T-group was not, certainly, a psychotherapeutic one. Such a notion and reaction on the part of these trainers struck this T-group participant as paradoxical when the same trainers in another context recommended the T-group experience as a useful procedure to change the behavior of a chronically overbearing and dominating business executive back home in the office of one of the participants in our T-group.

Some of the other trainers explained this apparent contradiction by stating that the group dynamics of the T-group was an educational experience, a learning experience which was in contrast to the experience occurring in psychotherapy. Apparently realizing that such a distinction is inadequate and that all psychotherapies have educational and, hence, learning features, other trainers stated frankly they did not see any clearcut distinctions between group psychotherapy (or individual psychotherapy) and T-group work with regards to the dimension of psychotherapy.

The pressure from trainers of T-group participants on participants to change their attitudes or behavior: In contrast to most psychotherapies in which an individual requests to be changed in some respect — to be relieved of some distressing symptoms or what he regards as some personality or behavioral deficiency — the T-group participant does not regularly frame his goal in such terms, but rather claims to want to learn about groups, his behavior in groups, and how to improve (in some way or another) his functioning in groups. When the T-group is under way, many T-group participants find that they are being induced to change in ways they did not anticipate. They find that the trainer and various group members are calling upon them to stop certain ways of behaving, talking, thinking and feeling, and different ways of behaving are being prescribed. The pressure of the group and trainer may not necessarily be in the same direction and this may be made explicit. Or the trainer's silence may be taken as a sanction and endorsement or recommendation for behavioral change, made by one participant with regard to another, when it is not meant to be so.

Some of the T-group participants may become seriously emotionally upset in getting such pressure to alter their identity, especially when they did not recognize this identity as a problem or difficulty and when they had not even thought of trying to modify some aspects of their identity.

The nature of the trainer's comments on the T-group process with special attention to the problem of consensus and accuracy. Time and again the trainers described what they thought was going on in the small and large groups, and their consensus with other members of the group was low, whenever time was taken to check out the impressions of other members of the group on this matter.

Another type of reliability check of the interpretive comments of the trainers was the comparative evaluation of two psychoanalysts who by chance were both members of the same group.* The two psychoanalysts almost always agreed in their appraisal of what was happening at any particular time, whenever they happened to confer on the subject after any small or even large T-group session. All discussions they had on such matters were haphazard and irregular, but, nevertheless, their joint impression was that they could agree with the trainers in their T-group only about 50 per cent of the time on the evaluation of the nature and

*Dr. N. B. Jetmalani and myself.

meaning of the human relations everyone witnessed and experienced. An attempt to analyze the nature of these interpretive differences suggested a number of possibilities. An obvious one was that theoretical persuasion draws the attention of different observers to different details. Another possibility, also due to theoretical approach, was that the psychoanalysts had views at variance with the trainers on the optimal timing of interpretive comments. Sometimes the trainer's comment appeared to the psychoanalysts to have more to do with the private fantasies and mental life of the trainer than the actual group behavior. Sometimes the trainer's statement revealed a selection of one behavioral trend or verbal content among many varied ones, and rather than the statement acknowledging this fact, the trainer attributed such behavior or processes to the total group. On these occasions someone in the group invariably spoke up to deny the generality of the statement. Sometimes one of several alternative generalizations was selected by the trainer when it appeared to be quite a justifiable prerogative of the trainer to focus on some aspect of the group process he considered to be of cardinal interest to the group members.

The most prominent area of diffculty for the two trainers in group #2 to handle was settling on whether cognitive or emotional issues were the foremost issues under discussion. It was obvious that the trainers wanted to call the group's attention to the problem-solving work the group had to do in the process of decision-making in the small (and large) T-groups. This was, indeed, a fascinating and instructive process to participate in and observe. However, the trainers seemed either to lose sight of or prefer to ignore or blind themselves to the powerful emotional swells unleashed by the T-group process. At a point where one group member was viciously criticizing another, it appeared inappropriate and unfitting to have one or the other of the trainers say, for example, "I don't think the group has agreed on how it is going to arrive at decisions." Such a response occurred, furthermore, at a point several times after the group had already given tacit evidence of agreement on acceptable decision-making procedures — for example, by not officially starting sessions until everyone was present and by stopping sessions approximately at designated times, using a flexible policy and basing its group action on nonverbal as well as verbal assent or dissent.

Not only did this kind of statement come forth after many informal yet precedent-making procedures for arriving at decisions had already been established, but also in one instance after the group actually came to a decision by taking a vote. On this occasion the whole group voted (with the trainers abstaining) to change its meeting place one evening to a cooler site on the lawn instead of in the meeting room. The majority vote was for moving outside. The insistence of the trainers at this point that the group had not agreed to use voting as a decision-making procedure, after the trainers had been quiet while the group worked at coming to a decision on this issue, appeared to be definitely out of order. Their move led to a temporary schism in the group, with four members leaving the meeting room to carry out the action positively voted upon. The other members who had voted for a temporary move remained with the two trainers — who did not budge from their seats when the group began to carry out the action which had been voted upon — and the most voluble of these group members complained to the trainers that they were using manipulative strategies by not going along with the vote. As in most of these group interactions and crises, a discussion and analysis of what behavioral and mental processes were actually involved in this episode never occurred; the group went on, the next day, to discuss only indirectly, and without specifying any threads of continuity, issues deriving from this episode and new matters (not of obvious relevance) introduced by group members. My impression was that the trainers saw the vote as a move to challenge their leadership and that they experienced the group action as a power struggle in which the authority they assumed (but recurringly denied experiencing) was challenged. Rather than acknowledge the strong emotional reactions they had about this situation or instead of questioning the motivations of the group members initially promoting the move and the vote, they chose to ignore the emotional implications of the group ferment at this point and weakly insisted that a cognitive issue — how to agree on decision-making procedures — was at stake.

Another point about the trainers deserves highlighting. This was a bit of behavior in which some trainers, at one time or another, often several times during the whole Human Relations sessions, stated that they did not want to be regarded or experienced by participants as trainers or any special persons by the group. Rather, they wanted to be designated as group members. The purpose of this maneuver in group dynamics was not clear unless it was principally prescribed as a technique of fending off recurring moves from other group participants to have the trainer give a lecture or take over strong, forceful leadership, solve some problem in the organizing of the group, or serve yet another purpose. The maneuver did oblige some group members to think and to specify what facts they were counting as evidence that the "trainers" had special functions in the group and what facts did not so count. It did help some participants see that they felt very anxious when no one assumed or took over definite leadership in a group and that such members needed a strong leadership in order to function rationally and comfortably.

However, some of the trainers carried the insistence to an absurd degree that they were the same in every respect as every group member. They overlooked that not only their official designation as "trainers" by the National Training Laboratories, but also their authoritative way of speaking and the content of their evocative behavior (designed like nondirective, client-centered, Rogerian therapy during its earlier phase of development[8] — to elicit the emotional and ideational aspects of an individual) earmarked their role as group members with a special teaching function and a prescribed type of behavior. Yet, quite often the trainers denied these functions, and this appeared to be unnecessary for the purposes of the National Training Laboratories but also inaccurate as well as confusing to the group members.

It is difficult to see what would be lost from the purposes of the Human Relations Laboratories if the trainers would acknowledge — when questioned by reality-testing, group participants — that they have a teaching function, a clarifying function, a theoretical frame of reference from which they operate which should become obvious and require minimal explanation if the other group participants remain alert and observant to what is going on in the group.

Discussion

Although the T-group has somewhat different goals and markedly different procedures from those of psychoanalysis, and although the T-group does not require that the members use free association and does not promise confidentiality or a long-term relationship with other group members, its short-term process somehow sets in motion reactions that also occur in the psychoanalytic situation. These reactions are called in psychoanalysis "transference reactions" and in more fully evolved form a "transference neurosis." Many derivative responses to the arousal of transference have been described, such as the defense transference, acting out of the transference, etc. In T-group theory and practice the reactions have, of course, not been classified according to such a terminology, for T-group work has not evolved directly from the psychoanalytic tradition, although some of its current theorists[5,11] show a psychoanalytic perspective. My rationale for extrapolating terminology from the psychoanalytic tradition and situation and applying it to an obviously different situation is that the behaviors and experiences of T-group members seem to have the distorted or irrational quality of transference-like reactions and also appear to have the potentially modifiable quality of transference reactions.

My conviction is that these reactions in the T-group are catalyzed by the trainer's tending to repudiate the usual leadership role in groups, providing no definite structure for the group's procedure or organization, and providing initially an absolutely ambiguous idea of the group's agenda and the preferred content of communication. These latter features of the T-group trainer's behavior are vaguely similar to the psychoanalyst's permissive, relatively nonjudgemental, nondirective behavior in psychoanalysis. It is my firm impression, however, that the T-group trainer's lack of structuring the process beyond a few initial expectant remarks accounts to a large extent for the evolution of transference-like reactions or their derivatives in the T-group. Many other features of the

Human Relations Laboratory — the physical setting, the official pre-lab propaganda, evangelical promotion by enthusiastic ex-T-group members, etc. — help shape these transference-like reactions occurring in the T-groups.

In this unstructured situation the T-group member projects his needs with regard to leaders (parents), anxiety about conflicts, and misperceptions with respect to authority figures.

My impression is that the T-group trainer may have inexpert knowledge or understanding about what is happening in the T-group. He is not inclined — by theoretical persuasion — to set limits on the speed of appearance and intensity of transference-like reactions. Rather, he behaves as if he trusts that the reactions of other members of the group will constitute a reality check for each other group member. The flaw in this hope is that every other group member, as well as the trainer, is capable of these indiscriminate generalizations of response, these transference-like reactions, to the point that the expression of some forbidden impulses is frequently met from some group member, with harshly suppressive, condemning, rejecting responses (superego reactions). Group members with high self-esteem and ego strength survive the impact of unfolding and exposing their irrational and rational selves and getting stepped on or of observing and participating in the harsh limit-setting of others. These T-group members report enthusiastically about having a growth or learning experience. The less well-integrated and insecure individuals are often severely upset by the T-groups, and in their shame they say little about their experiences.

There is a strong regular inducement to confession, to a religious experience, by some T-group members. Hearing such confessions produces intense anxiety in other individuals; some of the more reserved participants clam up and withdraw, and typically some group members berate these more guarded participants for not behaving in a more "open and trusting" way.

Especially in large T-groups reaching 100 people, the deep human craving for a deity is brought out in caricatured form as exemplified by the insistent, often desperate and pleading requests or demands of many T-group participants for leadership and guidelines, and for meaning, structure and purpose in the group enterprise. Other T-group participants repudiate and jibe at this performance.

A recently published book by Schein and Bennis,[6] who are well experienced in the T-groups approach, raises some of the same questions (and others) that have been highlighted here about the Human Relations Laboratory. The self-examining and critical point of view expressed, especially in chapter 18 ("Our Questions about Laboratory Training"), indicates that some of the leaders of this movement are aware of the problems that the procedure evokes.

Summary

The T-group is an educational and psychotherapeutic invention that merits more serious attention from psychiatrists, psychoanalysts, and behavioral scientists. In my opinion, it is a procedure and situation which should be studied more carefully, for it appears capable of inducing personality changes of at least brief duration and perhaps longer. Its application to the remedy of social and psychological problems, however, should be more strictly limited, and both its participants and trainers should be more carefully selected.

References

1. BLACKE, R. R. "Studying Group Actions," *T-Group Theory and Laboratory Methods. Human Relations Training News*, 7 (Winter, 1963–64), 4.
2. DEUTSCH, M., A. PEPITONE, and A. ZANDER. "Leadership in a Small Group," *Journal of Social Issues*, 4 (Spring, 1948), 31–40.
3. FRANK, J. "Training and Therapy," *T-Group Theory and Laboratory Method*, eds. L. P. Bradord, J. R. Gibbs, and K. D. Benne. New York: John Wiley and Sons, 1964.
4. HATHAWAY, S. "Some Considerations Relative to Non-Directive Psychotherapy as Counseling," *Journal of Clinical Psychology*, 4 (July, 1948), 226–231.
5. MASLOW, A. *New Knowledge in Human Values.* New York: Harper and Brothers, 1959.
6. SCHEIN, E. H., and W. G. BENNIS (eds.). *Personal and Organizational Change through Group Methods. The Laboratory Approach.* Ch. 18: "Our Questions about Laboratory Training." New York: John Wiley and Sons, 1965.
7. SEITZ, P. F. D. "A Report of a T-Group Experience." Unpublished paper.
8. SHLIEN, J. M., and F. M. ZIMRING. "Research Directives and Methods in Client-Centered Therapy," *Method of Research in Psychotherapy*, eds. L. A. Gottschalk and A. H. Auerbach. New York: Appleton-Century-Crofts, 1966.
9. STOCK, D. M. "A Survey of Research on T-Group," *T-Group Theory and Laboratory Method*, eds. L. P. Bradford, J. R. Gibb, and K. D. Benne. New York: John Wiley and Sons, 1964.
10. STORROW, H. A. "What Happened at Bethel: A Personal View of Human Relations Training," *Journal of Nervous and Mental Disease*, 138 (May, 1964), 491–498.
11. WHITMAN, R. M. "Psychodynamic Principles Underlying T-Group Processes," *T-Group Theory and Laboratory Method*, eds. L. P. Bradford, J. R. Gibb, and K. D. Benne. New York: John Wiley and Sons, 1964.

T-Groups
Selected Bibliography

Books

BENNIS, WARREN G. *Changing Organizations.* New York: McGraw-Hill, Inc., 1966.

———, KENNETH D. BENNE, and ROBERT CHIN (eds.). *The Planning of Change.* 2d ed. New York: Holt, Rinehart & Winston, Inc., 1969.

BLANK, LEONARD, MONROE G. GOTTSEGEN, and GLORIA B. GOTTSEGEN (eds.). *Confrontations in Self and Interpersonal Awareness.* New York: The Macmillan Company, 1971.

BRADFORD, LELAND P., JACK R. GIBB, and KENNETH D. BENNE (eds.). *T-Group Theory and Laboratory Method.* New York: John Wiley & Sons, Inc., 1964.

GIBB, JACK R., and LORRAINE M. GIBB. *Ways of Growth*, eds. Herbert Otto and John Mann. New York: Grossman Publishers, Inc., 1968.

KAPLAN, HAROLD I., and BENJAMIN J. SADOCK (eds.). *Comparative Group Psychotherapy.* Baltimore: Williams and Wilkins Company, 1970.

LUFT, JOSEPH (ed.). *Group Process: An Introduction to Group Dynamics.* Palo Alto, California: The National Press, 1963.

SCHEIN, EDGAR H., and WARREN G. BENNIS (eds.). *Personal and Organizational Change through Group Methods: The Laboratory Approach.* New York: John Wiley & Sons, Inc., 1965.

TANNENBAUM, ROBERT, IRVING R. WESCHLER, and FRED MASSARIK. *Leadership and Organization: A Behavioral Science Approach.* New York: McGraw-Hill, Inc., 1961.

Periodicals

ARGYRIS, CHRIS. "T-Groups for Organizational Effectiveness," *Harvard Business Review*, 42 (March–April, 1964), 60–74.

BASS, BERNARD M. "Mood Changes during Training Laboratory," *Journal of Applied Psychology*, 46 (October, 1962), 361–64.

———. "Reactions to *Twelve Angry Men* as a Measure of Sensitivity Training," *Journal of Applied Psychology*, 46 (April, 1962), 120–24.

BENNE, KENNETH D. "Some Ethical Problems in Group and Organizational Consultation," *Journal of Social Issues*, XV (Spring, 1959), 60–67.

BLANSFIELD, MICHAEL G. "Inside the Laboratory Trainer," *Journal of the American Society of Training Directors*, 14 (June, 1960), 20–25.

BLOOMBERG, LAWRENCE I., PAULA BLOOMBERG, and RICHARD MILLER. "The Intensive Group as a Founding Experience," *Journal of Humanistic Psychology*, IX (Spring, 1969), 93–99.

BRADFORD, LELAND P. "Am I a Good Group Participant?" *National Education Association Journal*, 45 (March, 1956), 168–69.

———. "National Training Laboratory in Group Dynamics," *National Education Association Journal*, 38 (February, 1949), 103.

——— and GORDON L. LIPPITT. "The Individual Counts in Effective Group Relations," *National Education Association Journal*, 43 (November, 1954), 485–87.

────── and STEPHEN M. COREY. "Improving Large Group Meetings," *Adult Education*, I (April, 1951), 122–38.

BUGENTAL, JAMES F., and ROBERT TANNENBAUM. "Sensitivity Training and Being Motivation," *Journal of Humanistic Psychology*, III (Spring, 1963), 76–85.

BUNKER, DOUGLAS R. "Individual Applications of Laboratory Training," *The Journal of Applied Behavioral Science*, 1 (April, 1965), 131–48.

CAMPBELL, JOHN P., and MARVIN D. DUNNETTE. "Effectiveness of T-Group Experiences in Managerial Training and Development," *Psychological Bulletin*, 70 (August, 1968), 73–104.

CARRON, THEODORE J. "Human Relations Training and Attitude Change: A Vector Analysis," *Personnel Psychology*, 17 (Winter, 1964), 403–22.

CLARK, JAMES V., and SAMUEL A. CULBERT. "Mutually Therapeutic Perception and Self-Awareness in a T Group," *The Journal of Applied Behavioral Science*, 1 (April, 1965), 180–94.

CULBERT, SAMUEL A. "Trainer Self-Disclosure and Member Growth on Two T-Groups," *The Journal of Applied Behavioral Science*, 4 (January, 1968), 47–73.

──────, JAMES V. CLARK, and KENNETH H. BOBELE. "Measures of Change Towards Self-Actualization in Two Sensitivity Training Groups," *Journal of Counseling Psychology*, 15 (January, 1968), 53–57.

────── and JOANN CULBERT. "Sensitivity Training within the Educational Framework: A Means of Mobilizing Potential," *Journal of Creative Behavior*, 2 (Winter, 1968), 14–30.

DAY, MAX. "The Natural History of Training Groups," *International Journal of Group Psychotherapy*, XVII (October, 1967), 436–46.

DELANEY, DANIEL J., and ROBERT A. HEIMANN. "Effectiveness of Sensitivity Training on the Perception of Non-Verbal Communications," *Journal of Counseling Psychology*, 13 (July, 1966), 436–40.

DELISLE, NORMAN E. "Bethel Comes to Connecticut," *National Education Association Journal*, 46 (January, 1957), 44–45.

FIEBERT, MARTIN S. "Sensitivity Training: An Analysis of Trainer Intervention and Group Process," *Psychological Reports*, 22 (June, 1968), 829–38.

FRIEDLANDER, FRANK. "The Impact of Organizational Training Laboratories upon the Effectiveness and Interaction of Ongoing Work Groups," *Personnel Psychology*, 20 (Autumn, 1967), 289–307.

GARWOOD, DOROTHY SEMENOW. "The Significance and Dynamics of Sensitivity Training Programs," *International Journal of Group Psychotherapy*, XVII, (October, 1967), 457–72.

GIFFORD, C. G. "Sensitivity Training and Social Work," *Social Work*, 13 (April, 1968), 78–86.

GOLEMBIEWSKI, ROBERT T., and ARTHUR BLUMBERG. "Sensitivity Training in 'Cousin' Groups," *Training and Development Journal*, 23 (August, 1969), 18–22.

GOTTSCHALK, LOUIS A., and E. MANSELL PATTISON. "Psychiatric Perspectives on T-Groups and the Laboratory Movement: An Overview," *American Journal of Psychiatry*, 126 (December, 1969), 823–39.

GRATER, HARRY. "Changes in Self and Other Attitudes in a Leadership Training Group," *Personnel and Guidance Journal*, XXXVII (March, 1959), 493–96.

GROSSMAN, LEN, and DONALD H. CLARK. "Sensitivity Training for Teachers: A Small Group Approach," *Psychology in the Schools*, IV (July, 1967), 267–71.

HAIGH, GERARD V. "A Personal Growth Crisis in Laboratory Training," *The Journal of Applied Behavioral Science*, 4 (October, 1968), 437–52.

HAIMAN, FRANKLYN S. "Effects of Training in Group Processes on Open-Mindedness," *Journal of Communication*, 13 (December, 1963), 236–45.

HALVERSON, CHARLES F., JR., and ROY E. SHORE. "Self-Disclosure and Inter-personal Functioning," *Journal of Consulting and Clinical Psychology*, 33 (October, 1969), 213–17.

HAMPDEN-TURNER, C. M. "An Existential 'Learning Theory' and the Integration of T-Group Research," *The Journal of Applied Behavioral Science*, 2 (October, 1966), 367–86.

HARRISON, ROGER. "Cognitive Change and Participation in a Sensitivity Training Laboratory," *Journal of Consulting Psychology*, 30 (December, 1966), 517–20.

HAVIGHURST, ROBERT J. "Workshop for Leaders of Groups: Third Session," *School Review*, 57 (April, 1949), 200.

HOUSE, R. J. "Leadership Training: Some Dysfunctional Consequences," *Administrative Science Quarterly*, 12 (March, 1968), 556–71.

JOHNSON, LYLE K. "The Effect of Trainer Interventions on Change in Personal Functioning through T-Group Training," *Dissertation Abstracts*, 27 (June, 1967), 4132–A.

KASSARJIAN, H. H. "Social Character and Sensitivity Training," *The Journal of Applied Behavioral Science*, 1 (October, 1965), 433–40.

KLEIN, DONALD C. "T-Group — Opening Moments," *The Journal of Applied Behavioral Science*, 4 (January, 1968), 125–27.

LOHMANN, KAJ, JOHN H. ZENGER, and IRVING R. WESCHLER. "Some Perceptual Changes during Sensitivity Training," *The Journal of Educational Research*, 53 (September, 1959), 28–31.

MILES, MATTHEW B. "Changes During and Following Laboratory Training: A Clinical-Experimental Study," *The Journal of Applied Behavioral Science*, 1 (July, 1965), 215–42.

MORTON, ROBERT B., and BERNARD M. BASS. "The Organizational Training Laboratory," *Training Directors Journal*, 18 (October, 1964), 2–18.

"National Training Laboratory in Group Development," *Educational Leadership*, 11 (February, 1954), 305.

"National Training Laboratory in Group Development to Be Expanded," *School and Society*, 71 (January 21, 1950), 44.

O'HARE, MARY RITA D. "Sensitivity Training in Teacher Education," *Teacher Education News and Notes*, 19 (May–June, 1968), 8–14.

OSHRY, BARRY I., and ROGER HARRISON. "Transfer from Here-and-Now to There-and-Then: Changes in Organizational Problem Diagnosis Stemming from T-Group Training," *The Journal of Applied Behavioral Science*, 2 (April, 1966), 185–98.

PARIS, NORMAN M. "T-Grouping: A Helping Movement," *Phi Delta Kappan*, XLIX (April, 1968), 460–63.

PETERSON, C. P. "What It's Like to Be a T-Group Trainee," *Wisconsin Journal of Education*, 95 (April 6, 1963), 12–16.

PROCTOR, JAMES O. "Delegate at Bethel," *Adult Leadership*, 10 (November, 1961), 136–58.

PSATHAS, GEORGE, and RONALD HARDERT. "Trainer Interventions and Normative Patterns in the T-Group," *The Journal of Applied Behavioral Science*, 2 (April, 1966), 149–69.

RAWLS, JAMES R., DONNA J. RAWLS, and ROLAND L. FRYE. "Membership Satisfaction as It Is Related to Certain Dimensions of Interaction in a T-Group," *Journal of Social Psychology*, 78 (August, 1969), 243–48.

SCHUTZ, WILLIAM C., and VERNON L. ALLEN. "The Effects of a T-Group Laboratory on Interpersonal Behavior," *The Journal of Applied Behavioral Science*, 2 (September, 1966), 265–86.

SMITH, PETER B. "Attitude Changes Associated with Training in Human Relations," *The British Journal of Social and Clinical Psychology*, 3 (June, 1964), 104–12.

SPIEGEL, HANS. "A Course in Human Relations: Some Group Methods and Techniques," *Adult Education Journal*, IX (April, 1950), 61–65.

STEELE, FRED I. "Personality and the 'Laboratory Style,' " *The Journal of Applied Behavioral Science*, 4 (January, 1968), 25–45.

"Summer Bargain," *National Education Association Journal*, 46 (February, 1957), 105.

TANNENBAUM, ROBERT, and J. F. T. BUGENTAL. "Dyads, Clans and Tribes: A New Design for Sensitivity Training," *Human Relations Training News*, 7 (February, 1963), 1–3.

THOMAS, HOBART F. "Self-Actualization through the Group Experience," *Journal of Humanistic Psychology*, IV (Spring, 1964), 39–44.

"Three Weeks Can Make a Difference," *National Education Association Journal*, 45 (April, 1956), 260.

TOLEA, MICHELE. "Effects of T-Group Training and Cognitive Learning on Small Group Effectiveness," *Dissertation Abstracts*, 28 (June, 1968), 5175-A.

TSCHIRGI, HARVEY D. "The Trainer's Role in Sensitivity Training," *Journal of the American Society of Training Directors*, 14 (May, 1960), 22–28.

"Yourself as Others See You: Sensitivity Training Program," *Business Week*, 1750 (March 16, 1963), 160.

ZWERDLING, PHILIP. "Student Human Relations Workshops," *Journal of Secondary Education*, 43 (February, 1968), 74–87.

Part Three
Attack Approaches

Introduction

Encounter is one of the most widely used and least clearly defined terms in sensitivity training. It is often used interchangeably with sensitivity training as a general term. Sometimes encounter refers to those groups which focus on "here and now" interaction between individuals, as compared to the T-group which places greater emphasis on the emerging structure of the group. Encounter is most popularly identified with what we call the "attack approach," an intense, aggressive confrontation between group members.

The attack approach originated at Synanon and is used in many self-help drug programs. In these therapeutic communities, ex-addicts live together in a group residential setting, functioning essentially as each other's "therapists" without much traditional professional help. Here, the group acts as a forum for treating individual problems or interpersonal conflicts. In addition to regularly scheduled group sessions, impromptu groups are called whenever any member feels the need for one.

The first selection, "The Dynamics of Synanon (IV)," is a chapter taken from Daniel Casriel's book, *So Fair a House: The Story of Synanon*. Casriel defines the synanon as "a form of leaderless group encounter for the creation of aggressive and provocative interchange."[1] Group interaction is often violent and hostile. A prohibition against physical violence is the only restriction given the expression of thoughts and feelings; any kind of verbal attack is permitted. One member will attack another for being a phony, or for not doing his job. Another will be attacked because a member finds the way he interacts destructive, disturbing or unpleasant. A confrontation will occur involving members who have had disagreements they could not settle between themselves. The theoretical assumption behind these violent exchanges is that they deepen the emotional involvement among group members, and help create a community of mutual personal concern and caring.

[1]Daniel Casriel, *So Fair a House: The Story of Synanon* (Englewood Cliffs, New Jersey: Prentice-Hall, Inc., 1963), p. 78.

In "Synanon and the Learning Process: A Critique of Attack Therapy," Walder questions this assumption. He holds that the attack methods are significantly less important than would appear in modifying an addict's behavior. What is crucial in the Synanon method is the supportive organizational structure, the community with its system of rewards. Walder relates traditional learning theory to the practices at Synanon. He points out that research in learning has established that while reward motivates change, punishment simply inhibits behavior temporarily. He explains that even the attack approach may constitute a reward for the ex-addict. He may experience verbal abuse as an expression of caring and concern for him by the attacker. Walder also warns against the potential destructiveness of the attack approach outside the context of a supportive therapeutic community.

In both articles the attack approach is described as a form of psychotherapy, rather than as a sensitivity training experience. Yet there is little in the literature to support its effectiveness either as psychotherapy or as sensitivity training outside of drug rehabilitation programs. In fact, this approach lends itself most to abuse and destructiveness when used indiscriminately by untrained leaders or irresponsible psychotherapists. Whether the attack approach can be a meaningful sensitivity training experience has yet to be demonstrated.

The Dynamics of Synanon (IV)

DANIEL CASRIEL

Daniel Casriel, "The Dynamics of Synanon (IV)," *So Fair a House: The Story of Synanon* (Englewood Cliffs, New Jersey: Prentice-Hall, Inc., 1963), pp. 78–91. Published by Prentice-Hall, Inc. Reprinted with permission of publisher and author. © 1963, Daniel Casriel, M.D.

The *synanon* is a form of leaderless group encounter for the creation of aggressive and provocative interchange. These group-therapy sessions of seven or eight members usually meet three times a week for an hour and a half. Synanons also take place once a week for the inmates of the Federal Penitentiary on Terminal Island, California, with a group of about fifteen Synanon members from Santa Monica in attendance. The Nevada State Prison also has the Reno Synanon members holding synanons for their prisoners. These synanons are conducted not only for former drug addicts, temporarily imprisoned, but for all antisocial performers.

Besides being leaderless and nonprofessional, the sessions differ from a more conventional group-therapy session in that in their "search for the truth" about themselves and each other, the members frequently become verbally violent and openly hostile. Each member is a "therapist," and each "therapist" is a member. There is complete freedom of feeling, thought, and language.

As Doctor Lewis Yablonsky wrote in his article "On the Anticriminal Society: Synanon" in the September, 1962, issue of *Federal Probation:*

> This form of group therapy is ideally suited for the overall Synanon community. The group sessions do not have any official leader. They are autonomous; however, leaders emerge in each session in a natural fashion. The emergent leader tells much about himself in his questioning of another. Because he is intensely involved with the subject or the problem in the particular session he begins to direct, he is in a natural fashion the "most qualified" session leader for that time and place. In short, the expert of the moment may be emotionally crippled in many personal areas, but in the session where he is permitted by the group to take therapeutic command, he may be the most qualified therapeutic agent.

Chuck* wrote in his paper, *Synanon Foundation:*

> By virtue of an empathy which seems to exist between addictive person-alities, they are able to detect each others' conscious or unconscious attempts to evade the truth about themselves.
>
> The temporary leader "leans heavily on his own insight into his own problems of personality in trying to help the members to find themselves, and will use the weapons of ridicule, cross-examination, hostile attack," as he feels inclined. The temporary inquisitor "does not try to convey to the other members that he himself is a stable personality. In fact, it may very well be that the destructive drives of the recovered or recovering addictive personality makes him a good therapeutic tool — fighting fire with fire.
>
> These "synanon sessions seem to provide an emotional catharsis and (appear to) trigger an atmosphere of truth-seeking which is reflected in the social life of the family structure. The sharing of emotional experience in the synanon sessions seems to encourage in the family structure a tolerance and permissiveness within rather loosely defined limits in which the addict who wants to recover feels sufficiently comfortable to stay and buy himself time."

*Chuck is Charles Dederick, who founded Synanon in 1958. — Ed.

A synanon can be called at any time — day or night — by any two members if they cannot settle their argument between themselves. In the early days of Synanon, these synanons were called more frequently. Physical violence excepted, there is no restraint put upon the members in how they express their feelings and thoughts. Anything goes verbally; the language is the language of the street. Members understand that the synanon is the only place where they may express themselves so freely.

Except to make sure there are one or two active and experienced members, as well as a cross-section of the membership in each group, no attempt is made to put the same members together in the same group; in fact, an attempt is made to change the groups constantly. At their requests, two or more members can be placed together on a particular evening. All members have equal rights in a synanon; anyone is permitted to question, attack, or probe anyone else. No one is allowed in the synanon unless he is willing to partake or to be verbally taken apart in the sessions. The following, a partial transcription of a tape recording, is what may take place at a typical synanon. The group is made up of eight people.

First its attention is directed at Gina and her hostility toward other members of the "club." Next to face the scrutiny of the group is Jim, who overreacted to Gina. This overreaction was traced to his relationship with his mother. Jim's attitude toward his mother is not uncommonly seen in people with severe maternal deprivation.

JOE: What was all that screaming in the coordinator's Office the other day, Gina?

GINA: I got a few remarks from Moe and Art. They told me a lot of things about myself, and I got insulted.

WILL: You got mad at both of them?

GINA: I didn't get mad at them really, I got insulted at what they said.

NANDY: What did they say?

GINA: Well, they said that I was inadequate, which is possibly true, and that I'm not capable in handling a lot of things.

NANDY: Is it true?

GINA: Possibly very true. That's what really struck me — that I was inadequate.

TOM: What brought all this on?

GINA: Well Art came down and said that Moe was coming into the office, that he didn't have a job. They had an idea that I was going to Reno and they wanted to get somebody started on my job. . . . I started feeling very let down, like Moe was taking over.

TOM: Then you all kind of lost your heads and called a synanon?

GINA: Oh no, Don called us all in the office. He closed the door and we let out a lot of feelings — things that were on our minds . . . which was very good. I didn't think it was so good at the time. I felt real hurt.

They both were yelling at me, but a lot of things were ironed out — I got out a lot of feelings.

JOE: I wonder when you're going to stop sounding so good in synanons. Every synanon that I'm in with you, someone asks you a question and you've got a beautiful book written. All made out about what went down and how you were wrong and how you realized you were wrong and all that kind of bull shit. When are you going to stop doing that?

How do you feel about Art?

GINA: I have nothing against Art.

WILL: You're a nut. Art hasn't got any damn sense. He's got you in there, yelling at you and Moe, and you've got everything so cool.

GINA: No, I feel he's very insecure in a lot of ways but that has nothing to do with me. . . .

JOE: You act like you're so goddamn understanding.

GINA: I was told to act as if I understand.

JOE: Well you're in a synanon now. You're not supposed to be acting like you're such a goddamn healthy person. Are you so well?

GINA: No.

JOE: Well why the hell don't you quit acting as if you were.

TOM: How do you feel about Art?

GINA: I like Art.

WILL: No! You feel he's insecure. Why don't you tell him about his insecurity; you're looking right into the sucker's face.

GINA: I told him about it. I let it all out the other day.

WILL: Tell it to him now.

GINA: It's ridiculous to tell him again. I told him that I think he's very insecure and that a lot of the things he was telling me were because of his feelings, and not really true. There were some that were, but there were a lot that weren't.

JOE: Like what?

GINA: Well, when he asked me to do something, I'd say, "Well, what do you want?" He said, I have a sick attitude behind it (i.e., in her voice). I don't feel I did — maybe I sounded as if I did and he built it up to be something big. But I don't feel like I had an attitude.

JOE: What kind of an attitude?

GINA: That I do anything for Don but I don't have the right attitude about doing things for him.

JOE: Well isn't this the way you feel?

GINA: No, Don is my boss. Anything that he gives me to do, I do. If Art asks me to do something, fine; but if Don has given me something more important at the time, I do it first. You know, there were times when I was sitting outside in the reception desk and Art asked me to do something and I'd say, "What do you want?" It's the way I said it, I guess.

WILL: You didn't know how he was taking it?

GINA: No. This is what he told me later.

JOE: Maybe your feelings about him were just showing? Maybe that's what was happening.

GINA: I don't dislike Art.

NANDY: Oh yeah! How about this. You're kind of an omnipotent kiss-ass anyway. Take Don. You'd do anything for him, but Art's a kind of a flunky in there. I can imagine your attitude or your tone of voice or anything else. I wouldn't need to hear you because I know. I've heard you talk to other people. You know he doesn't have a position and this is what's different in your gut. Only people with a position are important to you.

GINA: But he does have a position.

WILL: Then why the hell is it so hard for you to do something when he asks you to do something?

GINA: It wasn't hard for me to do it.

WILL: Well, what started the hassle. Don't lie to yourself. You got something in your gut going against Art. You said if Don tells you to do something, you'll do it. But if Art tells you to do something, you're going to find an excuse rather than do something for him.

GINA: Well, this is how it started. In the first place, it was early Monday morning. I said to Moe even before the morning meeting, "I hear you're coming into the office today." So he leaned across and said, "Oh, fuck you." So I went down to the office and . . .

WILL: Wait a minute, Gina, are you trying to say that you asked him with no malice and no feeling behind it?

GINA: Nothing.

WILL: You really believe that?

GINA: Really.

NANDY: With nothing else in your tone? I don't believe that.

GINA: Not a thing; this is what I said to Moe.

HARRY: Are you that shallow? Where did you get this Mickey Mouse thinking? What do you do in that office anyhow? All I see you do is make coffee all day long . . . and opening your big mouth. If you're going to Reno, they've got to have a substitute . . . ain't that right?

TOM: You said that there was no malice — nothing in your tone of voice — but a little earlier you said that you resented Moe coming in the office because you said he was a threat to you.

GINA: This was after he came in there and sat on the desk.

TOM: No! This is what he picked up, and this is why he said, "Fuck you." You copped on yourself a minute ago as to how you were feeling. You know Moe *is* a threat to you . . . you and your job. So when you asked him — I don't know how you asked him; I can imagine though — and he said, "Fuck you," you reacted to him. You did resent Moe being in there and evidently it showed.

GINA: It probably showed later on.

TOM: No, it showed right then — just give it a possibility.

JOE: Evidently you're working under some kind of delusion, Gina: that people don't see your attitude and your actions. When you live in this house people really get to know a person. I've seen you burst into the records office . . . not knocking, just burst in with some papers, throw them on the desk, and burst out again — I don't know what kind of roll you're playing.

GINA: You know, Joe, that's not true. You know that I knock when I come into that office, unless . . .

JOE: After you get told off about six times, you knock.

GINA: (disgusted) Oh man, that is bull shit.

JOE: What is bull shit about it?

GINA: About me bursting into the records office. I walk in there very unsure . . .

JOE: Baby, this is not your stick (i.e. way of behaving).

GINA: That's bull shit.

JOE: You are a pushy, omnipotent broad. This is what you are.

JUNE: What is the thing you're most consistently reminded of by the rest of us?

GINA: My attitude.

WILL: What is your attitude?

GINA: My tone of voice, the expression on my face, the way I walk, the way I look at people.

JUNE: These are all manifestations of what is inside of you. What is inside of you?

GINA: Bad feelings I guess — just plain bitchy . . .

JUNE: Yet you're sitting here in synanon, where you can get rid of some of this bitchyness, and you're rationalizing. You're explaining — you've got everything all figured out, and everything is fine with the world. All you have to do is get a little upset, sit down, talk it over and then it's finished; but you know it isn't. You're carrying all this stuff inside of you and it's got to burst out all the time in a thing that people call an attitude. Does this make sense at all?

JOE: Gina, how do you get along with the rest of the girls?

GINA: Pretty good.

WILL: How do you get along with this hostile broad right here? (Nandy)

GINA: I don't know.

WILL: You know. We all know Nandy. Nandy is as hostile as they come. You don't have nothing to do with her. You scared of Nandy?

GINA: No, I don't think so.

NANDY: You act like you are . . . 'cause I tell you the truth all the time. You don't particularly seem to dig it.

GINA: But, if you remember, I came to you for more of the truth. I asked you to come into the office and talk to me.

NANDY: It's this pushy attitude that you have. You assume that you're right all the time. You don't listen to people, Gina. You act like you know it already. You're spouting all this shit to these people. You don't know what you're talking about half the time. This thing with Art is the same thing that I pulled you up for the other day — telling someone what he is thinking. You don't know. I see you do it all the time. You're always misinterpreting what somebody means or what they think or what they say. It's not up to you to judge.

WILL: It's a goddamn attitude.

NANDY: You don't know any more than anybody else.

WILL: That was pretty goddamn omnipotent. You asked Nandy to come in the office and talk to *you!* You've been in here about two days. Nandy is a coordinator. She's been around here a long time.

GINA: You're mixing it up, really. It's *her* office, man.

JIM: What is your need to tell a guest something you know nothing about, Gina?

GINA: Oh . . .

JIM: I want to know what your reasons were . . . to walk over and stick your two cents into something you don't know anything about. When you make definite statements and make me look foolish, then you look foolish and Synanon looks foolish.

GINA: It so happens that just before you came over we were kidding around and I was telling him how . . .

JIM: Wait a minute, I was with that man . . .

GINA: No, you weren't. I was with him and his wife, man.

JIM: His wife! I was standing with that man. Don't tell me no story.

GINA: No, I'm telling you like it is . . . just like it is.

JOE: Say, Jim, what does she do to you? You came into the office damn near crying the other night.

JIM: She just makes little digs, anywhere, in front of anybody, and sticks her two cents into things she knows absolutely . . .

[*Turning the attention of the group from Gina to Jim.*]

WILL: Damn what she does. How come you react, whatever she does?

JIM: I don't know.

WILL: You don't know! But you come down here and throw hostility at her. Why are you so goddamn crazy that she can frown at you and you go into a thing?

JIM: I don't know.

WILL: You don't know and you're willing to drop it? Why the fuck don't you try to find out.

JIM: Yeah, I'll try.

JOE: Just like that.

GINA: What do you mean you'll try? I've been kissing your ass since Monday because they tell me you get hysterical, man . . . crying when I say something to you. What do you want me to do?

JIM: I'd like it best if you'd just stay away.

GINA: Crazy, I would do it if it would get me well. It won't. It'll get me well being nice to you.

WILL: You think he's in love?

HARRY: Yeah, I think there's something happening there . . . more than meets the eye.

WILL: If you have eyes for the broad, tell her. You're a man.

JIM: That's the last thing in the world.

HARRY: Why?

JIM: Because I couldn't possibly conceive of myself having eyes for her.

JOE: Oh, you stupid asshole. You're down here in a synanon in your humble, meek attitude when you're supposed to be yelling and screaming. The other day you were running around ranting and raving, roaring at the top of your lungs in the middle of the hallway.

TOM: Didn't you tell me you were going to make a conscious effort not to be an asshole?

JUNE: This is a bone he throws. He sits quietly in synanons.

TOM: Is any attention better than no attention, Jim? Isn't that where it's at?

JIM: Yes, I've considered this.

TOM: Did Gina really make you react or was it just an opportunity to get a little attention?

JIM: No, she bugs me, man!

TOM: What about anyone else.

JIM: Not as much as her.

TOM: She's the most, the worst?

JIM: No one bugs me continually like she does.

HARRY: Does she remind you of your mother?

JIM: Yes, in a lot of ways.

TOM: How.

JIM: I don't know.

TOM: That's a fuckin' story. That's very convenient.

HARRY: Is your mother big and fat?

JIM: She's heavy, yeah.

HARRY: Does she talk like Gina, with that Brooklyn twang? The same kind of values? The same conditioning? The same background?

JIM: A little of it. My mother has a lot more sense.

HARRY: Well, all right, I know you're fond of your mother. You can say that your mother has a little more sense. But if Gina reminds you of your mother, why do you react to her like this? Did your mother nag you, Jim? "Don't go out and shoot dope, now, Son."

TOM: That's where the identification comes in. His mother has never loved him, as Gina doesn't love him. She bugs him like his mother bugged him. Isn't this correct? Didn't your mother bug you all your life?

JIM: No.

TOM: Sure she did, she was never home. She put you in foster homes, orphanages, and hospitals. She'd commit you; you'd come out and she'd recommit you.

JIM: But she couldn't help it, man.

HARRY: What do you mean she couldn't help it? Why?

JIM: Because she was sick. My father went to prison. What could she do?

WILL: The gut doesn't know all that bull shit.

JIM: I was shooting junk. She remarried and my stepfather didn't want a dope fiend in the house. How could she help it?

WILL: Oh, that's sick, the gut doesn't know all that bull shit. You want a mama just like all the rest of us did.

JIM: (sarcastically): That's right, Mama is still with me.

JUNE: Mama *is* still with you . . . in your gut . . . and she still bugs you.

HARRY: She rejected you, so you must hate her. She kept you in these places. Weren't you jealous of your stepfather? She chose your stepfather instead of you. You like your stepfather? He doesn't want a dope fiend around, and you still like him? You're very decent, you're wonderful, and you like your mother for rejecting you. . . .

JIM: She didn't reject me, man.

TOM: The hell she didn't. She chose him over you. . . .

JIM: No, she didn't. She asked me when she was getting married what she should do. I don't think she would have gotten married if . . .

GINA: He probably threw a tantrum. I can just picture him banging his head against the wall.

TOM: She didn't want you around. As long as you were sleeping in some institution, it was all right. Isn't that the truth? How much does she love you?

JIM: Maybe she didn't want me out there killing myself.

JOE: Why don't you quit lying to yourself, Jim?

JIM: I'm not lying to myself, I can't see where my mother . . .

JOE: Do you feel your mother digs you more than anything else in the world?

JIM: Right.

JOE: Gut level?

JIM: Right.

JOE: You're a lying asshole.

NANDY: You're so full of shit, Jim, it's ridiculous. That's why you react to this broad, Gina, all the time.

HARRY: You know how bad you want your mother and your mother's love. You're always running to the phone, or to see if there's any mail. How old are you by now?

JIM: Twenty-seven. I didn't say it was good, but she loves me.

HARRY: She's got to prove that. Are you so sure that she loves you? Why do you come every time the telephone rings? If you're so sure of her love, why were you running to Arnold, a half hour after you were here asking for permission to call, to write.

JIM: I love her, too.

WILL: Well that's your sick need. You want her to love you, that's the need you've got.

TOM: You wanted her to (love you), because she never has.

HARRY: Unconditional love. You see, whatever little love she's given you was more than anybody else gave you. Gina doesn't give you that kind of thing, not even a little bit.

TOM: Jim, what do you mean when you say she loves you.

JIM: She always thinks about me. She always does what she can for me . . . money.

TOM: This means she loves you? Is that what you're saying?

GINA: This is her guilt. She has to give you money for cigarettes, man. . . .

HARRY: That's your measurement of love?

JIM: She's not a rich woman, Harry.

GINA: Yeah, but she's very guilty. She knows that she doesn't want you, but she knows that she should because you're her son. So she throws you this money and she's satisfied her soul.

HARRY: Or maybe she's ashamed of you.

WILL: You're whining and sniveling all the time.

TOM: She's paying like . . . what do they call that when they pay?

NANDY: Penance.

TOM: She's paying off to get rid of you, that's why she sent you commissary money and all that garbage. This is all you need to pacify you. She does this to keep you off her back.

JIM: Maybe she does.

HARRY: The important thing is, you don't understand this is a sick need.

JIM: Why should I blame her? You know I haven't been a model son.

HARRY: What is a model son? You don't understand your sick need. Through your childhood a set of values has been placed on you. Your brother is a lawyer, and another a dentist. She's thinking how come you're not a lawyer or a dentist.

JIM: I never heard that bull shit.

GINA: Yeah, but you know that she was thinking it. She never said it to her girl friends?

JOE: Hey, wait a minute, Jim. You dig attention. Do you think it's a sickness with you?

JIM: I know it is.

JOE: How does your sickness for attention show itself around here?

JIM: Probably in everything I do. It sounds stupid, but when I go thru a motion *not* to get attention, I get very lonely, even with crowds of people around.

HARRY: When did you start laughing like a hyena in heat? Is that laughing physical? We're sitting around in a group now and someone says something funny and everyone starts laughing. He starts laughing like a hyena. Everybody stops and looks at Jim. It goes over big. How do you train yourself? It must have taken years to laugh like that, did it? You don't have to laugh like that, Jim. You can laugh a little more normally like hahaha-hohoho.

JOE: If you wanted to, Jim, you could probably do 99 per cent of the things that you do around here, differently. Has any one of us suggested to you to try some constructive way of getting attention?

JIM: Joe, I . . .

JOE: No, wait a minute. Keep your mouth shut! The only way you can not manifest your insanity is to keep your mouth shut.

HARRY: He isn't going to keep his mouth shut. Look, do you know the difference between attention and approval?

JIM: Yeah.

HARRY: Which do you prefer?

JIM: I don't know, I never had much approval.

HARRY: Well, you see, you're looking for approval, but you think attention is approval. Look up those two words in the dictionary. You're looking for approval and you get attention. If you want people to laugh at you, fine and dandy. But what you want is approval, not attention.

From the foregoing, it can be seen how, in Synanon, the *constant* assessment required in the member's daily interaction with others fosters the consolidation of self-identity and self-evaluation. The member's self-estimation is under constant observation and attack by his peers, who are sensitive to and concerned about him. In the synanon, each is given a chance to see himself as others see him, and in the eyes of the newcomers he sees how he affects the image of Synanon.

Synanon and the Learning Process: A Critique of Attack Therapy⎯⎯⎯⎯

Eugene Walder, "Synanon and the Learning Process: A Critique of Attack Therapy," *Corrective Psychiatry and Journal of Social Therapy*, II, 6, 299–304, 1965. Reprinted with permission of publisher.

In a recent issue of *The New York Times Magazine* (3)* featuring an article on Synanon, the front page photograph was of a drug addict who was accepted back after he "split" and returned to drugs but paying the price with shaved head and ridiculing placard. The verbal "haircut" (4) is a form of "attack therapy" making use of ridicule and exaggeration and directed against undesirable behavior. In the synanons or group therapy sessions the techniques of exaggeration, caricature and ridicule are practiced with artistry and skill by other group members. The "fireplace scene" (4) is reserved for extreme cases of misbehavior where the transgressor is exposed to the verbal attacks of the entire membership. Attack therapy is considered by Synanon to be a necessary and valid method in the "cure" of the drug addict. Yablonsky states: "Behavior and thinking are modified by verbal-sledgehammer attacks. . . . The individual is blasted, then supported, and he seems to learn to change his behavior as a result of this positive traumatic experience." How crucial the attack methods are to the modification of the addict's behavior by Synanon is the subject of this article.

Despite Yablonsky's injunction against the professional presuming to use his own conceptual tools to understand "a new methodology and social structure," it is the author's contention that principles of learning theory sharpen, rather than distort, our understanding of the Synanon method. Humiliation, ridicule and sarcasm represent punishment of

*Numbers refer to References at the end of this article.

"bad" behavior. From the standpoint of learning theory, however, punishment is an ineffective means of eliminating socially undesirable behavior, serving to inhibit the disapproved habit without decreasing the strength of the response, encouraging conformity without the acquisition of internal restraints, and producing negative by-products of hostility, fear and frustration which stimulate antisocial actions (1). If within this framework attack therapy is based upon principles which are ineffective in the control and manipulation of behavior, it becomes necessary to understand the methods of influencing the addicts who are helped to remain "clean" and to lead constructive lives by virtue of the Synanon experience. It is the contention of this article that other methods employed by Synanon are essential to behavioral change and that attack methods perform only a subsidiary function.

Controlling Agent

Basic to the effectiveness of the Synanon method is the control and manipulation of behavior through primary and secondary rewards. In his review of learning mechanisms in psychotherapy, Bandura discusses the inappropriateness of techniques used with neurotics for the treatment of antisocial personalities:

> While counterconditioning, extinction, and discrimination learning may be effective ways of removing neurotic inhibitions, these methods may be of relatively little value in developing new positive habits. Primary and secondary rewards in the form of the therapist's interest and approval may play an important, if not indispensible role in the treatment process. Once the patient has learned to want the interest and approval of the therapist, these rewards may then be used to promote the acquisition of new patterns of behavior.

As a prerequisite to the exercise of the effective control of behavior, it is essential that the drug addict accept an authority figure in the role of controlling or reinforcing agent. Through the process of generalization members of Synanon at the top of the hierarchy borrow the director's reinforcing properties and act as surrogate controlling agents. Because of the organizational structure of Synanon, the directors and senior members are associated with the administration of primary and secondary rewards, strengthening their position as controlling agents. The newcomers' being "given a pass" (treated gently) is necessary since the entering members have not accepted Synanon as a positive reinforcer until they have the opportunity to experience the available primary and secondary rewards. If the addict were attacked in the synanons in this early stage, it is likely that he would respond to the punishment with hostility and "split." Within the Synanon framework, the drug addict is compelled to emit the desired operant responses by insistence upon his "going through the motions" (4) i.e., displaying approved behavior even though he does not believe in the Synanon system. A new response repertoire is acquired by the addict for which he is rewarded by the controlling agents. Isolation of the newcomer from past associations increases the strength of the Synanon family as a positive reinforcer by eliminating the influence of reinforcing agents who are rewarding competing behaviors; for example, the mother who complains of her loneliness and offers her son barbiturates if he would leave Synanon (4).

Reward

Reward is the most effective instrumentality employed by Synanon for effecting modification of behavior, without which the synanons, "hair-cuts" and "fireplace scene" would be experienced as rude and barbarous punishments. Administration of rewards begins as the new member enters the "paternalistic family structure" (2) where he is accepted into the Synanon "family." During the period when he is undergoing physiological detoxification the members provide food, eggnogs, massages and baths. Support of Synanon House is provided by local merchants who contribute supplies of food. The addict is accepted into a loving family relationship, associated with primary rewards and gaining secondary reward properties.

Status and rank in the hierarchy are strong secondary rewards used in manipulating behavior in a constructive direction. Status-seeking is consciously encouraged (2,4) and the new member can progressively move upward in the hierarchy, even some day reaching the position as director of a Synanon House.

Imitation

Children learn through imitation of parental figures. Bandura points out that "rewards promote imitative learning" (1). Primary and secondary rewards encourage acceptance by the addict of members above him in the hierarchy as "role models" (4) whose attitudes, values and behavior can be observed and copied. Synanon recognizes the importance of imitation and encourages the members to emulate a senior Synanist (4).

Punishment and Attack Therapy

Within the total process of Synanon, punishment as dispensed by attack methods serves the following functions. First, punishment inhibits undesirable behavior through the association of the impulse to perform the act with anxiety (1). Responses are suppressed which would compete with the operant responses emitted in "going through the motions" facilitating the reward of desirable behavior. Second, as Yablonsky (4) observes, the drug addict may experience verbal attack against "bad" behavior as rewarding, i.e., the members are really interested and care enough to be concerned about his disapproved behavior. Attack therapy, therefore, may owe much of whatever effectiveness it possesses, not to the negative effects of punishment, but to the positive rewards experienced. Whatever the value of punishment in Synanon, it is accepted only by virtue of the stronger rewards administered, since without these rewards attack would elicit negative motivations and cause the member to "split."

The synanon Outside Synanon

Adoption of attack therapy by other settings which are not in possession of the organized structure of Synanon, equipped to administer strong primary and secondary rewards, is bound to be a debacle. Reward, not punishment, is the sine qua non of therapeutic change. Brutal verbal attacks can only stimulate negative motivations if the therapist or other group members do not have secondary reinforcing properties. Similarly, to seize upon any of the features of the method such as the "haircut," indigenous leadership, the "hot seat," etc., is to be in the position of the blind men in the fable, each convinced that he has represented the elephant by describing only the limited part he has explored.

References

1. BANDURA, ALBERT. "Psychology as a Learning Process," *Psychological Bulletin*, 58 (March, 1961), 143–154.
2. CASRIEL, DANIEL. *So Fair a House: The Story of Synanon*. Englewood Cliffs, N. J.: Prentice-Hall, 1963.
3. SAMUELS, GERTRUDE. "Where Junkies Learn to Hang Tough," *The New York Times Magazine* (May 9, 1965).
4. YABLONSKY, LEWIS. *The Tunnel Back: Synanon*. New York: Macmillan, 1965.

Attack Approaches
Selected Bibliography

Books

CASRIEL, DANIEL. *The Concept: The Story of Daytop*. New York: Hill & Wang, Inc., 1971.
————. *Drug Addiction*. New York: Funk & Wagnalls, 1971.
————. *So Fair a House: The Story of Synanon*. Englewood Cliffs, New Jersey: Prentice-Hall, Inc., 1963.
YABLONSKY, LEWIS. *The Tunnel Back: Synanon*. New York: The Macmillan Company, 1965.

Periodicals

FRIEDENBERG, EDGAR Z. "The Synanon Solution," *The Nation*, 200 (March 8, 1965), 256–61.
GOLEMBIEWSKI, ROBERT T., and ARTHUR BLUMBERG. "Confrontation as a Training Design in Complex Organizations: Attitudinal Changes in a Diversified Population of Managers," *The Journal of Applied Behavioral Science*, 3 (October, 1967), 525–47.
GOWLAND, PETER. "Fred Schwab: Synanon Photographer," *Popular Photography*, 59 (October, 1966), 28+.
HAER, JOHN L. "Anger in Relation to Aggression in Psychotherapy Groups," *Journal of Social Psychology*, 76 (October, 1968), 123–27.
KOBLER, JOHN. "Second Coming of Synanon," *The Saturday Evening Post*, 242 (February 8, 1969), 32–34+.
LINK, WILLIAM E. "Psychotherapy Outcome in the Treatment of Hyper-aggressive Boys: A Comparison of Behavioristic and Traditional Therapy Techniques," *Dissertation Abstracts*, 29 (December, 1968), 2205–B.
MCKEAN, W. J. "Encounter: How Kids Turn Off Drugs," *Look*, 33 (April 15, 1969), 40–43+.
MASLOW, ABRAHAM H. "Synanon and Eupsychia," *Journal of Humanistic Psychology*, VII (Spring, 1967), 28–35.
"Mutual Aid in Prison," *Time*, LXXXI (March 1, 1963), 45.
O'QUIN, SALLY. "Close-up: Chuck Dederich, Mr. Synanon Goes Public," *Life*, 66 (January 31, 1969), 36–38.
PARSONS, OSCAR A., LAWRENCE B. FULGENZI, and ROBERT EDELBERG. "Aggressiveness and Psychophysiological Responsivity in Groups of Repressors and Sensitizers," *Journal of Personality and Social Psychology*, 12 (July, 1969), 235–44.
ROBINSON, LOUIE. "Drug Addicts Who Cure Each Other," *Ebony*, XVIII (February, 1963), 116–18+.
"S. S. Hang Tough," *Time*, LXXVII (April 7, 1961), 72+.
SAMUELS, GERTRUDE. "Where Junkies Learn to Hang Tough," *The New York Times Magazine*, CXV (May 9, 1965), 30–1+.
SMITH, ROBERT J. "A Closer Look at Encounter Therapies," *International Journal of Group Psychotherapy*, XX (April, 1970), 192–209.
"Synanon House: Where Drug Addicts Join to Salvage Their Lives," *Life*, 52 (March 9, 1962), 52–65.
"Testing Synanon," *Time*, XCII (July 12, 1968), 74.
WINSLOW, WALKER. "Experiment for Addicts," *The Nation*, 192 (April 29, 1961), 371–73.

Part Four
Psychodrama

Introduction

The creation and development of psychodrama is largely the work of one man, J. L. Moreno. In 1914, while attending the University of Vienna Medical Academy, Moreno would improvise plays with the children in Vienna's beautiful Stadt Park. Originally as a form of recreation, he would ask the children to choose parents with whom they wanted to act out stories. At first the children were timid and chose their own parents. After a while, becoming more spontaneous, they freed themselves from their actual parents and gravitated to certain individuals who appeared more attractive to them as parents. Out of this exercise Moreno developed the beginnings of his system for the measurement of interpersonal relations, Sociometry.

Many of the parents, particularly those not chosen by their children, or for that matter any children, were upset by this choice process. To explore the reasons for these patterns of choice, Moreno had the children reverse roles and play the role of their parents. The parents were indeed amazed to see how their children perceived them. From these original "role reversals," Moreno created the Theatre of Spontaneity, which, when transplanted to the United States, evolved into the present Theatre of Psychodrama.

Since that time Moreno's charisma and creativity have influenced many. The power of his psychodramatic method created much controversy at first. In recent years, however, it has had wide influence in psychotherapy, education and the encounter movement. As a method of therapy, psychodrama is utilized in institutions and by therapists in private practice throughout the world. Currently, near-psychodramatic techniques are evident in most sensitivity and encounter groups. All too often, however, these techniques are used piecemeal by leaders untrained in the method and its theory, frequently producing negative results.

The three articles in this section present psychodrama from different perspectives. Moreno's article, "Psychodrama and Group Psychotherapy," is a classic statement of psychodramatic method. Moreno describes the five main instruments of psychodrama: the stage, the subject, the director, the auxiliary egos, and the audience; and he discusses some of their theoretical foundations. "The Psychodramatic Approach to Sensitivity Training," by Ellen K. Siroka and Robert W. Siroka, is addressed primarily to those unfamiliar with the method. It is also designed to give the reader a grasp of psychodrama as sensitivity training. Using case material, they present the basic structure of a psychodrama and define some of its major techniques. Howard A. Blatner, in "Comments on Some Commonly Held Reservations about Psychodrama," discusses ten criticisms frequently leveled at psychodrama by those in the traditional mental health professions. These objections include the fear that the emotional intensity in psychodrama might cause the protagonist to have a psychotic break, and the charge that psychodramatic techniques are gimmicks which do not result in a genuine relationship between protagonist and director. Blatner assesses the validity of each objection carefully and replies. He recognizes the responsibility of those in the field to direct more research and inquiry into the nature and effects of the method. He spells out some of the common pitfalls of psychodrama directors, stating that an unskilled director, rather than the method itself, is most often to blame for problems.

Psychodrama and Group Psychotherapy*

J. L. MORENO, M.D.

J. L. Moreno, "Psychodrama and Group Psychodrama," pp. 249–53. From *Sociometry*, Vol. IX No. 2–3, 1946, J. L. Moreno, M.D., Editor, Beacon House Inc., Publisher.

Drama is a transliteration of the Greek word which means action, or a thing done. Psychodrama can be defined, therefore, as the science which explores the "truth" by dramatic methods.

*Read at the American Psychiatric Association Meeting, May 30, 1946, in Chicago.

The psychodramatic method uses mainly five instruments — the stage, the subject or patient, the director, the staff of therapeutic aides or auxiliary egos, and the audience. The first instrument is the stage. Why a stage? It provides the patient with a living space which is multi-dimensional and flexible to the maximum. The living space of reality is often narrow and restraining; he may easily lose his equilibrium. On the stage he may find it again due to its methodology of freedom — freedom from unbearable stress and freedom for experience and expression. The stage space is an extension of life beyond the reality tests of life itself. Reality and fantasy are not in conflict, but both are functions within a wider sphere — the psychodramatic world of objects, persons and events. In its logic the ghost of Hamlet's father is just as real and permitted to exist as Hamlet himself. Delusions and hallucinations are given flesh — embodiment on the stage — and an equality of status with normal sensory perceptions. The architectural design of the stage is made in accord with therapeutic requirements. Its circular forms and levels of the stage, levels of aspiration, pointing out the vertical dimension, stimulate relief from tensions and permit mobility and flexibility of action. The locus of a psychodrama, if necessary, may be designated everywhere, wherever the patients are, the field of battle, the classroom or the private home. But the ultimate resolution of deep mental conflicts requires an objective setting, the therapeutic theater. Like in religion, although the devout may pray to his God in his own chamber, it is in the church where the community of believers attain the most complete confirmation of their faith.

The second instrument is the subject or patient. He is asked to be himself on the stage, to portray his own private world. He is told to be himself, not an actor, as the actor is compelled to sacrifice his own private self to the role imposed upon him by a playwright. Once he is warmed up to the task it is comparatively easy for the patient to give an account of his daily life in action, as no one is as much of an authority on himself as himself. He has to act freely, as things rise up in his mind; that is why he has to be given freedom of expression, spontaneity. Next in importance to spontaneity comes the process of enactment. The verbal level is transcended and included in the level of action. There are several forms of enactment, pretending to be in a role, re-enactment or acting out a past scene, living out a problem presently pressing, creating life on the stage or testing oneself for the future. Further comes the principle of involvement. We have been brought up with the idea that, in test as well as in treatment situations, a minimum of involvement with other persons and objects is a most desirable thing for the patient. An illustration of this is the "Rorschach." The Rorschach situation is reduced to ink blots. In the Rorschach the subjects change but the situation is always the same. It is thought to be its greatest virtue that it is pure and therefore offers an "objective" test. The psychoanalytic interview in its orthodox form too, tried to be pure and objective, by reducing the involvement with the analyst to a minimum. In the psychodramatic situation a maximum of involvement with other subjects and things is not only possible but expected. Reality is not only not feared but provoked. Indeed, in the psychodramatic situation all degrees of involvement take place, from a minimum to a maximum. In addition comes the principle of realization. The patient is enabled not only to meet parts of himself, but the other persons who partake in his mental conflicts. These persons may be real or illusions. The reality test which is a mere word in other therapies is thus actually made true on the stage. The warming up process of the subject to psychodramatic portrayal is stimulated by numerous techniques, only a few of which are mentioned here: self presentation, soliloquy, projection, interpolation of resistance, reversal of roles, double ego, mirror techniques, auxiliary world, realization and psycho-chemical techniques. The aim of these sundry techniques is not to turn the patients into actors, but rather to stir them up to be on the stage what they *are*, more deeply and explicitly than they appear to be in life reality.

The third instrument is the director. He has three functions: producer, therapist and analyst. As producer he has to be on the alert to turn every clue which the subject offers into dramatic action, to make the line of production one with the life line of the subject, and never to let the production lose rapport with the audience. As therapist, attacking and shocking the subject is at times just as permissible as laughing and joking with him; at times he may become indirect and passive and for all practical purposes the session seems to be run by the patient. As analyst he may complement his own interpretation by responses coming from informants in the audience, husband, parents, children, friends or neighbors.

The fourth instrument is a staff of auxiliary egos. These auxiliary egos or therapeutic actors have a double significance. They are extensions of the director, exploratory and therapeutic, but they are also extensions of the patient, portraying the actual or imagined personae of their life drama. The functions of the auxiliary ego are threefold: the function of the actor, portraying roles required by the patient's world; the function of the therapeutic agent, guiding the subject; and the function of the social investigator.

The fifth instrument is the audience. The audience itself has a double purpose. It may serve to help the patient or, being itself helped by the subject on the stage the audience becomes the patient. In helping the patient it is a sounding board of public opinion. Its responses and comments are as extemporaneous as those of the patient, they may vary from laughter to violent protest. The more isolated the patient is, for instance because his drama on the stage is shaped by delusions and hallucinations, the more important becomes, to him, the presence of an audience which is willing to accept and understand him. When the audience is helped by the subject, thus becoming the patient itself, the situation is reversed. The audience sees itself, that is, one of its collective syndromes portrayed on the stage.

The stage portion of a psychodramatic session has opened the way to action research and action therapy, role test and role training, situation tests and situational interviews whereas the audience portion has become the common ground of the better known forms of group psychotherapy, as lecture methods, dramatic methods and film methods. Scientific foundations of group psychotherapy require as a prerequisite a basic science of human relations, widely known as sociometry. It is from "sociatry," a pathological counterpart of such a science that knowledge can be derived as to abnormal organization of groups, the diagnosis and prognosis, prophylaxis and control of deviate group behavior.

Now that we have described the five basic intruments required to run a psychodramatic session we may ask ourselves: to what effect? We will limit ourselves here to the description of a single phenomenon, mental catharsis (stems from the Greek, it means purging, purification).

Breuer and Freud were ignorant of the psychotherapeutic implications of the drama milieu to which Aristotle referred. It remained for psychodrama to rediscover and treat the idea of catharsis in its relation to psychotherapy. We picked up the trend of thought where Aristotle had left off. We too, began with the drama but *reversed* the procedure. It was not the end phase but the initial phase of the drama towards which we directed attention. *Mental* catharsis was when we entered the scene with our investigations to be found only in dramatic literature, in faded memories of Aristotle's old definition and the term itself practically out of circulation. The psychoanalysts, after a flare-up in the early 1890's, had pushed it aside. As practically every human activity can be the source of some degree of catharsis the problem is to determine in what catharsis consists, in which way it differs for instance, from happiness, contentment, ecstasy, need satisfaction, and so forth, and whether one source is superior in the production of catharsis to another source; indeed, whether there is an element common to all sources which operates in the production of catharsis. Therefore my aim has been to define catharsis in such a way that all forms of influence which have a demonstrable cathartic effect can be shown as positive steps within a single total process of operation. I discovered the common principle producing catharsis to be: spontaneity.

Because of the universality of the act and its primordial nature it engulfs all other forms of expression. They flow naturally out of it or can be encouraged to emerge, verbal associations, musical association, visual associations, color associations, rhythmic and dance associations, and every other stimulus which might arouse or inhibit the emergence of one or another factor, for instance, the use of psychochemical starters like sedatives, as barbiturates, sodium amytal, sodium pentotal; or shock methods as insulin, metrazol or electricity; or endocrinological medications as thyroid are fully within the scheme of total catharsis; they may condition and prepare the organism for psychodramatic integration. The need for the drama can be temporarily choked, for instance, by sleep or shock therapies. But the fundamental need for the realization of certain fantastic imageries can not be "shocked away." Unless the subject is reduced to a brain invalid by surgery or prolonged shock treatments, the temporarily scared patient is bound to relapse and reproduce the same type of mental syndrome he had before treatment began. It is into the stream of action catharsis that all the rivulets of partial catharsis flow.

The treatment of audiences has become an important alternative to individual treatment. The relationship of the audience to itself in a psychodramatic session, being treated by its own spokesman on the stage, gives us a clue as to the reasons of the cathartic effect of psychodrama. According to historians of the Greek drama the audience was there first, the chorus, musing about a common syndrome. There were "keynoters" among them but they remained within the chorus. Aeschylos is credited with having put the first actor upon a social space outside of the chorus, the stage, not speaking to them, but portraying the woes of their own hero. Euripedes is credited with having put the second actor on the stage, thus making possible the dialogue and interaction of roles. We may be credited to have put the psyche itself on the stage. The psyche which originally came from the group — after a process of reconversion on the stage — personified by an actor — returns to the group — in the form of the psychodrama. That which was most startling, new and spectacular to see and to feel on the stage appears to the participants after thorough exposure as a process which is familiar to them and intimately known — as their own selves. The psychodrama confirms their own identity as in a mirror.

Bibliography:

J. L. MORENO. *Who Shall Survive?*, New York: Beacon House, 1934, New Edition 1953.

———. *Group Psychotherapy.* New York: Beacon House, 1945 (Contains first Group Psychotherapy Conference, 1932).

———. *Psychodrama, Volume 1.* New York: Beacon House, 1946.

———. *The Theatre of Spontaneity.* New York: Beacon House, 1946 (First German Edition, 1923).

———. *The Words of the Father.* New York: Beacon House, 1941 (First German Edition, 1920).

———. *Sociometry, Experimental Method and the Science of Society.* New York: Beacon House, 1951.

The Psychodramatic Approach to Sensitivity Training_____

ELLEN K. SIROKA, M.A., AND ROBERT W. SIROKA, PH.D.

Psychodrama creates self encounter and self-other awareness on a variety of levels. In its fullest sense, as a method of psychotherapy, it is designed to help an individual explore himself, encounter himself in the past, present and future, yet all in the here and now.[1] He is helped to face parts of himself and of his life which may be troubling him. The goal is the resolution and understanding of such problems and the subsequent learning of new behavior patterns. At this level psychodrama is used in mental hospitals, clinics and in private practice, both by itself and in conjunction with other therapeutic methods. On another level, psychodrama is effective as a diagnostic tool. Its role playing and role training aspects are used with such people as prison inmates and hospital patients soon to be released, to determine if they are ready to be released or discharged by seeing how they actually react to environmental situations presented to them. Along the same lines, in education psychodrama is an effective method of training teachers to be more productive in the classroom and to handle individual encounters with their students. On still another level, the one we are primarily concerned with, groups of individuals come together to learn to understand each other better by sharing parts of themselves and their lives.

Through psychodrama a person can learn more about himself, especially in his interpersonal relations. Whether he is protagonist or audience member, he plays or watches scenes that involve relationships — relationships between friends, family, members of the opposite sex, etc. If a protagonist is concerned with his job or with school, he will most likely examine this in psychodrama through scenes between him and his boss, his teacher or fellow students. The emphasis is almost always on interaction between himself and people in his world. As the protagonist does

---

[1] Used most effectively as an adjunct method combined with other approaches.

this, the spectators may see parts of themselves reflected in him. If so, they may express this to him in the sharing period. When they do this, the protagonist sees himself reflected in their experiences. Thus different people see parts of themselves in each other; through interaction with others, there is self-encounter.

Psychodrama is a spontaneous drama created and experienced by group members. There is no formal script, only that which is presented through the intimate relationship of the director and protagonist, as representative of the group interest. The psychodramatic structure is in three parts: the warm-up, which involves the entire audience and out of which one person comes forth as protagonist; the drama itself, a presentation of aspects of a person's life; and the sharing, the time in which the audience "share" with the protagonist some of their life experience. In what the protagonist expresses about his life, the individual audience members see parts of themselves reflected and help the protagonist to re-join the group by sharing these.

We would like to try to create for you a picture of a psychodrama. At best it is difficult to do verbally, as the primary emphasis in psychodrama is on action — we try not to "talk about," but rather to "experience now." Perhaps you, the reader, would begin with a very basic psychodramatic technique and imagine yourself a member of a group of individuals coming together for a sensitivity experience in psychodrama. As audience you may be a large group or a single spectator. You may have something in common with each other, for instance you may work in the same place, or, you may not know anyone there at all. Psychodrama can be done anywhere, but ideally the setting is a good-sized room with a raised platform, and easy access to and from the audience. Simple theatrical lights are available to help create a desired mood or expression.

Psychodrama begins with a warm-up, something to help break the initial tension which arises when a group of individuals/strangers meet together. You have reservations about becoming involved in a personal experience, especially with so many people, or perhaps with people you don't know. Perhaps you aren't here yet emotionally: you may still be mulling over a fight with your family, an incident on your job, a pleasant or unpleasant recent interaction. As a result of the warm-up, audience members become part of a group and each group has its own distinct feeling. At the same time both audience and director warm up to each other.

We find non-verbal exercises are an excellent way to promote immediate interaction, but it is most important that a director use whatever warm-up techniques he feels comfortable with. Here are the thoughts of many individuals whom we have interviewed as they experience our warm-up process. We have combined them here and presented them as if they belonged to one person. The instructions from the director to the group are italicized, and the rest is what goes through this hypothetical individual's mind:

A large room with seats around the stage. People look smaller and hard to know. Lights make everything dimmer. I'm not sure why I came, but I don't want anyone to see. These people I came with (I don't feel I'm with them any more) wouldn't know me. I wouldn't know them. I think I'll stay out of it. How boring it would be not to do something. I don't want to miss anything. I could be great up on stage.

I'm on the stage, so is everybody else. This isn't how I imagined it. Everyone is talking. I'm talking to *somebody you don't know*.

I'm asking her a lot of questions in case she asks me one. She asks me why I'm here. I guess we're both here for the same thing, but I can't really say what. People look about the right size here on the stage, and there's a lot of laughing. The guy I'm talking to now is crazy. He's reading Ellis on "rational therapy." He says he tells himself there's no reason to be uptight in these things, so he isn't uptight. I guess it's the heat that makes him sweat.

Now we're making *two circles around the stage*. There's a girl I used to date over there. I'm getting in the same circle so I don't have to *get to know her without words*. The two circles face each other, like having partners. I feel as if we're going to dance.

Communicate without words. It's hard to communicate without words. The noises are mostly growls and it's easier to smother them. Difference between throat noises and stomach noises. Stomach noises change the facial expression: throat noises are more tentative and polite. *Move on to the next person, around.*

This time, communicate without words but eyes closed. Are you supposed to touch? I touch a shoulder, an arm, maybe a face or a hand. I'm glad my eyes are closed. I feel rather embarrassed, yet happy. There is a hand on my neck, I can feel it shaking a little. Maybe this person likes it, I don't know. We open our eyes. Now it's harder. It's over, and the circles break.

Look for a family among the people here on the stage. I don't need a family. It's a horrible word; I don't feel part of anyone, anything. Maybe I should find one anyway. I could find an attractive girl. Perhaps I'll let someone else pick me. But I want to be the father (a big lie). Other people don't seem to mind. There are a lot of families in the world. OK, I made it, I'm the father. I have children — the kid wants to be the son, that's his problem. Two good-looking daughters. A grandmother. Something missing? A wife, "mother," but only for the others. Anyway she seems to be running the whole show. I'll steal it from her later. Let her hang herself. *Instant sociometry.* She points her finger at me: she feels *least comfortable with me*. I feel *least comfortable* with her too. Actually I feel *most comfortable with* the guy. He's younger than me, at least on top. I wonder if he knows what's going on. He seems shy.

The other families are taking turns to stand up, while the other ones listen, seated around them. They are talking about their relationships in the new family. Everybody enjoys it so much. It is fun, though why? It's fun if you are shy and have to do something; you like the feeling of having "gone your turn." My voice sounds strange to me. I can make everyone laugh. I laugh. I feel better.

Now the group is alive; there is a feeling of warmth between people. At this time we find it a meaningful experience for the group to have each person say what they would explore if they were to be protagonist. In this way the group becomes separate yet together, as several main themes generally arise although each individual area of concern is unique. In this way too, the fears a person may have about becoming the protagonist and exposing parts of his life may be minimized as he listens to others around him expressing similar concerns.

Once the protagonist is chosen, emphasis switches from the group and group interaction, to individual encounter of each audience member with themselves through the individual "on the stage." The director's emphasis is now on helping the protagonist explore himself by externalizing his feelings and presenting them in structural form. The relationship between the director and protagonist is crucial; the protagonist must feel trust in the director and receive a feeling of acceptance from him. The director does not lead, he guides. To do this he must remain at all times in touch with the protagonist's feeling yet without creating an exclusive relationship that isolates the protagonist from the audience.

We begin by building a picture of the protagonist's life; we want to see who he is and what his world is like. Depending on the person, this may involve seeing his home, his office, meeting his friends, his family. It is important that the protagonist construct these life scenes carefully, expressing them actively, describing his room, for example, and setting it up with chairs, a table, symbolizing different objects. We want him to smell the smells in his room, to look out of the window and tell us what he sees, to read the book titles on his shelf. One effective way to help the person talk about himself is to ask him to role-reverse, to change places, that is, with something in his room — for example with what he seems to have some feeling for. He may become a favorite painting, or perhaps the house itself and in this role be more free to talk about the protagonist as "another" person.

To illustrate more clearly how we "get into" a psychodrama, here is a portion of a transcript of one of our sessions. The group is large, consisting of several hundred people; it is a community college in a former army barracks. The theme they have chosen to explore is "crises in black and white." The protagonist is a black woman, disturbed at an experience she had with a job interview. Rather than begin with the interview the director asks her where she was before she went to the interview. She replies, "home."

> D.: Can you show us what your home looks like?
> Mrs. T.: It's small, we have two rooms and . . .
> D.: Mrs. T., in psychodrama we try to "do" what we say and feel. Can you show us with your body and these chairs what your home is like?

(*Mrs. T. then begins to walk around the area using chairs to represent furniture, windows, etc. The director walks with her.*)

MRS. T.: Here's the couch, it's too little. Here's a big window; I often sit in front and just look out and think.

D.: What do you see when you look out? Look out now.

MRS. T.: Nothing much, some old buildings, but I can see a little piece of blue sky, I like that. Looks like it's going to rain.

Once we establish where and how Mrs. T. lives, she begins to "get into" the situation and experiences similar feelings to those she had before the actual interview. (At this point we moved toward the interview scene.) An important aspect of psychodrama is the use of audience members to portray those persons the protagonist is engaged with in the psychodrama. The people who play these roles are called auxiliary egos.[2]

D.: Mrs. T., I'm going to ask someone here to come up and be the interviewer. Is there someone here in the audience who reminds you of him?

MRS. T. (*looking around*): Well, not really. He didn't look like anyone here.

D.: There doesn't have to be a physical resemblance. Does anyone here give you some feeling like the interviewer?

Generally at this point the protagonist will choose someone but if it is still difficult, the director may choose. Often the protagonist will choose the director for a role, but this should be avoided as it may seriously disturb the director-protagonist relationship.

Once an auxiliary is chosen it becomes necessary for the protagonist to show the audience how he sees the interviewer. Remember that psychodrama is told through the eyes of the protagonist; roles must be played as he sees them. This is accomplished again through role-reversal, the basic technique in psychodrama. The protagonist "becomes" the interviewer, in this way showing the auxiliary how the interviewer talked, walked, sat, etc. as he, the protagonist, perceived him. After some moments they reverse back and the auxiliary picks up the role of the interviewer. Any time the protagonist indicates that the auxiliary is not in role, they reverse again so that the protagonist can "correct" the portrayal.

In psychodrama, it is not necessary to achieve duplication of an event or physical resemblance. The fact that things are happening in the here-and-now onstage means that to a certain extent this really is the first time that a scene has taken place. The psychodramatic scene between Mrs. T. and the interviewer is not an exact replica of the one that actually took place, but similar. In what Moreno calls "surplus reality," Mrs. T.'s life experience is enlarged; she can re-do the scene many times, she can end it a different way, or, she may learn, as was the case here, that even in psychodrama she was unable to fight for herself, to tell our auxiliary ego what she felt about his reaction to her. The same is true of the person selected to play a role in the protagonist's life-space, like the interviewer in Mrs. T.'s psychodrama. The existence of physical resemblance is not

[2]When using psychodrama in group psychotherapy, in our private practice, we prefer to choose the auxiliary egos in order to duplicate as much as possible the nature of the interactions between the protagonist and the person he is relating to, e.g. mother, father.

necessary. The auxiliary may possess some quality undefined even to the protagonist but sufficient to help him respond as he normally does to this person. The drama lies within the protagonist himself and it is the auxiliary's task to play the role as the protagonist sees it. Several auxiliaries may be onstage at once if several roles are required, and the protagonist will role-reverse with each one to instruct the auxiliary how to play the role. It is this procedure which makes it possible for the group to be involved in a psychodrama without prior knowledge of the protagonist. This technique of role-reversal is a basic construct in psychodrama and used in a variety of ways. Sometimes we ask a protagonist to reverse roles with a figure in his life that he expresses difficulty relating to. By "putting himself in this person's shoes" the protagonist is often able to see the situation more clearly. He *feels* what it is like to be the other person interacting with him. One particular auxiliary ego is called a double. The double attempts to put himself inside the protagonist and feel what the protagonist is feeling but not expressing. He actually becomes a part of the protagonist, verbalizing thoughts and feelings of which the protagonist may not be immediately aware. The protagonist may block these feelings because he, like most of us, has difficulty expressing the full range of his feelings to others, or because the presence of the audience and the conventions of psychodrama inhibit him. (The first factor is usually more significant than the second; after a while the protagonist tends to forget the spectators and lose his feelings of strangeness and embarrassment.)

To facilitate the integration, the double usually takes a position just behind the protagonist or slightly to one side, and attempts to take the same physical positions as the protagonist and make the same gestures or motions, moving when the protagonist moves. He becomes in effect, a shadow, reflecting different parts of the protagonist to himself. The relationship between the double and the protagonist is an intimate, important interaction in the psychodrama. The double becomes support for the protagonist.[3] He is no longer alone with the significant others in his life; he has an externalization of his self to help him. The double must be sensitive to the protagonist and be able to distinguish intuitively between his own reactions, which he must set aside, and the protagonist's. He must respond in the role of the protagonist. He is there to support, not lead; if the protagonist rejects something said by the double, it is not the double's role to argue or defend. The psychodrama springs from the

---

[3]The process of doubling as we have described it here, is reflective doubling. The double reflects to the protagonist unspoken parts of himself. Using psychodrama in group psychotherapy we make use of another technique, interpretive doubling. Here, in our opinion, the double should be a therapist or otherwise skilled professional with knowledge of the protagonist and the situation. Still as part of the protagonist, he may interpret thoughts and feelings of the protagonist, and even at times lead the protagonist in different directions. Here of course the relationship between the double and the director is equally crucial as that between director and protagonist.

protagonist, from his heart, through his eyes, with guidance from the director.

Here is another section of Mrs. T.'s psychodrama, illustrating one way in which a double functions. The interviewer has seen Mrs. T. at their appointed meeting place and Mrs. T. realizes that he didn't know she was black. He is hesitant to approach her.

> MRS. T.: That must be the interviewer. Why doesn't he come over to me? Maybe he doesn't see me.
> DOUBLE: Maybe he does see me.
> MRS. T.: I guess he does see me. Why doesn't he approach me?
> DOUBLE: I feel uncomfortable.
> MRS. T.: I am uncomfortable. Maybe I should go over to him.
> DOUBLE: I feel afraid to go over to him.
> MRS. T.: Yes, I feel afraid.
> DOUBLE: I'm beginning to get angry.
> MRS. T.: Oh, now it's clear. He didn't know I was black.

(At this point Mrs. T. with the double's help has approached the interviewer and is speaking to him.)

> INT.: I'm sorry, but we really don't have any opening.
> MRS. T.: Oh, well . . . .
> DOUBLE: Then why did you make this appointment with me?
> MRS. T.: I was told on the phone that there were some openings.
> INT.: Someone misinformed you; we filled the last one yesterday.
> MRS. T.: Oh, I see.
> DOUBLE: I see all right. It's because I'm black. Why can't I say something to this man? Why can't I tell him how I feel?
> DIRECTOR: Mrs. T., here in psychodrama you can say whatever you wish to Mr. Interviewer. He won't answer back. Tell him how you feel.

(This particular technique was used because Mrs. T. was apparently too threatened to interact with the interviewer directly, even in the psychodramatic situation.)

Each psychodrama is unique and it is impossible to predict how the director will use his skills to aid the protagonist. Certain techniques are used frequently in psychodrama, but do not apply to all indiscriminately. The names of some of the most frequently used techniques are: *soliloquy, mirror, future projection, magic shop* or *magic island, death scene, trial scene,* and *diabolic scene.* The basic aim of all these techniques is to help the protagonist gain a clearer perspective of his situation and express the full range of his personality. Each technique has its own specific result as well, which helps determine its use. In a *soliloquy* the protagonist talks out loud to the audience about what he is feeling at the moment in the psychodrama. It may happen that the director senses the protagonist is becoming overwhelmed in his interactions and needs a chance to breathe, to be with himself, and explore aloud what has happened so far. Often the double may join the protagonist and speak as a part of him, entering into his world as much as possible. This is particularly helpful when the protagonist is beset by ambiguous or conflicting, contradictory feelings which are confusing to him.

Another way for the protagonist to perceive himself is through the *mirror technique*. Members of the audience come onstage and "become" the protagonist, mirroring symbolically or literally how he has come across to them. They may use words or body-language. The protagonist is thus able to see himself through others' eyes.

Another technique which helps the protagonist gain perspective is the *future projection*. The protagonist steps into the future as he sees it in the present. The director and the protagonist walk around the stage, each step representing a unit of time. At different times the director will stop and ask, "What are you doing? What is your life like now?" The protagonist, in the present tense and in concrete terms, builds a picture of his life as he foresees it. After this the director may ask him to proceed to other points in time. Often the protagonist will allow problems or conflicts in his life to surface in the projected future. Thus he can begin to explore how to resolve them in the present.

The same is true of the technique called *magic shop* or *magic island*. Here the protagonist is asked by the auxiliary playing this scene to make a certain number of wishes for himself. The wishes he makes are granted, but payment is required. This payment, requested by the director or auxiliary, may include things he has but needs or wants to be rid of, such as anger, fear, withdrawal or grandiosity. Through the exchange the protagonist explores what behavior he must give up in order to have the life he wants.

The *death scene* is another scene in which the protagonist figuratively steps out of his life and takes a new look at it. He is asked to lie down and respond as if he were dead. Sometimes a funeral is staged at which people discuss him aloud, giving him feedback about himself. Other comparable events would be a funeral oration, obituary, or last rites. The protagonist has the opportunity to confront his life from the point of view of someone who has temporarily stepped out of it. He may have to choose between passivity and making the changes required to live as he wants.

A further way for the protagonist to overview his life is through the *trial scene*. In this scene auxiliaries play judge and, if required, jury and advocates. The protagonist reverses roles with the judge, and sentences the significant people in his life. Finally he is asked to pass sentence on himself. In this way he explores the values by which he judges others and himself, and may feel the need to reexamine both. He may also feel a desire to act on the judgments he passes on himself.

It is frequently difficult for some people to express anger. This is the concern of the *diabolic scene* in which an auxiliary ego playing the devil offers to hurt anyone against whom the protagonist has a grudge. Sometimes the devil has to use considerable coaxing and persuasion to have the protagonist admit he harbors such feelings. The role of the devil should be played without judgment; the protagonist should feel acceptance of his angry vengeful desires in order for them to reach full expression.

Sharing Period

When we feel the protagonist has reached a point of closure, the psychodrama changes focus. The protagonist remains onstage, and we ask the audience to "share" with the protagonist. Sharing in psychodrama consists of expressing similar experiences to those portrayed by the protagonist in the drama. The emphasis is on relating your own life rather than judging, analyzing, or giving advice to the protagonist.

It is frequently necessary for us to intervene and remind audience members to share rather than analyze. On occasion the audience finds it easier to talk about the protagonist than themselves. We encourage the audience to give something of their experiences as the basis for communicating with the protagonist. The aim is to find common ground on which to encounter each other. The protagonist benefits from this because he has no way of knowing during the psychodrama itself whether he is alone with his problems. It is reassuring for him to feel that others are like him, and have experienced some of the same things. He derives emotional support from this sharing, and interpretations of his behavior at this time are not helpful.[4]

Psychodramatic techniques are used in many fields of human relations, as well as in education and industry. All too often, however, those practitioners who employ them are not trained in psychodrama itself. This has a danger comparable to "wild psychoanalysis" and should be especially avoided. Psychodrama has been indeed influential, and people are not always aware of the power of some of its techniques.

Psychodrama can be applied to many learning situations, especially where it involves learning more about oneself. It is basically an educative method whose materials are the life-experience of every individual.

Psychodrama — is it a technique, therapy, theatre, encounter, sensitivity training? It is widely used throughout the United States and, indeed, the whole world, yet not always called by its rightful name. It is the acknowledged creation of one man, J. L. Moreno, intended to help many men encounter themselves and reach out toward the greater universe. What is psychodrama? It is all of these: a series of techniques adaptable to many varied situations, a method of psychotherapy utilizing the universality of the theater, fostering encounter between man and himself,

---

[4]In ongoing group psychotherapy, after sharing we may offer interpretation where necessary.

man and man. It is a way of bringing together groups of individuals and of helping them to better understand themselves and therefore each other, and to become aware of their feelings and responses toward others, their mutual interaction. In all of these the basic psychodramatic structure is similar, but the situation, the intention and aim of both the psychodramatist and the group differ. It is this last context, sensitivity training, on which this article has focused. We urge the reader to keep in mind, however, that the lines between these areas are fine and in many cases determined individually, by each practitioner.

Bibliography

MORENO, ZERKA T. "Psychodramatic Rules, Techniques and Adjunctive Methods," *Group Psychotherapy*, XVIII (March–June, 1965), 73–82.

ORTMAN, HARRIET L. "How Psychodrama Fosters Creativity," *Group Psychotherapy*, XIX (September–December, 1966), 201–12.

SIROKA, ROBERT W. "Psychodrama in a Therapeutic Community," *Group Psychotherapy*, XX (September–December, 1967), 123–26.

———. "Sociodrama and the Negro Family," *International Journal of Sociometry and Sociatry*, IV (September–December, 1964), 91–93.

——— and GILBERT A. SCHLOSS. "The Death Scene in Psychodrama," *Group Psychotherapy*, XXI (December, 1968), 202–5.

——— and ELLEN K. SIROKA. "Psychodrama and the Therapeutic Community," *Confrontation: Encounters in Self and Other Awareness*, eds. Leonard Blank, Monroe G. Gottsegen, and Gloria B. Gottsegen. New York: The Macmillan Company, 1971.

Comments on Some Commonly Held Reservations about Psychodrama___

HOWARD A. BLATNER, M.D.

Howard A. Blatner, "Comments on Some Commonly Held Reservations about Psychodrama," *Psychodrama, Role-Playing and Action Methods: Theory and Practice* (Thetford, England: Howard A. Blatner, 1970), pp. 157–61. Reprinted by permission of author. Available from: Howard Blatner, M.D., 3 Warren Close, Thetford, Norfolk, England

Professionals in the fields of psychiatry and related fields have been utilizing many new approaches to psychotherapy but they have had some reservations concerning the use of psychodramatic and action methods.

In this paper, ten of the frequently expressed objections will be presented and commented on. (5)*

The first reservation about psychodrama arises from the meaning of the use of action in therapy; is enactment equivalent to "acting out"? "Acting out" is generally conceptualized as an antitherapeutic discharge of neurotic tensions through behavior which repeats an unconscious psychic situation; one acts out instead of remembering fully with the appropriate attending emotions. Some people, however, may erroneously infer that the "remembering" must be *verbalized* instead of *enacted*, as the former seems to involve the "conscious" ego. The issue, though, is not verbalization vs. enactment, but whether or not the remembering is complete and done within a therapeutic framework. Thus, psychodrama is not equivalent to acting out because the enactment takes place within the self-observing context of individual or group therapy. The "acting" occurs *in* the therapy and would better be called "acting-in." This method is analogous to verbal free-association; both are forms of "regression in the service of the ego." The unconscious and pre-conscious material can be brought into awareness and examined by therapist and patient. Furthermore, there is a mutual and voluntary control of behavior and a willing submission to the limits of time and reality. The enactment has the further advantage of focusing on multiple sensory modalities, as well as the spheres of intuition and feeling; yet the drama remains subject to the observing and analyzing functions of the ego. (1, 2, 3)

The fear that enactment may lead to loss of control is based on a subtle norm of our culture which distrusts action and affect. In this society, enactment has the connotation of the "artificial"; it is associated with the theater, thus perceived as being somewhat frivolous and "unreal." The verbally-oriented psychotherapies of Freud, etc., were generated in a context that held these anti-dramatic values. Excitement and movement have been thought of as being part of a more childish and primitive area of life, an area which seemed to be the opposite of the cognitive and verbal spheres. The association of action in therapy with a more impulsive and infantile mode of thought and behavior is thus based on a group of questionable assumptions. (6, 7)

Considering the intensity of the catharsis or the expression of conflict which can occur in psychodrama, the second criticism is raised: will the "overwhelming" anxiety precipitate psychosis or violent behavior? Although this will have to be researched statistically, there is no reason to expect that it should. The experience of anxiety occurring in any form of psychotherapy is subject to the context of the therapy and the individual's "social field." If the experience is associated with a sense of abandonment or a sense that others also fear that he may lose control, the anxiety becomes magnified. In the psychodrama, support arises from

*Numbers refer to References at the end of this article.

the presence of the group and the confidence and skill of the therapist. In this context, the idea of avoiding upsetting a patient is anti-therapeutic. As in verbal therapies, the problem is not whether to generate anxiety, but rather how to structure this essential process in therapy. The channelling of anxiety is done through the use of proper timing and the maintenance of some effective coping strategies which are available as alternatives to the old patterns that must be renounced. The presence of the group lends further support to the protagonist, for it communicates to him that others will stay with him in his desperations. A cohesive and confident group can also be reassuring to the protagonist who fears loss of control. The phenomena of action and emotion are thus channelled to become strengths rather than liabilities in therapy.

The third objection to psychodrama is that it seems too unnatural; that is, as a form of therapy it is quite different from what patients and some therapists may expect from a "medical model." What may not be realized is that all therapies are to some extent different in the nature of their context from the harsh and shallow everyday experience of the patient. Yet, one way of viewing psychotherapy is that it helps the patient re-experience his life and interactions in a new light. If we consider the verbal and content-oriented dialogue as one context, then the use of self-examined enactments may be considered another. These contexts could then be thought of as two different media; the world of verbal interchange is more familiar to most people, but involvement in the media of action methods opens new worlds of experience. As Marshall McLuhan suggests, "The hybrid or the meeting of two media is a moment of truth and revelation from which new form is born. For the parallel between two media holds us on the frontiers between forms that snap us out of the Narcissus-narcosis. The moment of meeting of media is a moment of freedom and release from the ordinary trance imposed by them on our senses." When an individual uses action methods, however "unnatural" they may seem at first, he begins to see into the richness of the world of action, emotion, and imagination.

Indeed, it is surprising that the common form of psychotherapy seems so natural. The image of help arising from two people conversing in a quiet room fits many recent individual-centered norms in our society, but it is not similar to any cross-cultural "archetype" of therapy! It may be that since real lack of empirical or solid theoretical justification for any form of psychotherapy exists, and since there is a conservative tendency to follow the medical maxim of "Primum non nocere," ("First, do no harm."), therapists often retreat to the least active form of therapy that is compatible with a medical model.

The needs of the therapists are perhaps reflected in the choice of a passive, conversational, and non-directive model whose roots lie in a respectable "scientific" origin of the psychoanalytic tradition. The patients must give some validation to this overtly "medical" approach, for it is not too different (at first) from their expectations of their other doctors. These are only a few of the factors which have contributed to the norm of what is "natural" in psychotherapy in this culture.

In the light of these norms, some people might expect that it is difficult to participate in psychodrama; either in entering the enactments or taking assigned roles. Those who observe psychodrama for the first time are often impressed with how readily participants can naturally enter roles and become quickly involved. Of course the smoothness of this process will also depend on the adequacy of the warm-up and the skill of the director. Afterwards, rather than feeling that they have done something "different," participants report that their experience had been simply recreated, without having been subjected to any sense of artificiality. A further criticism is that psychodrama is "directive," implying by this that the therapist uses "tricky techniques" in an authoritarian effort to manipulate the patient's statements, so that they will fit into some preconceived theoretical bias. In answer, it should be noted that to be "directive," in the sense of requesting that the protagonist try out some activity, is not at all the same as being "directive" in the sense of imposing a focus of investigation or some interpretation on a patient. Within the drama, there remains a great deal of flexibility in the unfolding of the action, and a mutuality of choice exists as to the direction of investigation. The well-trained therapist has trust in the protagonist's creative ability to learn from the group and the enactment process itself, and will not have to spend time trying to get "points across" to the patient. Thus, it is quite possible to fully respect the protagonist's choice of what he feels ready to explore in even the most structured of psychodramas.

A fifth issue questions the usefulness of applying action methods to clarify group process. (4) The assumption may be that a group should deal with all intragroup conflicts by verbal discussion, with the implication that this is the most "direct" way of approach. In a group with communications difficulties, however, each member works from a particular perceptual and emotional frame of reference. Often only a *shared* experience can provide an object of focus to which all can relate and against which different expectancies and attitudes can be clarified. The use of an action technique in this context can facilitate the group's verbal analysis of their conflict.

A sixth objection to the use of psychodrama is that the use of "techniques" by a therapist is incompatible with an "honest and genuine relationship" with the patient. The phrase it is a "gimmick" has been used by some critics. Insofar as a therapist is not aware of his method of operating and is pretending not to be using techniques — or is unclear as to what they are — then he could justifiably be called "non-genuine." On the other hand, if the technique is used in an open manner, is explicit as to its nature, is time-limited, and is related to the enactment and not the therapeutic relationship, then the therapist is being neither insincere nor ambiguous.

A seventh criticism of psychodrama arises from some observers who have observed the method directed by directors who have had insufficient training. These observers state that the enactments were boring to the audience, awkward for the participants, and destructive of the self-esteem of the protagonists. These criticisms relate not to psychodrama, but to three common pitfalls of directing described below.

If the director himself is inactive, and demands only a verbal interchange with an occasional role-reversal, the enactment will seem physically and psychologically sluggish. The participants as well as the observing group will feel "bogged-down." Yet the reason for this feeling of constriction in the process may be hard to recognize, for many people in our culture do not realize how action, expression, and the nuances of non-verbal communication are intrinsic to the sense of spontaneity, excitement, and involvement in our lives. Thus, to create an effective psychodrama, the director must use a proper "warm-up"; this involves, among other things, the use of a great deal of physical movement — a concept essential to the theory of action therapy. (4)

A second failure in technique arises from the director's assigning roles to the participants which are unfamiliar and/or too emotionally loaded. The enactment will then seem awkward, because the participants will feel embarrassed and unsure of the behavior expected of them. To avoid this, a director must first build a sense of cohesion in the group, develop permissive norms of behavior, and properly "warm up" the participants.

The third pitfall involves directors who feel that the therapeutic element of the psychodrama arises from interpretation. As in individual or group psychotherapy, confrontations without a context of support, or poorly-timed interpretations can lead to a distressing loss of self-esteem in the protagonist. Because psychodrama can lead to even more exposure of the participant's feelings and fears, and allows the group to comment on his non-verbal behaviors which cannot then be denied or rationalized, there is a correspondingly greater vulnerability to ego-deflating remarks. The therapist must ensure a supportive response after the enactment in order to minimize the sense of destructiveness which can be felt by groups in the post-enactment discussion (e.g. using techniques of "sharing," "ego-building," etc.). Often the drama itself has provided a great deal of "confrontation" to the protagonist, and the skillful director will make the fullest use of this without having to resort to intellectualized interpretations.

Related to the improper use of interpretation by the director is the pitfall of subtly altering the goal of the psychodrama towards ends not desired by the protagonist. For example, if the task of the group is to increase skill-training (e.g. in teaching, nursing, counselling), it would be inappropriate for the leader to allow a focus on the personal problems of those in the role-playing enactments.

If the unskilled director falls into these errors of technique, it should be noted that it is not the method of psychodrama that is to blame.

An eighth criticism of psychodrama is that any use of "roles" is artificial and is contributing to a "phony" and "game-like" mode of behavior. This view arises out of a growing confusion about the meaning and implications of "taking roles." There is a growing bias against "superficiality," and many cultural tendencies which have created a distrust in the idea of roles. (It is not appropriate here to deal fully with an enumeration of the factors which have led to this bias.) Let it suffice to say that the concept of "role" has many aspects and has roots in psychological and sociological as well as psychodramatic theory. It is not a concept which need imply "phoniness," but is compatible with a model of man as an involved, spontaneous, and fully self-actualizing being.

The ninth question arises from a suspicion that enactment creates distortion of the protagonist's conflict, thus rendering the method invalid. This criticism can also be directed at the verbal psychotherapies; the reconstructions of past events is subject to the censorship of the patient. However, the introduction of action leads to a mobilization of somaesthetic cues which in turn stimulate a host of memories. This immersion in the sense-memories of the protagonist leads to his further involvement and a reduction of defensive maneuvers which would distort the revelation of the historical event. Indeed, the criticism of "distortion" might be less relevant to psychodrama than to other therapies.

The last reservation about psychodrama that will be commented upon is that the method awaits the validation of properly-controlled outcome studies. Although this problem is relevant to other forms of psychotherapy, there is nonetheless a responsibility of serious workers in the field to continue to subject their activities to rigorous theoretical and empirical research.

In summary, this paper has presented an attempt to answer ten commonly held reservations about the use of the psychodramatic method in psychotherapy. The author hopes that this commentary will stimulate further dialogue about the indications and applications of these different techniques.

References

1. BROMBERG, WALTER. "Acting and Acting Out," *American Journal of Psychotherapy*, 12 (1958), 264–268.
2. DEUTSCH, FELIX. "Analytic Posturology and Synesthesiology," *Psychoanalytic Review*, 50 (Spring, 1963), 40–67.

3. GREENWALD, HAROLD (ed). *Active Psychotherapy*, N.Y.: Atherton Press, 1967. Many varied articles on methods which demand active intervention in therapy — recommended for any therapist who wishes to get good eclectic approach.
4. KIPPER, D. A. "On Spontaneity," *Group Psychotherapy*, 20 (March, 1967), 62–73.
5. KRIETLER, HANS, and S. EBLINGER. "Psychiatric and Cultural Aspects of the Opposition to Psychodrama," *Group Psychotherapy*, 14 (1961), 25.
6. MORENO, JACOB L. "A Psychodramatic Frustration Test," *Group Psychotherapy*, 6 (January, 1954), 145–173.
7. ———. "Actual Trends in Group Psychotherapy," *Group Psychotherapy*, 16 (1963), 117.

Psychodrama
Selected Bibliography

Books

BLATNER, HOWARD A. *Psychodrama, Role-Playing and Action Methods: Theory and Practice.* Thetford, England: Howard A. Blatner, 1970.

GREENBERG, IRA A. *Psychodrama and Audience Attitude Change.* Beverly Hills: Behavioral Studies Press, 1968.

HAAS, ROBERT BARTLETT. *Psychodrama and Sociodrama in American Education.* Beacon, New York: Beacon House, Inc., 1949.

KLEIN, ALAN F. *Role Playing in Leadership Training and Group Problem Solving.* New York: Association Press, 1956.

MORENO, J. L. *The First Psychodramatic Family.* Beacon, New York: Beacon House, Inc., 1964.

———. *Psychodrama.* 3 vols. Beacon, New York: Beacon House, Inc., 1946–69.

———. *The Theatre of Spontaneity.* Beacon, New York: Beacon House, Inc., 1947.

———. *Who Shall Survive? Foundations of Sociometry, Group Psychotherapy and Sociodrama.* 2d ed. Beacon, New York: Beacon House, Inc., 1953.

———. *The Words of the Father.* Beacon, New York: Beacon House, Inc., 1941.

SHAFTEL, FANNIE, and GEORGE SHAFTEL. *Role-Playing for Social Values: Decision Making in the Social Studies.* Englewood Cliffs, New Jersey: Prentice-Hall, Inc., 1967.

SIROKA, ROBERT W., and ELLEN K. SIROKA. "Psychodrama and the Therapeutic Community," *Confrontation: Encounters in Self and Other Awareness,* eds. Leonard Blank, Monroe G. Gottsegen, and Gloria B. Gottsegen. New York: The Macmillan Company, 1971.

Periodicals

ALLEN, DORIS TWITCHELL. "The Essence of Psychodrama," *Group Psychotherapy,* XIII (September–December, 1960), 188–94.

BRIND, ANNA B., and NAH BRIND. "The Tragic Origins and Countertragic Evolution of Psychodrama," *Group Psychotherapy,* XIX (March–June, 1966), 94–100.

BRONFENBRENNER, URIE, and THEODORE M. NEWCOMB. "Improvisations — An Application of Psychodrama in Personality Diagnosis," *Sociatry,* I (March, 1948), 367–82.

DEL TORTO, JOHN, and PAUL CORNYETZ. "How to Organize a Psychodramatic Unit," *Sociometry,* VII (May, 1944), 250–60.

ENNEIS, JAMES M. "Establishing a Psychodrama Program," *Group Psychotherapy,* V (April–July–November, 1952), 111–19.

FEINBERG, HENRY. "The Ego Building Technique," *Group Psychotherapy,* XII (September, 1959), 230–35.

FINE, REIKO, DENNIS DALY, and LEON FINE. "Psychodance: An Experiment in Psychotherapy and Training," *Group Psychotherapy,* XV (September, 1962), 203–23.

FREEDMAN, JONATHAN L. "Role Playing: Psychology by Consensus," *Journal of Personality and Social Psychology*, 13 (October, 1969), 107–14.

HAGAN, MARGARET, and MARION KENWORTHY. "The Use of Psychodrama as a Training Device for Professional Groups Working in the Field of Human Relations," *Group Psychotherapy*, IV (April–August, 1951), 23–37.

KATONA, ARTHUR. "Sociodrama," *Social Education*, 19 (January, 1955), 23–26.

LIPPITT, RONALD. "The Psychodrama in Leadership Training," *Sociometry*, VI (August, 1943), 286–92.

———, LELAND P. BRADFORD, and KENNETH D. BENNE. "Sociodramatic Clarification of Leader and Group Roles, as a Starting Point for Effective Group Functioning," *Sociatry*, I (March, 1947), 82–91.

LIPPITT, ROSEMARY. "The Auxiliary Chair Technique," *Group Psychotherapy*, XI (March, 1958), 8–23.

———. "Psychodrama in the Home," *Sociatry*, I (June, 1947), 148–67.

LIVERGOOD, NORMAN D. "Roles People Over-Act," *Psychotherapy: Theory, Research and Practice*, 5 (December, 1968), 248–53.

MANN, JOHN. "Didactic Use of Sociometry and Psychodrama," *Group Psychotherapy*, VII (December, 1954), 242–48.

MORENO, J. L. "The Concept of Sociodrama: A New Approach to the Problem of Inter-Cultural Relations," *Sociometry*, VI (November, 1943), 434–49.

———. "The Dilemma of Existentialism, Daseinsanalyse and the Psychodrama: With Special Emphasis upon 'Existential Validation,' " *International Journal of Sociometry and Sociatry*, I (September, 1956), 55–63.

———. "On the History of Psychodrama," *Group Psychotherapy*, XI (September, 1958), 257–60.

———. "Role Theory and the Emergence of the Self," *Group Psychotherapy*, XV (June, 1962), 114–17.

———. "The 'United Role Theory' and the Drama," *Group Psychotherapy*, XV (September, 1962), 253–54.

MORENO, ZERKA T. "Note on Spontaneous Learning 'In Situ' versus Learning the Academic Way," *Group Psychotherapy*, XI (March, 1958), 50–51.

———. "Psychodramatic Rules, Techniques, and Adjunctive Methods," *Group Psychotherapy*, XVIII (March–June, 1965), 73–86.

———. "A Survey of Psychodramatic Techniques," *Group Psychotherapy*, XII (March, 1959), 5–14.

ORTMAN, HARRIET L. "How Psychodrama Fosters Creativity," *Group Psychotherapy*, XIX (September–December, 1966), 201–13.

PARRILLI, ANNE, and FRANCIS SCAVULLO. "Guidance through Drama," *High Points*, XLIII (November, 1961), 76–77.

RIESSMAN, FRANK. "Role-Playing and the Lower Socio-Economic Group," *Group Psychotherapy*, XVII (March, 1964), 36–48.

SACKS, JAMES M. "The Judgment Technique in the Permanent Theater of Psychodrama," *Group Psychotherapy*, XIX (March–June, 1966), 29–31.

SCHWEBEL, MILTON. "Role-Playing in Counselor-Training," *Personnel and Guidance Journal*, XXXII (December, 1953), 196–201.

SHAFTEL, GEORGE, and FANNIE SHAFTEL. "Language Plays a Role," *Elementary English*, XXVII (May, 1950), 297–305.

SHEATS, PAUL H. "Sociodrama as an Aid to Large Group Communication," *Sociatry*, IV (March, 1948), 431–35.

SIROKA, ROBERT W. "Psychodrama in a Therapeutic Community," *Group Psychotherapy*, XX (January, 1967), 123–26.

———. "Sociodrama and the Negro Family," *International Journal of Sociometry and Sociatry*, IV (September–December, 1964), 91–93.

——— and Gilbert A. Schloss. "The Death Scene in Psychodrama," *Group Psychotherapy*, XXI (December, 1968), 202–5.

SPEROFF, B. J. "Empathy and Role-Reversal as Factors in Industrial Harmony," *The Journal of Social Psychology*, 37 (February, 1953), 117–20.

TOEMAN, ZERKA. "Clinical Psychodrama: Auxiliary Ego, Double, and Mirror Techniques," *Sociometry*, IX (May–August, 1946), 178–83.

VON WIESE, LEOPOLD. "Role Playing as a Method of Academic Education," *Group Psychotherapy*, V (April–July–November, 1952), 73–77.

WEINER, HANNAH B. "The Identity of the Psychodramatist and the Underground of Psychodrama," *Group Psychotherapy*, XX (September–December, 1967), 114–17.

——— and JAMES M. SACKS. "Warm-Up and Sum-Up," *Group Psychotherapy*, XXII (March–June, 1969), 85–102.

ZANDER, ALVIN F. "Role Playing: A Technique for Training the Necessarily Dominating Leader," *Sociatry*, I (June, 1947), 225–35.

ZELENY, LESLIE D., and RICHARD E. GROSS. "Dyadic Role-Playing of Controversial Issues," *Social Education*, 24 (December, 1960), 354–58.

Part Five
Marathons

Introduction

A marathon group is differentiated from other group forms by its length. This method, first developed by Dr. George R. Bach, consists of a group process which continues essentially uninterrupted anywhere from six hours to three or four days. The purpose of extending the time is to intensify and accelerate the process of emotional self-exposure. The deliberate building of group pressure over time, combined with the effects of fatigue, helps resistant participants to lower their social masks and defenses.

Although this approach is used extensively in growth center programs, literature on the marathon as sensitivity training is very sparse. The articles in this section are all written by psychotherapists who use marathon techniques as part of their therapy, or as an adjunct to therapy.

Bach ("The Marathon Group: Intensive Practice of Intimate Interaction") discusses the psychological processes and therapeutic effects of this method. He outlines Ten Marathon Commandments, a set of ground rules he feels are important for the effectiveness of all marathons. Bach believes the marathon is most beneficial to the individual whose fear of behavioral change is manifested in such extreme resistance that it demands the extended time and consequent heightened intensity of this process.

Elizabeth Mintz ("Time-Extended Marathon Groups") is concerned primarily with the phases of the marathon group process. In the opening phase, participants get acquainted. Next, in the hostile phase, feelings of anger and boredom are openly expressed. In the dependency phase, participants express the need to be loved and their accompanying fears of rejection. This is a period of intimacy when group members accept and comfort each other. The final phase involves, along with warmth and cohesiveness, feelings of anxiety at the coming termination of the group.

While the first two articles deal more generally with the structure and process of the marathon group, Paul Bindrim ("A Report on a Nude Marathon") treats a specific factor, physical nudity, as it affects the group process. Since the aim of marathon members is to disrobe emotionally,

Bindrim feels that physical nudity heightens and stimulates this process. Bindrim describes the structure of the group and the reactions of participants, presenting transcribed sections of the actual verbal interaction. Reactions ranged from fear to a feeling of freedom. In the process of the marathon, the group moved from mistrust to trust, from polite acceptance to honest critique, from dependency to autonomy and from autocracy to democracy. Bindrim concludes that nudity facilitated open discussion of feelings about sex and increased participants' self-acceptance. His conclusions are tentative and he points out the need for more experimentation with this technique.

The Marathon Group: Intensive Practice of Intimate Interaction[1]

GEORGE R. BACH

G. R. Bach, "The Marathon Group: Intensive Practice of Intimate Interaction," *Psychological Reports*, 18: 995–999, 1966. Reprinted with permission of author and publisher.

Summary. — Briefly are described the schedule, contents, the psychosocial processes, and the therapeutic effects of Marathon Therapy which is a living-in, intensive interaction experience in which so-called "patients" and so-called "psychotherapists" involve each other as persons in reciprocal influence-pressures to improve their styles of life.

I

Like all effective group psychotherapeutic programs, the *Marathon* is a group practicum in intimate, authentic human interaction. One of the unique aspects of the Marathon technique is an intensification and acceleration of transparency and genuine encounter by a deliberate instigation of group pressure focused on behavioral change.

[1]The information contained in this paper was presented May 5, 1964, at the 120th annual meeting of the American Psychiatric Association in Los Angeles, California and then prepared in manuscript form on October 6, 1964. Although much clinical work and a great deal of research have been done since that time, the need for a description of the basic procedure seems still needed, hence, the manuscript in its original form is made available.

In the course of conducting over 12,000 therapeutic group hours with a great variety of patients, it is clinically observable that for many patients the 50-minute individual hour or the 1- to 2-hour group sessions are not long enough for either patient or therapist to take off their social masks, i.e., to stop playing games and start interacting truthfully, authentically, and transparently. It takes a longer session for people in our culture to switch from the marketing stance of role-playing and image-making, which they must practice in the work-a-day world, to feel free to "come out" straight and strong, not hidden behind oblique "sick" roles or other so-called "resistance."

Clinical experience has shown that *group-pressure*, rather than the therapist's individual interventions and interpretations given privately, is a major vehicle which can move people effectively and quickly from impression making and manipulative behavior toward honest, responsible, spontaneous *levelling* with one another. But it takes time for the therapeutic group to generate influence-pressure in intensity and work-oriented kind, sufficient to produce behavioral change. It takes time, also, for group members to display their individual ways of acting within the group which simulates their ways of being and acting in the world. It takes time for therapists and peers to discern the potential for therapeutic change in each person and then to focus on this potential and to suggest change. Finally, it also takes time to experience the change, experiment with it and practice it here and now while participating in shaping the learning culture of the therapeutic group. All of this, becoming transparent, levelling, exposing to influence-pressure, attempting changes and practicing new behavior, we believe, is a *natural Gestalt*, i.e., *a unit* of learning experience which should not be broken up into bits and pieces but should occur as a whole, mediating a significant turning-point, a big step toward becoming what one can be!

Customary schedules of group therapy tend to break up this experiential learning unit. One-, two-, or even three-hour office meetings are not enough therapeutically, although staff time and fee economics make them universally accepted schedules. We have tried long hour groups and also week-end retreats and closely spaced groups (every other evening). With each of these schedules we noticed that there are always a few patients who "slip by" the experience, always waiting and ready to level truthfully with their peers, but never quite coming out openly transparent in time for the group to get hold of them fully for feedback, confrontation, and pressure to change. These brief interrupted groups rarely generate the right amount and kind of *influence-pressure* to make a crucial impact on the resistant learner. The brief group is an ideal playground for time-wasting, psychiatric games, such as diagnosing (labelling) safaris into phantasias, psychological archeology, playing psychoanalysis with "transference" interpretation, collusive acceptance of people's irrational self-propaganda as to "who is the best therapist," "best patient," etc., etc.

Searching for a practical solution, we were delighted to discover last year (in 1963) that a group of younger colleagues (Roger Wickland and Frederick Stoller) had independently developed in a psychiatric hospital setting all-day-long types of group therapeutic sessions which were effective in producing therapeutic changes in "difficult" patients. Adopting this approach to our private practice patients, we re-activated our old week-end retreat program but with a new twist: no interruptions, continuous meetings for 2 days, no sub-grouping, no socializing, minimal breaks, clear-cut ground rules, and admission of people seriously interested in changing themselves rather than the universe. The revision is a success thanks to our consultant, Dr. Frederick Stoller, who working as my co-therapist in the very first Marathon ever done with private patients, has helped me significantly to improve our old week-end live-in program.

Currently, our *Marathon* group therapy retreats take place in a secluded private setting where a selected group of 10 to 14 participants can stay together for 2, 3, or 4 days.[2]

The actual schedule of a particular Marathon varies, depending on setting and the members' goals and values. In the standard procedures members meet non-stop throughout the first night, i.e., without sleeping for 24 hr. or longer. The Marathon terminates in non-verbal, silent communication exercises, conducted in pairs. This is followed by a "closure-party" in which sub-grouping is resumed. Thus, a gradual re-entry into the conventional social atmosphere is reluctantly made. The entire session may be recorded and a feedback follow-up is scheduled 4 to 8 weeks later, which is designed to reinforce those decisions for change which have been emerging during the Marathon itself. In our Institute practice the Marathon retreats for private patients are systematically integrated with the regular group therapy program. Most patients are first seen individually (briefly) and then assigned to a regular 2- to 4-hour weekly therapy group. Marathon retreat experiences are interspersed at intervals of 3 to 6 months. Some Marathons are "specialized" for marital couples, executives of business organizations, or an advanced training session for group psychotherapists or social science researchers.

We conceptualize the Marathon therapeutic process as a practicum in authentic communication, based on freedom from social fears conventionally associated with transparency.

The unique opportunity of participating in honest encounter on a day-and-night basis produces psychological intimacy among the participants.

---

[2]The enrollment fee, which includes room and board, ranges from $90.00 to $300.00 per participant depending on duration, setting, and staff. The minimum fee per actual group therapy hour is $3.00.

This gives them a taste for what can be achieved with significant others everywhere.

As subjective truths are shared, irrational and ineffectual behavior appears incongruent, to be dropped in favor of new, more intimate, and competent behavioral patterns. The latter emerge and are practiced in the course of the Marathon. Orientation is ahistorical, emphasizing "what" and "how now" rather than "why" and "where from."

The genuine productivity of every group member is the therapist's mission which he procures by whatever means at his disposal. One of the other missions of the therapist is to maximize group feedback and enhance the opportunity for genuine encountering of and exposure to group pressure. For these reasons the Marathon is not unlike a "*pressure cooker*" in which phoney steam boils away and genuine emotions (including negative ones) emerge. The group atmosphere is kept focused every moment on the objectives at hand: to produce *change in orientation* and new ways of dealing with old crucial problems (creativity).

Every member is a co-therapist and co-responsible for the relative success or failure of any given Marathon meeting. Thus, the two or more professional co-therapists will, if and when they genuinely feel it, take their turns to participate "patient-wise," that is, as whole persons rather than just in a technical role-wise form. Decisions for change and serious commitment to follow through in life action are frankly elicited. Follow-up sessions will inquire into their validity.

Concerning *selection*, prospective Marathon participants are not sorted out in the traditional psychiatric-diagnostic sense, but rather on the basis of (1) attitudes toward self-change and (2) group constellation. Before admittance "Marathonians" must convince one and preferably both professional co-therapists that they are anxious to make significant *changes* in their customary ways of acting and being in this world. This presumes some degree of basic self-understanding of what one *now* is and what one can potentially become. The purpose of the Marathon is to awaken and strengthen further feelings for new directions and *movement* toward self-actualization in mutual *intimate concert* with others who are growing also. Marathons create a social climate for inter-peer growth stimulation, a sort of *psychological fertility!*

The Marathon group-therapeutic experience is most fully effective with those who wish to exchange their own ways of acting and being in this world and who are ready to quit blaming others and environment for their present unsatisfactory lot. New patients who initially tend to play the psychiatric game: "*I* am sick — *YOU* cure me" may be admitted to *initiation types* of *Marathons* whose specific mission is to knock out blamesmanship and other false, irrational, socially destructive operations (Bach, 1954) by which people preserve, cuddle, and justify their sick-roles. A patient who has given up his game of "I am sick — You, Doctor, and you-all (group) do something and take care of me" is a person ready to behave like a problem-solving adult. Such an individual can quickly learn to accept rational group-pressure as a useful means of strengthening his still weak and new "character." Therapeutic group pressure need not be misused irrationally (Bach, 1956) and immaturely as a substitute for individuality or as some social womb into which one may regressively crawl and hide there in fearful alienation from the big, bad competitive world of adult "fighters!" The regressive tendency to depend on the group is counteracted by the demand for *everyone to act as therapist to everyone*.

The work-burden of trying to be an effective co-therapist and agent of change to others *fatigues* all Marathonians over the long work hours. It takes devotion mixed with CONSTRUCTIVE AGGRESSION to get people to take off image-masks and put on honest faces. It takes patience and energy to break down resistances against change which all well-entrenched behavioral patterns — however irrational — will put up as part of a person's phoney "self-esteem." The exhaustion and *fatigue* produced by the Marathon procedure leads to refusal to spend any energy on 'acting up' or 'acting out.' Tired people tend to be truthful! They do not have the energy to play games.

Therapeutic Effects of Marathon Therapy

It also takes disciplined, concerted group-cooperation to create properly *focused* selective group pressure. Behavioral change is not created by uni-lateral influence, or chaotic, disorganized "free-for-all," cathartic "group-emotions" *per se*. Marathons are *not* tension-relieving, cathartic acting-out groups. They generate rather high levels of emotional tensions which stimulate cognitive re-orientation for their relief! Generally two new modes of acting, feeling, and being emerge during a Marathon: (1) *transparency of the real self*, which (being accepted and reinforced by the peer-group) leads to (2) *psychological intimacy* within the peer-group. This sequence from transparency to intimacy is a natural development because what alienates people from one another are the masks they put on, the roles they take, the images they try to create, and many of the games they play. Parenthetically, there are a few intimacy-producing games played by explicit mutual awareness and consent. These inter-personal stances alienate because they make it harder to know a person and to know where one stands with him. Inter-personal uncertainty is experienced as psychologically dangerous and anxiety-evoking until authenticity and transparency are reciprocally practiced. One or both parties may have hidden ulterior motives which usually turn out to be exploitive or destructive. Unless a person displays himself transparently, one never knows when to come on with him and when to get off or when to give, when to get or when to give up! One must remain alienated, on guard against the possibility of *psychological ambush*, i.e., to be seduced into spilling one's guts, to expose one's vulnerability, to get one's expectations up, only to be let down, even 'destroyed.' The con-artist's use of the double bind, i.e., you are damned if you do and damned if you don't, is psychologically lethal, for friends have no effective defenses against the double bind.

In the course of the long work hours of Marathon therapy, a transition from this self-defensive alienation and exploitive game-playing to psychological intimacy is revealed for everyone present to see.

II [3]

Entering a Marathon group implies submitting to a set of *ground rules*. The importance of these rules is such that they have been termed *Ten Marathon Commandments*. How explicit these rules are made depends upon the sophistication of the particular group; many participants grasp them without their having to be concretely outlined. However, there are groups which require that the rules be clearly laid out, and individual participants may behave in such a manner as to force the rules to be spelled out. In any case, these rules must be crystal clear in the minds of the group leaders and will act as a guide for their direction of the sessions. The following, then, are the basic group rules of the Marathon.

The Ten Marathon Commandments

(1) To stay together in the same place and not leave until the group breaks or ends at its prearranged time. Everyone communicates with the *whole* group. Everyone attends to and reacts to how each individual acts in the group situation. This means that there must be *no sub-grouping*, such as is common at ordinary social gatherings and parties. Only during official group breaks and at the end of the session do people break up into sub-groups.

(2) Creature comforts are to be taken care of on a self-regulatory basis. Eating will be done within the rules of the group, usually on a buffet basis *without disrupting the continuity of the group proceedings!* Participants can move about to different chairs, lie down on the floor, indulge in exercises within the sights and sounds of the group arena. Brief breaks for exercising, sleeping or changing clothes will be decided on by each group as a whole. There will be no alcohol or drugs taken during the Marathon proper. At the conclusion, most groups treat themselves to a "closure-party" and some groups schedule a follow-up meeting.

(3) The group leader is bound by the same rules as everyone else, except that in order to keep his services alert he has the privilege, during

[3]Part II was drafted by Dr. Bach and edited by Dr. F. Stoller after both had worked together and also independently with Marathon groups for 2 years.

every twenty-four hours of work, to rest up to four hours away from the group. During his absence, the group continues the meeting on a self-regulatory basis with every group member responsible for the uninterrupted continuation of the group proceedings and the enforcement of the ground rules. (A group leader in top physical condition may become so involved in the proceedings that he may choose not to exercise his resting privilege.)

(4) All forms of physical assault or threats of physical violence are outlawed. Attacks must be confined to verbal critiques. However, there are no limits as to the straight-forward use of Anglo-Saxon words or slang.

(5) Legitimate, professionally correct group procedures such as Psycho-Drama, Awareness-expansion Exercises, "Sensitivity Training," Transactional Games Analyses, etc., may be used temporarily during a Marathon, but only under *very* special circumstances. We have found that the use of a "technique" may retard rather than facilitate the slow, natural emergence of trust, transparency, and intimacy. Any routine use of any group-process "technique," however valuable it may be in other settings, is definitely contra-indicated in the Marathon group situation.

(6) The encountering experience is a four-phase process. Individual expressions are (a) reacted to, and (b) these reactions are shared in a "feedback." (c) The "feedback" in turn generates counter-reactions (d) from the original expressors as well as from the rest of the group. Members are expected to facilitate each of these phases by active participation in the following manner.

(6i) Members share true feelings as clearly and transparently as possible. The expressor is himself responsible for drawing and keeping the full attention of the group onto himself. No one should wait to be "brought out." Every participant is expected to put himself voluntarily into the focus of the group's attention, to seek out the group and to turn attention to himself, preferably a number of times. This applies to *everybody* including the official group leaders. There are *no observers*, only active participants!

By being an attentive audience, the group rewards the expressor. The expressor will remain in focal-position (or "hot-seat") until his feeling-productivity wanes and/or until the expressor himself has had "enough" of the "hot-seat," or until group-interest and group-pressure are dissipated.

(6ii) In the "feedback" reactions to the expressor, no holds are barred! Candid "*levelling*" is expected from everyone, which means participants explicitly share and do *not* hide or mask their here-and-now, on the spot reactions to one another! Tact is "out" and brutal frankness is "in." Any phony, defensive or evasive behavior (such as playing psychiatric games or reciting old "lines") is fair game for the group's critique and verbal attack. "Ought's-manship" (advising others how to solve their problems) can deteriorate into a time-consuming, dulling routine which suppresses spontaneous encounter. Excessive advice-giving is, therefore, undesirable.

(6iii) Trying to make people "feel better" is *NOT the purpose of the Marathon.* Self-appointed, tactful diplomats, amateur "protectors," and "Red Cross nurses" distract and dilute the levelling experience. Any kind of protective "cushioning" or cuddling spoils (for the central "hot-seat" person) the experience of standing up alone to the group, as he must to the world. Cushioning interventions should be held in abeyance until a participant has had the opportunity to express the full range of his Being in the group and to feel the group's reaction to him.

(7) "SHOW ME NOW . . . DO NOT TELL ME WHEN" is *the* Marathon Leitmotif. Owning up to feelings *here and now* and sharing them is *the* mode of participation. Telling the group about how one behaves outside the group and how "he" then and there reacted in bygone times and other places, back home or back at the office — is only warm-up material. The thing to do is for each member to let himself feel his presence in the group and let the *currently active impact* of the others get to him!

The modes of participation recommended in the four paragraphs above (6i, 6ii, 6iii, and 7) provide each group member with the opportunity to become better aware of how he *IS* in the group and in what directions he may want to *change*, and to try out new ways of being in the group.

(8) "AS YOU ARE IN THE GROUP, SO YOU ARE IN THE WORLD." As the members learn to exchange feelings in the group, a pattern of participation automatically emerges which the group will mirror back to the individual member. In the long hours of a Marathon one cannot help being seen for what he really is and to see what he may become. The Marathon group simulates the world of emotionally significant others; and the ways in which the member relates to this world reflect the core pattern of his Being. The group members' reactions give cues as to the effect his behavior patterns have on the world. He has the option to try out new, improved ways of Being.

(9) Group members' changes and improvements in participation will be attended to by the group. Giving affectionate recognition to growth and new learning is as much in order as cuddling, defensive behavior is out of order (cf. Rule 6iii). Reinforcement of new learning is the loving side of critical levelling (cf. rule 7 for the "attack" part).

(10) While nothing is sacred within the group, the information gained during a Marathon week-end is confidential in the nature of professionally privileged communication. Nothing is revealed to anyone outside. Objective research reporting in anonymous format is the only exception to this "rule of discretion."

The "Ten Commandments," the ground rules for Marathon participants given above, are not arbitrary "rules" or "conventions." Rather, they emerged gradually and painfully in years of clinical experience with interaction groups generally and with Marathon groups in particular. Respecting these basic ground rules does not necessarily guarantee success for a given Marathon. But, we do know that respecting the work-spirit of the situation facilitates the exciting metamorphosis of an assembly of role-playing strangers into a creatively intimate, authentically sharing communion. Since the Marathon leader likes to facilitate and partake of this metamorphosis, he has a vested, professional and personal interest in keeping anybody from distracting him and the group from this beautiful and valuable experience.

References

BACH, G. R. *Intensive Group Psychotherapy*. New York: Ronald, 1954.
BACH, G. R. "Pathological Aspects of Therapeutic Groups," *Group Psychotherapy*, 9 (1956), 133–148.
BACH, G. R., & ALEXANDER, S. *Fight Training Manual*. Dubuque, Iowa: Kendall-Hunt.
Accepted May 1, 1966.

Time-Extended Marathon Groups_____

ELIZABETH E. MINTZ

Elizabeth E. Mintz, "Time-Extended Marathon Groups," *Psychotherapy: Theory, Research and Practice*, 4: 65–70, May, 1967. Reprinted with permission of author and publisher.

There is a favorite fiction theme: a number of people (typically 5 to 8, about the usual number in a therapy group) are cast away on an island, a mountain peak, a lonely castle, or somewhere else where there is no communication with the outside world. They have two common tasks: first, surviving; next, re-entering the world. The way they meet these tasks, and the intense drama of their relationships, have enthralled readers for centuries.

In the past two years the writer has conducted 24 time-extended "Marathon" groups[1] in which the participants (usually 8 in number) meet once only for an encounter lasting 28 hours. The circumstances are strikingly similar to those of free-association in the classical Freudian style, in that outside stimuli are minimized. For two days the participants relate to one another without stimulation from their outside lives.

As a therapeutic technique, marathon groups are experimental. Participants usually leave the groups glowing with enthusiasm, and there is considerable anecdotal material indicating that therapeutic gains are often permanent. Yet there are many purportedly curative experiences which can elicit warm testimonials although their objective value seems dubious. Objective measurements for the lasting value of marathons are lacking, and the power of contagious suggestion is especially difficult to rule out in such a group. Consequently, this paper will only offer a description of how a marathon group functions, what behavior patterns have been observed, and what special techniques have been found useful.

The Participants

With the exception of special groups conducted for therapists, groups are now composed of self-selected participants interested in dealing with their emotional problems. The earlier groups were carefully selected for ego-strength plus experience in individual and group therapy. As my confidence increased, I accepted referrals from colleagues and subsequently from participants who wished a friend or a spouse to undergo the experience, and gradually I abandoned the requirement of previous experience in group therapy.

If the referral came from a non-professional source, one or more initial get-acquainted interviews were scheduled, and it was made clear that if the patient did not already have a relationship with a therapist, either myself or a colleague would be available for any follow-up work on an individual basis which might be needed. Thus far, no emergency follow-up work for people not in ongoing treatment has been requested.

Colleagues have sometimes voiced concern about the possibility of traumatization by a marathon. Thus far, no adverse effects have been noted or reported, although two participants (in different groups) left the marathon after the first day. Both were patients in ongoing therapy; in both cases, therapist and patient were aware of the possibility of the patient's being overwhelmed by a group of this type, and felt that the ongoing therapeutic relationship gave adequate protection.

[1]The technique of time-extended groups was developed by Dr. George Bach, and was first encountered by the writer as a participant in one of his groups. The warmest gratitude is due to Dr. Bach for his bold creativity and for his generous encouragement. Special acknowledgement is also due to Benjamin S. Brody, with whom most of these groups have been conducted.

As yet, the writer has not ventured to admit into a marathon anyone whose reality-testing was substantially impaired. Such a participant could probably be protected from cracking under group pressures, but would drain the time and energy of the group disproportionately.

The Setting

Participants remain in one room, except to visit an adjoining bathroom. They are advised to wear comfortable, informal clothing. Liquor is not served. Coffee, soft drinks and snacks are continually available. Meals are brought in. No observers or outsiders are present in any capacity. Cushions are placed on the floor, and the therapist often sets an example by being the first to lounge informally. When one participant rises to stretch or get coffee, another is likely to take his seat, since there is a physical need to vary position over such a long period of time. This continual shifting of position helps to prevent the tendency of any group to congeal into rigid poses or mutually-protective dyadic relationships.

The beginning time (around noon on Saturday) is set by the therapist. The ending time (late Sunday afternoon) must also be firmly established beforehand, because most groups are reluctant to separate and might drag on to an inconclusive ending, thus missing the therapeutic advantage of a clearly-timed, definite separation. The group makes its own decision on when to break up for sleep, and what time to re-assemble for morning coffee. Typically they choose to work until three or four a.m. Sunday, and convene again around ten. They arrange their own sleeping accommodations near the writer's office.

Typical Phases and Special Techniques

Although there are many exceptions among individual participants, these groups as a whole tend to pass through a sequence of phases: an initial phase which is primarily on an ego-level and in which the participants exhibit their characteristic defense systems; a phase in which anger is freely expressed and which may be seen as corresponding to a regression to Freud's anal-sadistic stage of development; a phase in which unsatisfied dependency needs of past and present are intensely experienced, and which may be seen as corresponding to a further regression to Freud's oral-dependency stage of development; a phase of enhanced self-acceptance and acceptance of others in which nearly all participants show heightened spontaneity and mutual warmth, seen as corresponding to Freud's mature genital stage of development; and a final phase in which the group deals with separation anxiety. An effort will be made to describe these phases, along with the special techniques which must be used and the problems which must be faced by the therapist.

The Beginning Phase

The first feeling reported by most participants is frank anxiety.[2] One participant expressed it in a poem, of which one couplet was: "In thirty hours, can I conceal / The secret feelings that I feel." Some participants succeed in repressing this anxiety and present the group with a mask of poise and self-confidence, or in some instances resort quickly to putting other participants on the defensive.

Participants tell one another about their outside lives, their problems, and sometimes their early backgrounds, partly in an effort to get acquainted, partly in an effort to avoid the fear produced by intimacy with a group of strangers. Here, as in general throughout the life of the group, the therapist refrains from making interpretations, but instead tries to reach the immediate feelings behind these defenses.

A specific defensive measure often used in this beginning period is semi-social one-to-one conversations. The therapist utilizes this to make clear a basic requirement that the group must at all times function as a group.

This requirement is quickly taken over and enforced by the group itself after the therapist has said two or three times "You're leaving the group" or "Please stop talking in sub-groups — I want to hear everything."

One-to-one encounters on a feeling level within the group setting, however, are facilitated in much the same way as in conventional therapy groups, although a heightened intensity is aimed for. Here appears an advantage of the marathon situation; the therapist need have less fear that group members will be overwhelmed by intense intra-group transference and counter-transference reactions, since there is ample time to work them through. Thus, when two members begin to relate but are afraid of an intense encounter, the writer might say in a conventional group, "You're talking to Joe, but I don't see you looking at him." In a marathon, she might say, "You're talking to Joe, but actually you're avoiding him. What if you went over and stood in front of him, or even put your hand on his shoulder?"[3]

Fairly often, the defensive conventionality of the beginning phase is broken when a participant, after struggling painfully with his fear of rejection, forces himself to share with the group a secret which he has long regarded as painful or shameful (and which in two instances he had not shared even with his individual therapist). These secrets, often touch-

[2]The writer well remembers her apprehensiveness at entering Dr. Bach's marathon, and her efforts to convince herself that transportation arrangements could not possibly be made. As with other forms of therapy, it is desirable for the therapist to begin with a personal experience, and the first-hand experiencing of this anxiety is helpful in understanding what the participants experience.

[3]This technique, along with several other nonverbal techniques described here, were adapted in part by the writer from her experiences in the National Training Laboratory at Bethel, Maine, at which her "trainer" was Dr. William Schutz.

ingly and dramatically presented, are so meaningful to the participant that even long afterward the writer would not feel free to describe them, but they are invariably memories of guilt-laden actions which in themselves seem trivial to the group, and which are found to carry guilt-feelings from quite different sources. The working through of this displacement of guilt, which the courageous member is usually able to do with the help of the group, and the consequent moving together of the group into a more intimate relationship, is often the first important therapeutic movement which takes place.

The Hostile Phase

The next two phases, open hostility and open dependency, are broadly distinguishable, but there is often considerable overlapping or a pendulum swing back and forth in which dependency may be used as a defense against hostility, or vice versa, depending upon the dynamics of the individual. Nevertheless, most individuals tend to release hostility first.

When acute resistance appears in a marathon, it has — in the writer's still-limited experience — invariably preceded the phase of hostility, and has invariably taken the form of boredom and a sense of futility. "What are we all doing here anyway?" "Look at that sun outside — I could be playing tennis!"[4] Usually this is the only phase when there may also be prolonged silence.

The boredom may be accompanied by open criticism of the therapist's competence or personality. If these criticisms are transference distortions, their correction can usually be left to the group or to the exposure to reality offered by the prolonged time. Transference interpretations are rarely made at this period, as the insight — "My mother was like that — now I can't really see you any more as being that way — " seems to have more impact when achieved spontaneously.

Outright anger, sometimes appearing intensely and dramatically, may break through at this point, between two men, two women, or a woman and a man. Any characteristic of the target, whether perceived realistically or distorted, may evoke the anger — assertiveness, submissiveness, seductiveness, withdrawal, or superficiality. The "assistant therapist," who uses intellectualization as a defense, is of course a favorite target. The intensity of anger observed in these groups goes far beyond what has been observed in conventional groups. The writer was once or twice frankly afraid of an outburst of physical violence between two men.

The therapeutic management of openly-expressed anger depends on so many variables that only a few possible techniques can be described. When the anger is exaggerated, or indicates a gross perceptual distortion, the group

[4]All quotations offered in this article are taken verbatim from remarks made by participants in various marathons.

can be depended upon to stay with reality, offering alternate ways of perceiving the anger-evoking participant, or offering interpretations — usually valid — of unconscious reasons for the anger, having to do with family background ("Didn't you say your father was submissive too? Maybe that's why you're so burned up by his submissiveness,") or with projection ("Well, frankly, you impress me as kind of effeminate, yourself. I think you're sore at him because you're sore at you.") The angry participant may then temporarily shift his anger to whoever makes the interpretation, and thereafter often spends some time in a silence, perhaps assimilating the experience. Surprisingly often, the silence ends in friendly overtures to the participant who originally elicited the anger.

When the anger is accompanied by intense anxiety over the possibility of loss of control, the therapist prefers to be more active. The angry participant may be asked to carry fantasy as far as possible. ("What would you like to do to him? No, don't explain any more why you feel angry. Would you like to hit him, strangle him, or what?") In one group, where the participant's fear of his own anger was directed toward the male co-therapist, and where anxiety over loss of control seemed excessive and unrealistic, the angry man was asked to cross the room and place his hands around the throat of the male co-therapist. He complied after much anxiety and hesitation, and to his own surprise found that the fantasied destructiveness became a gentle touch. Such an episode often ends in an outburst of relieved, delighted laughter.

When the anger takes the form of intensely competitive feelings, along with the surface fear of being defeated which often masks an unconscious fear of winning, the competitive participant may be asked, "Who in this room would you most like to compete with? Or who are you most afraid of competing with?" The therapist may then suggest the non-verbal technique of arm-wrestling, which is quickly picked up by the group and utilized spontaneously as an auxiliary technique thereafter. This involves the competitors placing their two right arms together on the floor or on a table, elbow to elbow, and each attempting to force down the arm of the other. Nearly always, both competitors become intensely involved in it, and as yet the defeated competitor has never seemed to experience any resentment. Usually there is a mutual sense of exhilaration which spreads to the group. Often there are sudden, spontaneous insights as to the meaning of competition. ("I wanted to win, but God, I think I threw the match. My God, am I afraid of winning?") ("It scared me to beat him.") ("I felt as if I'd die if I couldn't win. Didn't know how set I'd be on winning.")

This conventionalized, almost ritualized form of direct physical competition has various advantages. It is a safety valve for anger, rather than a temptation to express the anger inappropriately. The participants do not get carried away, as they might in less-restricted forms of physical competition. Yet it gives an excellent opportunity to elicit feelings about competition and to channel and express anger in a harmless way. (It is almost impossible for anyone to get hurt in arm-wrestling, provided someone present knows how to direct the placement of the arms.) Finally, it offers the participants an opportunity for a kind of experience almost unique among adults in our society — direct physical competition, with bodily contact, without the necessity for a formal learning or practicing situation as in gymnasium wrestling or judo. Women as well as men may find themselves dealing with conflicts about competition in a more relaxed and open way after arm-wrestling. In one group, the writer used arm-wrestling to help dissolve a transference distortion of a long-term private patient, a mother-dominated man who actually believed that a husky, athletic, 30-year old male might be vanquished by a sedentary middle-aged female analyst, and who was completely astounded when, with an ease foreseen by everyone except himself, he defeated his omnipotent mother-substitute.

The Dependency Phase

When most (not necessarily all) of the participants have expressed and partly worked through some of their competitive or hostile feelings, a new atmosphere appears in the room. Sometimes the new feeling begins very late in the evening of the first day; sometimes it appears when the participants reassemble in the morning after the night's interruption. Physical fatigue perhaps plays a part in the emergence of the new feelings — a natural toxin, which can be naturally handled by the body, and is not open to some of the objections which can be raised to pharmacological aids to treatment. In any case, all groups thus seen now begin to show some of the most basic human feelings — the longing to be loved and cared for, and the accompanying dread and pain of rejection. Most often, these feelings emerge with vivid memories of early childhood experiences, which appear to lack the complaining, grudge-bearing quality and self-pitying sentimentality so often heard when a patient recalls early deprivation.

> Examples may make this phase clearer. In one marathon, a 30-year old man with three years of intensive individual treatment behind him, who had spoken often but rather unemotionally of his mother's lack of emotional warmth, finally spoke of it with true feeling — and, for the first time since his boyhood, was able to weep bitterly. Afterwards he experienced a sense of great release. In another group, a woman of 40, by no means immature either socially or emotionally, had spoken earlier with great bitterness about her late mother's indifference and mistreatment; now she acknowledged with intense feeling that she had loved her mother, who was in many ways a good person despite her faults; and she also experienced in her weeping a true mourning for her mother, leading to a sense of relief and freedom.

This is perhaps the most intense phase of a marathon group. With the natural sensitivity with which all group therapists are familiar, a group does not intrude upon a participant who is undergoing this deeply-felt sense of loneliness and desolation, but accepts his feelings with warm silence. Almost invariably, one person, usually but not necessarily the therapist, offers physical comfort. When a mother-figure or a father-figure seems to be needed as the comforter, the writer or her male colleague may put an arm around the shoulder of the grieving member, or clasp a hand. In other instances, a fellow-participant is a more appropriate comforter.

> For instance, a mature man who had been dealing earlier in the group with feelings of hatred toward an elder brother now began to experience, with weeping, his deeper feelings of affection and remorse. Another man in the group, who had earlier been the the first man's brother-substitute and had

consequently received transference feelings of antagonism, crossed the room and remained next to the weeping man, with an arm around his shoulders, until his grief was spent.

The question has been raised legitimately by colleagues as to whether this type of physical contact does not imply a direct libidinal satisfaction which may sidetrack the group from its therapeutic purpose, or lead to undesirable acting-out. In the writer's opinion, physical contact under these circumstances is neither a direct sexual gratification nor an evasion, but rather a genuinely-therapeutic corrective emotional experience. In our emotion-alienated society it is rather easy to find sexual contacts, even though they may be meaningless; but our tradition is quite consistently opposed to physical contact between adults which expresses affection, sympathy, support, or even simple human comradeship.

In this same phase of the group, physical contact of a counter-phobic nature is often apparent. Thus, in one group a man was describing the physical distance which his mother kept between her children and herself, and his conviction that this distance had contributed to his difficulty in having physical experiences with girls which were emotionally-meaningful. The writer approached him, sat down close by, and said to him "Touch me." The embarrassment and awkwardness of his response made his intellectual convictions about his problem into an immediate, vivid emotional experience, and he laughed with pleasure and relief when he was finally able to embrace his therapist-mother.

In another group, a homosexual girl spoke of her physical distaste for men, which she could overcome only by heavy drinking; a friendly man said to her, "I'd like to put my arm around your shoulders, but I'm afraid you wouldn't like it." She responded, "I'll meet you half-way." They met in the middle of the room, sat down close together, and remained together until the girl grew frightened by the closeness, moved away, and began to explore some of the reasons for her fear.

The incidence of sexual relationships occurring after encounters in marathon groups is about the same as in conventional ongoing groups; in the writer's 24 marathons, only three sexual relationships have been initiated by the group situation. In one, a fairly-mature man and woman, both desperately lonely, found one another so congenial that they began a relationship which was satisfying to both and which has now lasted almost a year. In another group, two young people, both chronically possessed by the need for conquest, picked out one another as "the coolest man" and "the cutest girl" in the room, and went off together after the group. The sexual experience, which in this instance was unquestionably acting-out, was disappointing to both; they did not meet again, but instead tried to work out their motives in individual therapy. As a result of this last incident, which was disappointing but not damaging to the couple, the writer has adopted a policy of suggesting that, if two participants in the marathon wish to see each other again for any reason, they should exchange phone numbers and wait for a week before getting in touch with one another, to avoid the possibility that the emotional intensity of the marathon situation would lead them to form unrealistic relationships.

The Final Phase

As the allotted time draws toward a close, the group members begin to experience and express a deep appreciation of one another. Participants seated side by side may reach out and clasp hands. In one marathon, the group members spontaneously pushed their chairs into a close circle, so that all shoulders were touching, creating a feeling of sitting around a campfire.

If there is a group member who has remained comparatively aloof and defended, the group as a whole turns to him at this time, and works hard and often very skillfully to draw him out and help him experience his feelings. Such a member is then sometimes able to express dependency and grief; if he continues to need his defenses, the group shows striking perceptiveness in deciding when to leave him alone, and it is very rarely necessary for the therapist to intervene if it seems necessary for him to keep his defenses.

Simultaneously, separation anxiety may begin to appear. More often than not, some group members will ask, "Why don't we go on a few more hours?" In other groups, there will be a request for the same group to meet again for another marathon. The writer responds by saying that, if all participants feel the same way a few weeks later, another marathon can certainly be arranged. Thus far, although about ⅔ of all marathon participants request membership in a second or even a third marathon, the eventual decision is, "I want another marathon, but after all I guess I'd rather have it with a different group of people." Participants seem to sense, and in some instances express consciously, the value of working out their defenses with a different group of potential transference-figures.

The last moments of a marathon, for which adequate time-warning should be given, are extremely touching. One woman participant said "People are so beautiful when you know them." A man whose rigid defenses had remained intact until the last few hours asked the group to join hands around its circle before parting.

Then with surprising ease the group moves toward the outside world, putting on coats, paying fees, and exchanging very warm good wishes.

Discussion

As noted above, participants almost unanimously speak of marathons, immediately afterward and a year afterward, as a worthwhile and moving experience. The words "I felt reborn" are often uttered. At the very minimum, this type of group has the stimulating and enriching impact of any intense emotional experience shared with other people.

There is only anecdotal evidence as to the value of marathons. ("I went home and felt closer to my wife than in years." "I left feeling so strong; I still feel so strong." "I went home and discovered my kids don't really hate me." "I've taught school for years and all the students always hated me. Ever since the marathon they like me. They come up to my desk and ask me questions.") In the absence of objective measurements, notoriously difficult here as in other forms of psychotherapy, one may legitimately question the enduring benefit of an experience lasting only two days.

The phases of a marathon group have been compared to the stages of psychosexual development in Freudian theory; there is also an analogy to a religious revival, in which confession is followed by a sense of divine forgiveness (in this situation represented by social acceptance by the group) and a renewed feeling of self-acceptance and well-being.

Finally, because the intensity of the interaction in these groups places special demands on the therapist, it should be stressed that it would be unwise for any therapist to conduct such a group without considerable experience in ongoing group therapy, and preferably not without personal experience as a participant.

A Report on a Nude Marathon:

THE EFFECT OF PHYSICAL NUDITY UPON THE PRACTICE OF INTERACTION IN THE MARATHON GROUP

PAUL BINDRIM

Paul Bindrim, "A Report on a Nude Marathon," *Psychotherapy: Theory, Research and Practice*, 5: 180–88, September, 1968. Reprinted with permission of author and publisher.

While this paper is factual, being based upon tape recordings of the entire session, it must also be regarded as highly tentative. It concerns only one experience with a nude group which may prove atypical, and has been prepared by an author whose past experience as a therapist does not qualify him as an expert on nudity or sexology and to whom these fields represent a minor area among his wider interests.

It hardly need be said that researching the effect of nudity on psychotherapy is highly controversial and is not suited to all therapists in all communities and in all professional settings, or to all participants, but should be approached in a cautious and sensitive manner by interested individuals, particularly during this early phase when knowledge is sparse, prejudice is strong and acceptability highly dependent upon the circumstances and the persons involved.

In the group to be described here, therapeutic interaction occurred with the same frequency as would be expected in a clothed marathon. In this regard extensive discussion has been omitted in the interest of conveying an overall picture of the new vector of nudity.

Theoretical Constructs Leading to the Experiment

The basic concept of the marathon is a minimum period of twenty-four hours of intimate, intensive, authentic human interaction, uninterrupted by sub-grouping, structured activities, and the routines of eating and sleeping (Bach 1966; Mintz 1967). It is hoped that this round-the-clock pressure will lead the participants to take off their social masks, stop playing games, and start interacting authentically and transparently. Theoretically, the group moves from mistrust to trust, and from polite acceptance to honest critique, from peeping-Tomism to participation, from dependency on the group leader to autonomy, and from autocracy to democracy. During this trial by intimacy, it is anticipated that layer by layer, roles, masks, and pretenses will peel away, leaving a more authentic revelation of oneself and of others. Many innovations have been introduced around this basic format, such as lengthening the period of interaction, allowing periods for sleep, and the use of structured activities such as video playback, movement and sensory awareness techniques.

Over a period of seven years the author noted that there was a growing tendency to disrobe as emotional intimacy and transparency developed between the group members. On a few occasions, when a pool or hot baths were available, the participants spontaneously engaged in nude swimming after the marathon had ended. These spontaneous excursions into nudity seem to increase interpersonal transparency, remove inhibitions in the area of physical contact, decrease the sense of personal isolation and estrangement, and culminate in a feeling of freedom and belongingness. It seemed quite possible that the inviolable sense of privacy that man maintains by wrapping himself in a tower of clothes, or retreating to the castle of his home might not only serve to safeguard his individuality, but also perhaps, in effect, be a self-imposed padded cell through which he can limit his contact when he basically distrusts and fears interaction with other persons. It seemed that disrobing might constitute a symbolic attempt to open this cell of isolated psychological privacy to healthy group interaction and intimacy. If a participant disrobed physically he might, by this gesture, gain the freedom to also disrobe emotionally. If this were true, it might be desirable to first disrobe and then interact, thus shortening the process and intensifying the beneficial results. At this point, the author read Maslow's (1965) *Eupsychian Management*, in which he stated: "After all, these training groups are a kind of psychological nudism under careful direction. I wonder, as a matter of fact, what would happen as an experiment, if these T-groups remained exactly as they are but only added a physical nudism. People would go away from there an awful lot freer, a lot more spontaneous, less guarded, less defensive; not only about the shape of their behinds, or whether their bellies are hanging or not, but freer and more innocent about their minds, as well. If I can learn not to be conscious about the fact that my ass is hanging or that my belly sticks out too much, if I can throw off this fear, this defense, maybe this act of freedom will enable me thereby to throw off a lot of other defenses — maybe the defense of looking ignorant, or uncontrolled, or something like that."

While this paper is tentative, and subject to the fallacies of clinical judgment, it reports what to the author's knowledge is the first attempt to explore the value of nudity as a facilitator of human interaction in a therapeutic group. I hope it may serve as a guide to others who are willing to risk the negative social and professional pressures that are inherent in conducting an experiment of this type.

It is a common experience in interacting groups that persons hesitate to touch each other. If full body contact of disrobed individuals were to be encouraged, this might well result in a deeper sense of intimacy. If, at this stage, sexual expression was not permitted, this sensory intimacy of skin contact might then be expected to deepen into more meaningful emotional intimacy. This emotional level of intimacy and transparency might then, in some instances, further develop into a sense of intensified personal identity and core unity with all life, which has been described as peak experience, self-transcendence, or the basic spiritual experience of at-one-ment. In structuring the marathon, it was hoped that each individual could be helped to move a little bit further along this chain of increasing authenticity and interrelatedness.

Composition of the Group, Location, and Living Arrangements

Announcements of the proposed nude marathon were sent to psychologists, marriage counselors, participants in group and individual therapy, and persons who had attended previous marathons. Dr. William E. Hartman, professor of sociology at California State College (Hartman & Fithian 1967), acted as co-therapist with the author. Dr. Hartman was assisted by Marilyn Fithian, A.B., a college instructor of folk-lore and marriage classes. The author was assisted by Sara McClure, B.S., a dance therapist. Twenty participants registered for the marathon and were initially screened by telephone interviews. A small reduction in fee was extended to married and unmarried couples, in an attempt to keep an even balance of sexes. This was felt to be important, since it was anticipated that the initial effect of nudity would be expressed in terms of sexual curiosity, which made it desirable that there be an equal number of men and women in attendance. Since more males than females registered, a few single women were offered reduced rates as an inducement for them to attend the marathon, thus maintaining the balance of the sexes, namely ten males and ten females. Minors were not admitted.

The occupations of the persons attending included three engineers, two school-teachers, four clinical psychologists, a pharmacist, two magazine editors, two social workers, an artist, and a number of housewives. Two of the participants were referred by clinical psychologists who felt that their problems were of a sexual nature and that their symptoms would be helped by the experience of social nudity. A few of the participants had prior experience with social nudity at nudist camps, but the majority either had had no prior experience, or their previous experiences had been limited to one or two occasions when they experienced nudity with a small group of their own selection. Two of the participants were a married couple; others were married but came without their mates; and the majority were single.

The location was Deer Park Nudist Camp near Escondido, California. Deer Park occupies an entire valley between two mountain ranges, is approximately four hundred acres in size, affords privacy, a beautiful natural setting, with abundant fruit trees and wildlife, and is equipped in a comparable fashion to a high-class resort hotel. It had just closed its operation to the general public so that the marathon group had complete privacy on the grounds. Its facilities included a large swimming pool, surrounded by cabanas, and a Jacuzzi bath, which was kept at a temperature of 102 degrees, and was large enough to accommodate the entire group. The group brought sleeping bags and air mattresses and slept in the open around the pool and in the surrounding cabanas. Meetings were held indoors and outdoors, depending on the weather. Climatic conditions were at times unfavorable, occasionally requiring the wearing of clothing for comfort. Meals were served cafeteria style while the group remained in session.

Ground Rules and Scheduled Activities

The participants agreed to conform to the following ground rules:

1. Remain with the group for the entire session and avoid sub-grouping;
2. Participate in all scheduled activities;
3. Remain in the presence of persons who would be nude, and feel free to remove their own clothing or to continue to wear their clothing as they wished;
4. Be known by their first name only, if this was their desire;
5. Refrain from any use of alcoholic beverages and drugs throughout the session;

6. Refrain from photography or overt sexual expression which might prove offensive to other participants in the group. Overt sexual expression was defined as any activity which would be socially inappropriate in a similar group wearing clothing. For example, hugging and kissing would be permissible, but intercourse or the fondling of genitals would not be considered appropriate behavior in a group setting.

The leaders reserved the right to refund tuition to any individual if they felt that the experience would be detrimental to his best interest or to that of the group.

It was suggested that the participants bring with them the things that they enjoyed smelling the most, touching the most, tasting the most, looking at the most, and hearing the most, for use as stimuli in a sensory saturation experience designed to induce a peak state of experiencing, which is perhaps best described as a mild "turn-on."

The group was in continuous session from 9 P.M. Friday evening until 3 P.M. Sunday afternoon, with six hours out on Friday evening and six hours out on Saturday evening for sleeping.

The group met on Friday evening with all members clothed. They were asked to share with the group the anxieties, anticipations, and fantasies that they were experiencing as they contemplated nudity. They were again reassured that they did not have to remove their clothing and that our primary interest was the exploration of their emotional attitudes toward clothing and nudity. The interaction took a little over an hour; the group was then informed that the session would move to the Jacuzzi bath and that they could bathe in the nude or wear bathing suits as they chose. They were also informed that following the session in the Jacuzzi bath, there would be an experience with colored lights in the main meeting-room. This would consist of colored patterns being projected on their bodies from a 35 mm slide projector. Those who wished to participate actively could stand in front of the lights and observe the esthetically beautiful patterns and colors in a full-length mirror, while those who preferred to observe could sit quietly in the darkened room.

Following the Jacuzzi bath and the lights, the group retired for the night and was awakened the following morning with the playing of a Bach Brandenburg concerto. They then had orange juice and coffee, and took a one hour walk around the grounds to enjoy the natural setting. Breakfast followed and the session continued out of doors. After lunch, another encounter was held in the Jacuzzi bath, which was followed by approximately one hour of movement and sensory awareness work, led by Sara McClure. As the weather was becoming colder, the session moved indoors for the evening. There was another brief period in the Jacuzzi bath prior to retiring.

The Sunday morning session included one hour which was devoted to meditation, facilitated by sensory saturation with peak stimuli. In this procedure, the participants chose partners of the opposite sex by gazing into each other's eyes for a few moments and then selecting the person with whom eye contact was the most comfortable and relaxing. They were then seated close to and facing the person of their choice. They were then asked to close their eyes and to keep them closed until asked to open them, following which, they were given suggestions conducive to relaxation. Each participant was asked to simultaneously taste, touch, and smell the items which he enjoyed the most and had selected for the experiment (Bindrim, 1966). For example, one participant simultaneously touched velvet, ate chocolate, and smelled a rose. These items were, of course, different for each participant. During this period, the prelude to Tristan Isolde, by Wagner, was played on a record player. This process of sensory saturation led to a mild drugless "turn-on" or peak state of experiencing. In this state, the participants were asked to re-experience in fantasy whatever event in their lives they considered to be the best moment that they had ever lived; a time when they flowed freely in the joy of living and felt close to the core of their being and at one with life. When they each had completed this fantasy recall of a peak experience and were "turned on" within the limits of their capabilities, they were asked to touch the fingertips of both hands with their partners and to quietly gaze into each other's eyes without movement or distraction, allowing themselves to open to each other and experience a growing sense of intimacy and at-one-ment. During this time, the Love Death from Tristan and Isolde was played. After twenty minutes of this eye-centered meditation, they were asked to place their chairs in a circle and share their experiences.

A brief period of evaluation preceded the closing of the marathon at 3 P.M.

The Emerging Dynamics of Adaptation to Nudity as Expressed by the Participants

In less than one hour and a half from the beginning of the marathon on Friday evening all participants were bathing nude in the Jacuzzi pool. Although two participants had been referred to the marathon specifically because of anxieties relating to sexuality and nudity, it may be assumed that most of the participants who were willing to attend the marathon were, by and large, ready for the experience. Permitting individuals to remove their clothing if they wished to, but not requiring them to do so, also eliminated issues that normally would be involved. The setting in which nudity was encouraged was a functional setting in which it was natural to remove one's clothing before bathing.

The preliminary ventilation of anxieties regarding nudity also desensitized areas which might have inhibited individuals, had they not been openly expressed and discussed by the group. The following quotes from the tape recording of the session held prior to removal of clothing are typical in this respect:

KEN: This is entirely new to me. I've never had any occasion with a group of people to be nude, and I'm scared to death. I think that Lou said it better than I could say it — that I was not so much inhibited as I'm scared of my reaction to other people, and of course scared to death of having an erection.

GREG: I've never tried it before, and I'll say that I have some inhibitions about it, mild to moderate.

LEE: I feel quite sensitive, both from the standpoint of being looked at and more so from the standpoint of looking at other people. I don't know exactly why I should, but that's what I want to find out.

TED: As I mentioned to Vicky earlier, I wasn't going to be the first, but I wasn't going to be the last one, either.

JOAN: This is my first experience in anything like this, including therapy, but I feel kind of included in the group; I'm not sure though if one weekend is quite enough.

The presence of people in the group who had already experienced social nudism also helped. They could allay some of the fears expressed by others. For example:

LEO: I had an experience seven months ago, just one experience in group therapy which became a nude session. It was a big hurdle, but once I said, 'Oh, the hell with it,' well, it's all over, and everybody's nude and who cares?

KATHLEEN: I had my first experience with social nudism about three years ago — it gave me a great feeling of exhilaration.

KARL: I've probably been nude longer than any of you here. I can't ever remember not having wanted to be in the nude, because I can remember when I was a very small boy in Germany, we used to swim nude. I look upon people who choose to dress when they don't have to as the odd ones. If, after I met a person at a nudist camp, you asked me under oath whether they were dressed or undressed, I couldn't tell you; it's because it's the normal thing. Nudity is a normal way of life and not something to be consciously made a goal.

ELIZABETH: We regularly have an open house, and at 9:30 the open house becomes a closed house. Everybody continues the conversation, but they take off their clothes. We've been doing this for a number of months and we find that when they remove their clothes, people seem to remove a layer of hypocrisy. The conversation seems to become more meaningful.

Saturday morning participants were asked to share what they had experienced when going into the Jacuzzi nude and when standing in front of the lights on the previous evening. The reports quoted from the tape recording of the session may be grouped under the following headings:

1. A sense of pleasure derived from the freedom to look at other persons' bodies and to be looked at:

LEE: I enjoyed looking at the lovely female bodies last night.

JACK: It was like one of my fantasies come into reality — all these girls — especially your body, Anita.

SUNNY: I was kind of hesitant, I didn't want to stand up in front of as many people as were there, I felt that was kind of exhibitionistic, and yet I really wanted to.

WALT: I did find it very difficult to look at people; in there in the light show of course it was easy. I was sitting there in the dark and nobody was looking at me and I could look at anybody, but it's very difficult to look directly. I thought a lot of the women were very attractive and I wanted to look at them directly but I didn't feel able to.

MURRAY: I particularly enjoyed looking at the bodies of the women, at their genitals and their breasts.

VICKY: The thought crossed my mind last night — what a shame it is that this wonderful structure, this human body, created by Nature, has to be covered up for a whole lifetime.

2. A personal sense of comfort, exhilaration, and freedom:

VIRGINIA: I felt very much more comfortable in the nude.

ANITA: I felt very much more comfortable being undressed than dressed. When dressed, I feel I have to sit up straight, keep my back up and all that. Undressed, I feel it's all open and so I feel very good, being undressed.

TED: I felt very exhilarated, not to the point that I was excited, but I just felt good about the whole thing.

3. The desire to touch and experience skin contact and a sense of being inhibited in this respect:

LEE: I enjoyed the lovely female bodies last night. Many of your breasts — I wanted to touch them, feel them, put my face against them.

TED: I was constantly thinking about just this idea of wanting to touch — why can't I touch?

4. Pleasure arising from the sense of group closeness and the relaxed expressions on the faces of the other participants:

EVELYN: I've been attending weekly therapy sessions, and I think it's remarkable how much closer I feel to the people here than I have felt in these other encounter groups which I have attended.

RICHARD: The pleasure of seeing people in their first experience in nudity — they don't find it a problem — it was enjoyable.

KATHLEEN: There seemed to be such a change in personality as the people got into the water. I think everyone who did get into the pool seemed immediately to relax, and to be comfortable.

LOU: I'd like to tell Jack what a marvelous look of pleasurable wonderment I saw cross his face when he hit the water in the pool last night. I haven't seen an expression like that except on a child's face when something marvelous happened and everything's all right.

5. A sense of the naturalness of the nude condition, and a feeling of relief at not having reacted inappropriately:

KEN: Just before going to bed I was walking around nude for a few moments, just to get my own reactions, and there were no reactions — the lack of a reaction was my only reaction.

LEE: My reaction was, 'What's all the goddam fuss about,' and I was pleased and a little bit surprised at my willingness.

GREG: It seemed like a very normal situation, particularly in swimming, a very comfortable situation, because it seemed for a purpose.

JACK: And speaking of erections, I looked at a girl, especially your body, Anita, and I could catch myself concentrating on this and I could feel a tickling in my genitals and I found that if I concentrated, if all my thoughts were on this, then I could have an erection very easily, but if it is diffused, it's just like going about everyday life, and I found it quite pleasurable.

TED: I had the feeling, "Why don't I have an erection, why don't I have this sensual urge that I might get when I see somebody in a bikini?"

6. The experience of being high or unable to sleep for most of the remainder of the night.

JERRY: Something very strange happened. After we got in the sleeping bags and I fell asleep, after about five minutes, all of a sudden I woke up, and I had this tremendous erection and I felt as if someone had taken this big heavy blanket off me, just pulled it off, and for the next two or three hours, I don't know what a trip is, I don't know what it is to be high, but what a time, my God!

TED: I laid awake the entire night. The stimuli that had been created by the nudity, I think, allowed a great deal of thought in my mind all night.

7. A sense of concern about one's physical body when comparing it with other members of the group.

WALT: . . . and the other reaction that I was aware of was feeling that my genitals perhaps weren't as large as the other men's, and this was a matter of some concern, although I didn't think about it much, but as I sit here now I know I was concerned.

PETER: When you were moving with Sandra, Jack, I felt jealous. I thought, "I'm not as good-looking as this guy is — look at his body, and I'm getting kind of paunchy and aged."

SUNNY: I found myself thinking, "Do I look as good as her?", comparing, and I didn't particularly like that reaction, and I felt like kicking myself for doing it, but I was doing it, and I thought, "I'm kind of fat here, and this and that, and do I want it to be out in the open and out in the light and have someone looking at me and thinking the same things about me?" — this kind of bothered me, especially when I was looking at Anita. She has such a beautiful body.

ANITA: The funny thing is that I have the same kind of negative feelings about my body.

At first, the experience of colored light patterns on nude bodies permitted the overt expression of voyeuristic and exhibitionistic tendencies. As the marathon continued, the tendency to look excessively or to experience self-consciousness when being looked at diminished to a point where many of the participants would have probably been unable to report whether others were or were not wearing clothing. Full body contact became more spontaneous and less sexually centered. In these respects, physical contact in the warm water of the pool was largely responsible for overcoming the inhibitions that most participants experienced in terms of skin contact in the initial phases of the marathon. Movement work and dance therapy in couples also furthered the process. Overt sexual expression was undoubtedly inhibited by the presence of the group and the ground rules, to which all participants had agreed. The beneficial effect of emotional openness, on the other hand, continued to enhance the depth of interaction in the marathon.

In the sensory saturation meditation and eye contact period on Sunday morning, emotional openness was even more intimate Perhaps it is best described as a group peak experience or a sense of spiritual at-one-ment. Most participants felt that this was the most profound experience they had in the marathon:

> MURRAY: I found it to be a very tranquil experience. I got out somewhere on the stream of the universe.
>
> KATHLEEN: . . . then in the eyeballing it was as if I were looking into my own eyes. I felt he was very with me — practically every moment — there were times when we were just grabbing for each other — trembling — and it was very difficult to withdraw.
>
> VIRGINIA: I think the high point was the experience I had this morning. . . . I felt a terrific warmth and tingling sensation up the spine and sometimes a sexual sensation with it — and as the experience built, I again saw the two experiences that I had in your office: the violet eyes followed by the light.
>
> GREG: Sometimes I would have a hard time telling whether your face was your face or whether I was there — rather that it was myself, rather than any extension or anything else — just merely the self in the same way as any other part of oneself. In many ways there was kind of a relaxing feeling, almost like being asleep for three years.
>
> EVELYN: (after a period of time on the floor, going through labor pains and the movements of giving birth): I feel as though I'm in labor . . . I feel like I created something — it didn't just happen to me . . . I guess God is always right here — I hadn't really believed it before. I gave birth but I feel purged at the same time; it's like they're both the same . . . I'm shook up but boy, do I feel good . . . I feel like laughing and crying and everything all over.
>
> TED: I've pulled away all my life from people — pulled away. I pulled away from Lou just now — or I felt I did. I don't know whether it's pulling away or whether it's a sort of feeling that I'm standing on my own two feet. I used to have to hold on to somebody because I couldn't stand up. I came closer to seeing God (shouting and weeping). He must be there — why do I shut Him out? I'm seeing God (sobbing) (long pause) . . . (opens eyes) I think I see better without my glasses on now.
>
> SANDRA: I was looking at the sky and I thought — I've never been here before and I haven't seen it, and my heart started pounding. And I looked around and I haven't seen any of you, I haven't seen the floor. And at this point I thought "I'm really tripping out" and then the beauty of the whole thing came through. I feel like a kid!

The Apparent Permanent Gains as Expressed by the Participants at a Post Session

Fifteen of the twenty participants attended a post session five weeks following the marathon.

The general consensus of opinion of both professional and lay participants was best expressed by Murray, a clinical psychologist, who stated:

> I've been telling people that asked me about what happened that I felt
> there were some people that were helped a great deal, and I didn't see any-
> body who was harmed. I think that when in a group of twenty-four people
> you have twenty or twenty-two who were really benefited, and no one really
> harmed, you have held an effective marathon.

The following comments made by participants are transcribed from the
tape recording of the post session:

LEE: For a period of several months I've been in a kind of metamorphosis.
I guess I can call it for lack of a better word, an emerging. If we can think
about my emerging like this (*gestures, indicating slow uphill plane*) our time
together kind of did this (*indicates rapid upswing*), a kind of zoom. Virginia
too has been emerging. For the first time in years we talked to each other
about things that are important. We're becoming friends for the first time in
many years. Virginia and I are divorcing — not as a result of this marathon —
but I think as a result of our re-emerging and finally discovering that we can
like each other, we can be friends, very good friends, but we just can't be
husband and wife any longer.

And after the meeting of the Humanistic Psychology Forum the other
night, this sour old bastard colleague psychiatrist with whom I had tangled
violently every time we got together came over to me with a great big smile
on his face, put his arms around me, patted me on the back, and said, "You
narcissistic old son-of-a-bitch, you've always been in love with yourself, and
I'm delighted that you recognize it." And George (a psychologist) who is
always kind of stand-offish, did almost the same thing. I'm alive again!
I don't feel as old as I am by a damn sight, and as a therapist I'm many times
more effective.

I ran a marathon with seven couples out of my practice a weekend or two
ago. I was open and free, and what I did came from way down deep inside,
not from thinking, as I used to — she's thinking this, he's thinking that, now
what would be the best way to get at it. I do think that the nakedness, the
feeling, what the hell have I got to hide now, might as well let the rest of it
come out, I think that this facilitated a lot of it."

VIRGINIA: On Tuesday night following the marathon I said to Lee, "This is
ridiculous. You're not happy with me and I'm not happy with you. We're
making each other miserable. Let's get this divorce," and from there on it
went ahead, and as he said, we have been friends. As he said, this is probably
the most friendly divorce anybody ever saw. We can talk together now. It's
as though somebody had to make the decision that set all of us free, including
our children. It was the best thing I've ever done in my life.

LEO: At the marathon one of the guys, I forget just who it was now, told
me I had a good-looking body, and this surprised the hell out of me, especially a man telling me that I've got a good-looking body. I had not thought
much of myself before this, in fact, I felt pretty much ashamed of myself.
I felt I was worthless and all this sort of thing. But I think that, along with a
number of other things, has caused me to experience a much greater acceptance of myself since the marathon. Now I don't care too much if I make a
mistake or if I'm wrong, or if somebody thinks I'm wrong. It's just too bad.

And I think I must have had a sort of dependency kind of thing with any
woman that I'd go with. I think I'm losing this dependency thing now. If this

woman I'm going with doesn't want to go with me, all right, and I didn't feel that way before.

I've felt a good deal more courage in facing anything that came along since the marathon, more confidence, and steadiness, rather than being all jumpy. And then as a result of this I moved into areas that I avoided because they were too traumatic. I'm just taking on bigger challenges now.

JACK: I seem less hostile to women, and more natural around them. I feel more open and less afraid of being attacked by them. I have been to two previous clothed marathons and I do believe nudity played a large part in my reaction.

ANITA: The most wonderful thing that happened to me at the marathon was that everybody thought that I was beautiful, and I had never really accepted this because of my relationship with my husband.

And the marathon also did something to my relationship with my husband. I saw what was going on between he and I. I've been open to him as far as my feelings are concerned. I always felt I had to kind of play my female role — I don't have to do this any more. If I say *no* it's *no*. My husband's been very dependent on me. I don't want to be a mommy, I want to be a female. He said, "I was looking at you as a mommy, and I was finding faults with your body like you were my mother." He catches himself now when he calls me mommy, and I pinch him, you know, to make him aware of it. I'm sick and tired of playing mommy. It's becoming much better now.

WALT: Sunday morning showed me that I can't open up and relate. I didn't interpret it that way for about two days. I had a whole case built up that it wasn't my fault. But then I became aware that, what the hell, all this came out of me, so I decided to start working on it. I discovered that what I'd been doing all my life was avoiding relationships. My mother died when I was seven and my father started chasing around with women. I saw all these women as bad. They were sexy as hell and I probably wanted them, but I saw them as bad and my grandmother told me they were bad. I think I fabricated stuff about women ever since in order to avoid getting close to them. I married a woman who didn't want to get close, and we're working that through now, but it's seventeen years later. I used to sleep in my mother's bed when my father was working nights. I think I've been true to my goddam mother all this time, and it's ridiculous, but that's what I've been doing. My father certainly wasn't, so somebody had to be. All the opportunities I've wasted! I've just been in constant turmoil for three weeks. I run to the john and I cry at work and I cry over everybody I can get to listen to me. I can talk to my wife, though, and she understands it completely, and I understand it.

BOB (*commenting on the telephone conversation that he had just had with Ted, who was not present*): Ted felt the marathon was beneficial in some ways. He said he's been in therapy for seven or eight years and he's never been able to work through his relationship with his father before, and he thought that was the most significant thing that happened at the marathon. He said people are so painful to him, and it's so hard to come and meet them and say goodby. He felt that if he came here tonight he would be in a sense reliving the painful experience of the marathon, so he decided he would not come. He said the religious experience on the last day was very positive for him. It gave him a great feeling of inner spiritual worth and value, not from the standpoint of formalized religion but in terms of personal strength. He said he'd like to go to another marathon, but people are there, and while he likes this group as well as any group, this group is still people, and people frighten him.

VICKY: Since the marathon I find myself smiling every once in a while, and I think the reason is the memory I have of how I so easily related to the men, without any fear of being rejected. It's really a big thing for me, even though I feel as though I'm doing it very naturally. For many years I've been very stiff, and I haven't related to men at all. Being in the nude did a great deal for me in this respect. I am still a little anxious when I see people clothed.

Conclusion

Nudity apparently facilitates group interaction in a marathon. Seventeen of the twenty participants felt that the factor of nudity increased their ability to open up to each other emotionally and to achieve a greater degree of authenticity and transparency. The group integrated and seemed to become therapeutically functional more rapidly than clothed marathon groups.

Nudity in a group which encourages skin contact seems to be therapeutic in itself. This is perhaps needed to compensate for the sensory isolation experienced by the individual in his normal clothed state. It may be assumed that the social world outside of the home is frequently experienced as a jungle of polite estrangement where physical and emotional contact is prohibited by walls, locked doors, clothing, status roles, and a variety of other masks. Perhaps this is why individuals frequently lack a developed sense of social responsibility and love for their fellow men and are seldom strongly motivated to give of themselves generously and work for the common good. It may also explain why family life at times disintegrates under the extreme emotional demands made by individuals whose relationships with a depersonalized society leave a famine in their hearts and a hunger that cannot be filled by any one person, not even, at times, by their mates. If this is true, nudity in itself may represent a symbolic and factual lifting of the mask which constitutes an invitation to tribal unity and which is most effective when a reversion to the established pattern of private paired relationships is inhibited by blocking sexual expression and sub-grouping.

Nudity is apparently of considerable help in dealing with specific problem areas, which often remain unexplored when participants are clothed. On leaving, Ted indicated that he was considerably less self-conscious when looking at, or being looked at by, other persons. This symptom was probably intensified by nudity and would have been less apparent in a clothed marathon. In addition, it manifested in a more basic sexual form, simplifying therapeutic intervention, which moved to an exploration of his sense of potency and manliness, and to an apparent resolution of an Oedipal complex which had prevented him from identifying with his father, who objected to his being physically close to his mother. In this respect, it would be interesting to see if voyeurs and exhibitionists and other sexual deviates referred by the courts might benefit by a nude marathon.

Self-acceptance, in many cases, is associated with body image. In this respect, much can be accomplished by the open discussion of what the individual feels are his undesirable physical characteristics. These are frequently distortions in his own thinking which can best be remedied by open exposure to group reaction, thus increasing his ego strength and mobilizing his deeper emotional conflicts.

The inhibition of overt sexual expression during the marathon is probably beneficial to individuals who would employ sexual activity as a defense against emotional closeness. For other sexually inhibited participants, it is perhaps unfortunate that our present social mores prevent a more generous sexual attitude in the therapeutic group.

In our society sensual body contact is generally considered to be an invitation to sexual intimacy. The inhibition of sexual intimacy by our mores thus also inhibits body contact. Since body contact is frequently essential to emotional expression, this taboo of touch blocks a vital avenue of communication. This is most clearly observable in relationships between males who are inhibited in their expression of love, since they may not embrace or experience tender body contact without the implication of homosexuality. The nude marathon seems to eliminate this confusion by encouraging sensuality while inhibiting sexuality, thus increasing the range of permissible emotional expression for both sexes. Most of the participants in the marathon were pleasantly surprised to find that they could enjoy sensual pleasure without sexual involvement. The author also observed that when participants in the nude marathon returned to ongoing clothed therapy groups they were more spontaneous in terms of body movement and physical contact. One somewhat inhibited female participant reported that following the marathon men were asking her for dates for the first time in years. Apparently her increased freedom to express emotionally and sensually made her more attractive to the opposite sex. We may tentatively conclude that nude marathons help to differentiate between sensuality and sexuality, thus increasing emotional expressiveness and furthering communication.

The nude marathon apparently requires two steps:

1. A permissive group setting in which participants express their reactions to intimacy which they inhibit in society and in clothed marathons. For example: voyeuristic and exhibitionistic tendencies, the need to touch and to be touched, and the anxieties relative to body image and sexual potency.

2. Once these factors which limit intimacy and authenticity are openly expressed and mobilized in their most basic forms, they are open to the therapeutic intervention of the therapist and the group. This process proceeds in most respects as it would in a clothed marathon.

It is also apparent that the nudist movement itself could contribute more to society if it permitted physical contact and encouraged the formation of encounter groups which would permit the continuation of what has begun as a symbolic removal of defenses in the form of clothing to proceed to the more significant emotional levels of basic human interaction.

References

BACH, GEORGE R. "The Marathon Group: Intensive Practice of Intimate Interaction," *Psychological Reports*, 18 (June, 1966), 995–1002.

BINDRIM, PAUL. "Cultivating Peak Experience," *Ways of Growth*, eds. Herbert A. Otto, and John Mann. New York: Grossman, 1968.

————. "Peak-Oriented Psychotherapy: An Approach to Self-Actualization through the Cultivation of Peak Experiences." Mimeographed, 1966.

————. "Peak-Oriented Psychotherapy: Case Histories and Taped Transcriptions of Therapy Sessions." Mimeographed, 1966.

HARTMAN, WILLIAM E., and MARILYN FITHIAN. *Nudism in America: A Social Psychological Study*, to be published.

MASLOW, ABRAHAM. *Eupsychian Management: A Journal.* Homewood, Illinois: R. D. Irwin, 1965, p. 160.

MINTZ, ELIZABETH E. "Time-Extended Marathon Groups," *Psychotherapy: Theory, Research, and Practice*, 4 (May, 1967), 65–70.

Marathon
Selected Bibliography

Books

MANN, JOHN. *Encounter: A Weekend with Intimate Strangers.* New York: Grossman Publishers, 1970.

SHEPARD, MARTIN, and MARJORIE LEE. *Marathon Sixteen.* New York: G. P. Putnam's Sons, 1970.

Periodicals

BACH, GEORGE R. "Marathon Group Dynamics: II. Dimensions of Helpfulness: Therapeutic Aggression," *Psychological Reports*, 20 (June, 1967), 1147–58.

———. "Marathon Group Dynamics: III. Disjunctive Contacts," *Psychological Reports*, 20 (June, 1967), 1163–72.

BINDRIM, PAUL. "Nudity as a Quick Grab for Intimacy in Group Therapy," *Psychology Today*, 3 (June, 1969), 25–28.

DEMOS, GEORGE D. "Marathon Therapy: A New Therapeutic Modality," *Psychotherapy and Psychosomatics*, 15 (1, 1967), 14–15.

GUINAN, JAMES F., and MELVIN L. FOULDS. "Marathon Group: Facilitator of Personal Growth?" *Journal of Counseling Psychology*, 17 (March, 1970), 145–49.

LAWRENCE, STEPHEN B. "Video Tape and Other Therapeutic Procedures with Nude Marathon Groups," *American Psychologist*, 24 (April, 1969), 476–79.

LEWIS, RICHARD W. "The Effect of Long Group Therapy Sessions on Participant Perceptions of Self and Others," *Dissertation Abstracts*, 28 (March, 1968), 3879–B.

MINTZ, ELIZABETH E. "Marathon Groups: A Preliminary Evaluation," *Journal of Contemporary Psychotherapy*, 1 (2, 1969), 91–94.

STOLLER, FREDERICK H. "The Long Weekend," *Psychology Today*, 1 (December, 1967), 28–33.

Part Six
Buyer Beware

Introduction

The articles in this section evaluate sensitivity experiences with caution, warning the readers of some dangers and limitations. Each author presents concerns about sensitivity groups from a different perspective. The result is a critical evaluation of the field. The articles range from the personal experiences of participants to the theoretical considerations of psychotherapists.

John E. Drotning ("Sensitivity Training: Some Critical Questions") points out that sensitivity training has strong dynamic similarities to psychotherapy. Serious emotional problems may be exposed when participants are stripped of defenses indiscriminately. Drotning cautions potential participants not to allow their enthusiasm to lead them into an experience with which they may not be able to cope. He suggests a screening procedure as one means of reducing the chances of traumatic, destructive experiences. In relation to business and industry, Drotning questions whether participants are able to transfer their learning from the group to the job. He offers for consideration the possibility that personal exposure among co-workers may make working relationships more difficult. Drotning suggests that T-groups focused on group decision-making, not on personal growth, may be more effective in business and industrial settings. He affirms the need for more research.

"Sensitivity Training: Cult or Contribution?" by T. C. Greening, is largely a critique of the critics. According to Greening, opponents of sensitivity training often base their criticism on misconceptions rather than on scientific data. He answers some criticisms and suggests several safeguards against the critics' worries. These include the screening of applicants, collecting more data about what actually happens in the group, and clarifying trainer standards. He calls on trainers to evaluate their own work, using the reactions and impressions of participants in their appraisal. Greening concludes that sensitivity training critics should themselves be more involved in this concrete evaluation process.

Max Birnbaum ("Sense and Nonsense about Sensitivity Training")

distinguishes clearly between two types of training groups — those
geared toward organizational change, and those designed to stimulate
individual growth. Birnbaum sees sensitivity training as an important
vehicle for introducing emotions into education. He stresses its creative
potential for influencing organizational change, but warns against the
assumption that groups aimed at emotional confrontation and personal
growth will miraculously yield organizational benefits. He, too, cites the
dangers of inadequately trained trainers and deplores the lack of responsible leadership standards.

In "Interpersonal Skills — A Rejection of Empathy Concept and T-
Group Methodology," Allen R. Solem discusses interpersonal sensitivity
as essentially a biological process of intuition based on sensory cues. Lack
of sensitivity, then, is due to obstacles such as emotional blocks, frustrations, values, or preoccupations, that deter reception of these cues.
Although Solem views certain techniques as valuable for developing
sensitivity, he rejects sensitivity training in general as an effective method.
He feels that the changes which occur in T-groups reflect conformity
resulting from group pressures, rather than any significant new freedom
from anxiety or frustration.

George R. Bach ("Marathon Group Dynamics: I. Some Functions of
the Professional Group Facilitator") stresses the need for professional
leaders trained in the art of the marathon. He is concerned with the clear
delineation of valid leadership practices such as screening participants
and focusing feedback. He makes a strong case for the value of legitimate
groups with responsibly trained leaders, but cautions firmly against the
dangers of "wild marathons."

Sensitivity and encounter groups are instruments with tremendous
potential. However, as we have indicated, risks are involved. Fantastic
claims on brochures about groups should not be bought lightly; the
potential buyer must take the same responsibility here that he would
for any other important decision. The motto *caveat emptor* or "let the
buyer beware" is understood by most consumers. This warning also
applies to group workshops and weekends. Before exposing himself to
an experience as powerful as sensitivity training, the prospective group
member should do some careful comparison shopping.

Because of the wide variation in quality and type of groups available,
a person wanting a sensitivity experience should seriously examine his
needs and expectations, and the nature of the particular group he is
considering, before plunging in to be "sensitized." This section is designed as a form of consumer education to aid you in the difficult task of
evaluating a group. To help matters, we are including our "Consumers'
Guide to Group Processes" which presents our classification of the major
kinds of groups, what should be expected from these groups, and what
we feel are the necessary qualifications for leadership.

CONSUMERS' GUIDE TO GROUP PROCESSES

I HUMAN RELATIONS GROUP

A. *Laboratory Training*

Individuals meet to explore their reactions to each other in a group setting. The experience is designed to assist them in understanding their own behavior, others' reactions to their behavior, and the group process. The leader should be trained in behavioral science and group dynamics.

B. *Organizational Development Workshop*

This workshop involves members of an already existing group which meets for the purpose of effecting organizational change. Goals are the examination of interpersonal relations, the facilitation of communication processes, and the understanding of role relationships. The leader should be trained in behavioral sciences specializing in organizational development.

II PERSONAL GROWTH GROUP

This is a group of individuals who meet for the expressed purpose of enhancing their growth through an intensive emotional experience involving new behavioral risk-taking and the sharing of personal intimacies. The leader should be a psychotherapist trained and experienced in leading groups.

III GROUP PSYCHOTHERAPY

This group focuses on the networks of existing interpersonal relations, projected intrapsychic patterns, and repeated and persistent behavior related to personality development. The purpose is to achieve corrective emotional experience, *personal* insight and change, and provide an opportunity for group support and reinforcement of new productive behavior. Group psychotherapy is utilized in conjunction with individual consultation or as a separate mode of treatment. The leader should be a trained group psychotherapist.

IV THERAPEUTIC COMMUNITY

Individuals meet for group psychotherapy (above) who also choose to integrate their life style and their networks of social relations. The community becomes an ongoing, supportive, social interaction laboratory, which provides the reinforcement, nurture and form necessary for the individuals' personal growth and social development. The leader should be a trained group psychotherapist with experience in a therapeutic community setting.

We are also including an individual checklist — questions which the prospective participant should ask himself before he joins a sensitivity group.

1) What are my reasons for joining this group? What do I want and expect from the experience?

2) What is the purpose of the group? What are its stated goals?

3) Are my goals and the group's goals similar?

4) Who is the leader of this group? What is his theoretical orientation, experience and training? Can I have an interview with him before the group? (These are vital considerations. Perhaps the most serious dangers in sensitivity training result from "wild" groups, haphazardly organized and run by individuals with few personal or professional qualifications.)

5) Is there a screening process for group members?

6) Is there any provision for follow-through? Will the leader make himself available for consultation after the group?

7) Am I hoping to resolve long-standing emotional problems? If so, psychotherapy, not sensitivity training, may be what I need.

Sensitivity Training: Some Critical Questions

JOHN E. DROTNING

John E. Drotning, "Sensitivity Training: Some Critical Questions," *Personnel Journal*, 45: 604–6. November, 1966. Reprinted with permission of publisher.

There have been few critics of laboratory training with the notable exception of George Odiorne of the University of Michigan.[1] T-Group adherents proselytize this technique with a fervor which might have surprised even Kurt Lewin, the progenitor of sensitivity training. Their

[1]George Odiorne, "The Trouble with Sensitivity Training." *Training Directors Journal*, October, 1963.

cult-like devotion to collaborative group decision making and the quasi psychoanalytic laboratory training preceding it have taken management and some business schools by storm.[2] But aren't there some aspects of laboratory training that ought to be discussed before accepting it with open arms? The T-Group is an extremely powerful behavioral tool and the probability that no dysfunctional results follow its use are certainly not zero. In addition, are participants willing and/or able to transfer learning from the lab to the job? And should selection criteria be used to screen potential participants? Or should anybody be allowed to involve himself in sensitivity training?

The T-Group is designed to expand one's awareness at the conscious and pre-conscious level; to let one look inside one's self in order to learn more about one's own behavior and its impact on others. Some argue that T-Groups are not psychoanalytic, but rather, a distinctly different technique of behavioral change. Yet this is hard to believe. For example, Maslow comments,[3]

> I even have the suspicion that there are some kinds of things that can happen in these T-Groups that can "never" happen in the individual psychoanalysis, no matter how long it takes.

This hardly leads one to think that the T-Group is non-psychoanalytic. And since T-Groups involve elements of psychoanalysis, they ought to be employed with great care.[4] Potentially, sensitivity training may do great damage to a participant's mental health, especially if there are no standards for participation in the training.

The trigger for the sensitivity training group is its lack of structure. Most of us are programmed to some degree and the unstructuredness encountered in the opening moments of a laboratory group generates tremendous tension which can be alleviated only through intimate inter-action among group members. This kind of intimacy may be foreign to the American culture, and opening one's self up or subjecting one's self to group criticism may literally tear one apart.[5] In one T-Group, the writer watched the members bear down on one individual's apparent inadequacies as a plant manager. He was shorn of his normal defenses (which we all have to some degree) and subject to intense personal criticism. He appeared to suffer tremendous internal stress — hands shaking, dry lips, and at times near tears. Suppose this internal conflict is not resolved in a week long session. What kind of permanent damage could follow this

[2]See George Strauss & Leonard Sayles, *Personnel*, revised edition, 1966. Recently, the Sloan School of Industrial Management introduced a sensitivity training course for all degree candidates.

[3]Abraham H. Maslow, *Eupsychian Management* (Homewood, Illinois: Richard D. Irwin, Inc., 1965), p. 159.

[4]I'm using T-Group, laboratory group, sensitivity training, interchangeably. Some feel that sensitivity training differs from T-Groups in their focus in individuals, rather than the group.

[5]Maslow, p. 161.

rather futile attempt to liberate the man from his inadequacies by means of group pressure. Should we view this as management development?

The T-Group attempts to get its members to rid themselves of all defenses — healthy as well as neurotic. But we may need healthy defenses in our world; we may need them within our own families; in fact, we may need them even with our ministers and priests, if we are to preserve internal stability. We have our private worlds that we may not want to share with any but a few selected people in our lifetimes. Would it be mentally healthy to share these private worlds with a group of strangers in a T-Group? While sensitivity training attempts to focus on the here and now, there is a real danger that the trainer won't be able to "contain" the violent emotions experienced by some members. After all, all laboratory training is not always conducted by the best possible men. For example, Odiorne points out the example of a group of business school professors willing to work with any company in week long programs. Imagine the damage that could be done to the plant by really opening up men who must interact daily in a work situation after the professors leave.

Laboratory training may be a tremendous behavioral tool, but it may also be totally inappropriate for many of its present applications. Does it make sense to think that a large firm can be turned into one "big happy family" by means of laboratory training? Managers must manage; they must hand out both rewards and punishment.[6] And the possibility of handing out punishment is a strong barrier to open, frank, and trusting interaction between superiors and subordinates. Moreover, sensitivity training implies non-authoritarian or permissive management. And permissive management relies on each individual's desire to self-actualize. Self-actualization is the capstone need in the hierarchy of needs underlying Maslow's motivational theory.[7] This is the need for self-fulfillment, "for realizing one's own potential, for continued self development, for being creative in the broadest sense of that term."[8] In simpler and more direct language, self-actualizers are the doers, the drivers, the achievers, the people who finish jobs assigned to them, *not* the free loaders, the hangers on or the talkers.[9]

[6]See Roger Harrison, "Cognative Model for Interpersonal & Group Behavior: A Theoretical Framework for Research," (National Training Labs, Washington, D.C., 1965). This is the only theoretically analytical treatment of the dynamics of sensitivity training I've seen. It may serve as an excellent basis for empirical research.

[7]The need system involves physiological, safety, social, ego, and finally self-actualization drives. See Abraham Maslow, *Motivation and Personality* (New York: Harper & Bros., 1954). Douglas McGregor, *The Human Side of Enterprise* (New York: McGraw-Hill Book Co. Inc., 1960), pp. 36–40. Also see Arthur H. Kuriloff, "An Experiment in Management," *Personnel*, Nov-Dec. 1963, pp. 8–17. Alexander Winn, "Laboratory Training in Industry," *Personnel Administration*, 27, No. 3 (March-June 1964), 6–11.

[8]Paul R. Lawrence & John A. Seiler, *Organizational Behavior and Administration*, Rev. Ed. (Homewood, Illinois: Richard D. Irwin, Inc., 1965), p. 448.

[9]Abraham Maslow, *Eupsychian Management* (Homewood, Illinois: Richard D. Irwin, 1965), p. 5.

Yet all men may not self-actualize. Do hourly paid employees self-actualize at all?[10] And if they do, will it be in the way top management hopes or will it be off the job actualization, e.g., in the family? Maslow comments on the "various students and professors who 'wanted to work with me on self-actualization'. Most of them are starry eyed dilettantes — big talkers — who do little — who won't work like the devil on unimportant tasks — who won't see the job through to its end."[11]

Suppose most men and women in the U.S. are doing jobs they would quit at once, if they weren't paid. The tasks they perform, the hours, etc. are fixed for them as conditions of employment. And even if they were "free," what proportion would voluntarily work extra hours because of the meaningfulness of their jobs? Even many college professors with low teaching loads — leading the "ideal free life" — end up as non-achievers who use free time, not for reading and research, but for daydreaming, gabbing, long lunch hours or other personal enjoyment.

Real self-actualizers are in very short supply and it makes little sense to hope for revolutionary results from a management philosophy based on an imaginary, generalized drive for self-actualization.

These comments are critical; maybe too much so! Sensitivity training is an intense emotional experience which may be put to good use. But if this is to happen, it ought to focus on the processes of group decision making rather than on individual or personal growth. Perhaps the T-Group ought to work with real conceptual problems rather than focus only on emotional learning. Moreover, it would seem advisable to carefully screen participants before subjecting them to what may be a tortuous experience.

Finally, we should do more research on the effectiveness with which positive laboratory learning is transferred to the plant. Then we will have a better understanding about the utility of laboratory training as a management development technique.[12]

---

[10]See George Strauss, "Some Notes on Power Equalization" in *The Social Science of Organization*, edited by H. J. Leavitt (Englewood Cliffs: Prentice-Hall Inc., 1963), pp. 45–54.

[11]A. Maslow, p. 5.

[12]A good example of this is: Matthew B. Miles, "Change During, and Following Laboratory Training: A Clinical Experimental Study," *Journal of the Applied Behavioral Sciences*, Vol. I, No. 3.

Sensitivity Training: Cult or Contribution?

Thomas C. Greening

Thomas C. Greening, "Sensitivity Training: Cult or Contribution," *Personnel*, 41: 18–25, May–June, 1964. Reprinted by permission of the publisher from *Personnel*, May–June 1964. © 1964 by the American Management Association, Inc.

Sensitivity training is a complex human venture that arouses intense emotions in its participants, critics, and defenders. Consequently, it is usually difficult to discuss it with any appreciable degree of detachment, let alone the empirical evaluation it deserves.

Typical of the opposition sensitivity training encounters are the attacks of two of its most vociferous opponents — Malcolm McNair and George Odiorne. Both, it should be noted, have made important criticisms of human relations training in general and sensitivity training in particular.

In so doing, they have claimed that their intention is to stir up "useful" controversy. In expressing their views, however, both have tended to make extreme, judgmental statements and to draw pessimistic conclusions without due recourse to scientific method. Thus, neither has offered documentary excerpts from representative samples of behavior in specific training programs or sophisticated research evidence to support his criticisms. In both cases, their attacks have been based on anecdotal, selective impressions and have taken the form of emotional, value-laden assertions.

Thus, in his well-known blast at human relations training, McNair averred:

> Too much emphasis on human relations encourages people to feel sorry for themselves, makes it easier for them to slough off responsibility, to find excuses for failure, to act like children. When somebody falls down on the job or does not behave in accordance with accepted codes, we look into his

psychological background for factors that may be used as excuses. In these respects the cult of human relations is but part and parcel of the sloppy sentimentalism characterizing the world today. . . . Undue preoccupation with human relations saps individual responsibility, leads us not to think about the job any more and about getting it done but only about people and their relations. . . . Will power, self-control, and personal responsibility are more than ever important in a world that is in danger of wallowing in self-pity and infantilism. . . . Such courses lead to a false concept of the executive's job. There is a de-emphasis of analysis, judgment, and decision making. . . . Putting so much explicit emphasis on the emotional and irrational makes the student feel it is all important.[1]

And *Business Week*, in a report on sensitivity training, quoted Odiorne:

[Sensitivity training] sets up nothing but a stress situation. . . . "This is nothing more than an experiment to test your toleration for frustration," he said. In such an emotional binge courtesy goes by the board. . . . Odiorne admitted that group dynamics is a good thing, but he said the small group efforts of Lewin had been perverted by the sensitivity training cult into a sort of personal therapy.[2]

Public pronouncements of this kind, using such emotionally loaded phrases as "sloppy sentimentalism," "self-pity and infantilism," "emotional binge," and "perverted by the sensitivity training cult" hardly seem calculated to generate the dispassionate and thoughtful discussion needed for a sound evaluation of sensitivity training programs. It is inevitable and appropriate that we should have emotions and values about this kind of training, but these are not in themselves an adequate basis for evaluating so complex a development in our culture. We need thoughtful criticisms as well as defenses of sensitivity training that have been empirically substantiated. Sensitivity training is too powerful, too potentially dangerous as well as beneficial in its effects, to be attacked or defended with the techniques of propaganda, or caught up in the provocation of controversy for its own sake.

For example, let us briefly consider one criticism of sensitivity training that crops up again and again. These programs, their opponents charge, are naïve and unilateral attempts to make people more open, more trusting, and more sensitive to the feeling of others, and to increase egalitarian democracy in business without regard for the realities of business life.

Actually, this criticism is based, for the most part, on misinterpretation of the goals of sensitivity training. In fact, most sophisticated trainers now go out of their way to avoid championing any one particular mode of behavior by the participants. It's true that early leaders in the group dynamics field did place somewhat excessive emphasis on democratic permissiveness as a panacea; but few workers in this field cling to the

---

[1] M. P. McNair, "What Price Human Relations?" *Harvard Business Review* (March-April, 1957), 15–22.
[2] "Yourself as Others See You," *Business Week* (March 16, 1963), 160–162.

simple belief that sensitivity training should aim solely at bringing about increased openness, trust, harmonious human relations, and egalitarian cooperation. Rather, the view now is that laboratory training can help to increase the participants' capacity to select more flexible and more realistic modes of behavior on the basis of discerning assessment of their own goals and needs and the interpersonal and task situation that confronts them.

Chris Argyris has explained this point very well:

> If we examine the available data, we find that directive leaders who learn at a laboratory do not tend to throw away their directive skills. Rather, they seem to use other leadership patterns that they may have developed at the laboratory. Indeed, in a highly authoritarian, competitive, politically oriented situation, the individual would be seen as "weak" if he attempted to be more open, to trust, and to show concern. In other words, rather than reject one leadership pattern, they actually add a new one and increase their range of choices.
>
> It cannot be emphasized too strongly that there is nothing in laboratory education that requires an individual to throw away a particular leadership pattern. The most laboratory education can do is (1) help the individual see certain unintended consequences and costs of his leadership and (2) help him to develop additional leadership styles *if* he wishes.[3]

In fact, independent analysis of situations, judgments, and decision making are crucial for participation in a sensitivity training program. Attempts "to feel sorry for oneself," "slough off responsibility," "find excuses for failure," "indulge in emotional binges," and "act like children" usually meet with varied reactions from other members of the group, and at least some of these reactions will be critical. Thus, individuals who do show these tendencies are provided with a learning situation in which they can come to recognize their possession of them and how they affect their relations with others. Peering into one's psychological background for factors that might be used as excuses rarely gains much acceptance in a laboratory group, though a healthy respect for the influence of past experience on present behavior often does develop.

Sensitivity training has also come under the gun for reasons that seem based on a misunderstanding of psychoanalytic theory and its use in human relations. For example, McNair has asserted that human relations is "headed the wrong way because of its fairly heavy dependence on Freudian psychology." He naïvely misinterprets Freud as promoting wholesale cracking of "veneer," morbid introspection, and lack of strong moral convictions. Actually, Freud's own life and his theoretical statements advocate none of these things. Though he helped discover the royal road to the unconscious, Freud never suggested making the

---

[3]C. Argyris, "In Defense of Laboratory Education." Unpublished manuscript, distributed by National Training Laboratories, Bethel, Maine.

unconscious king; instead, one of his basic principles was, "Where id is, there shall ego be." And it was Freud, in his clinical formulation of the obsessional neurosis, who gave us our basic understanding of "morbid introspection" as a neurotic defense mechanism.

Interpretation of Freud

Actually, though McNair sees himself as being in opposition to Freudian psychology, his tendency toward fatalistic acceptance of man's divided nature and his view that "intellectual and moral veneer" must cover but cannot alter man's essentially savage nature constitute essentially the same position as Freud took in his more pessimistic writings, such as *Civilization and Its Discontents*.

Thus, on some issues he seems unknowingly to subscribe to Freud's views; on others his disagreement with Freud is based on a misunderstanding of him. In any case, the charge that human relations is especially dependent on Freudian psychology is open to question. It is more likely that sensitivity trainers are closer to subsequent psychoanalytic thinking (e.g., Hartman and Erikson) and the neo-Freudians (Horney, Sullivan) than they are to Freud himself.

Perhaps one of the difficulties in all these discussions arises from the common tendency to reach for simple definitions of man's nature. One school of thought holds that man is basically good, self-actualizing, and cooperative, if only we can help him let down his barriers. On the other hand, there are those who argue that man is basically an amoral, irrational animal who must be kept in check by external restraints and a self-deluding veneer. Personally, I prefer the position I once heard Martin Buber take in a discussion with Carl Rogers: "Man is basically good — and bad."

The purpose of sensitivity training groups is to provide an existential setting in which the participants can intensively review and possibly revise their basic views about man's nature, group behavior, and the roles and procedures necessary for accomplishing tasks with others.

In such an existential setting, the people who feel that they cannot benefit from a further confrontation of themselves and others may be those whose views of man are so unrealistic that they cannot endure the threat of having them revised; or, at the other extreme, those whose views of man are so satisfying to them that they see no need to revise them. Members of the first group should not risk close involvement with real human beings in sensitivity training or anywhere else; those in the second group can be counted as fortunate in possessing a highly satisfying and functional view of human nature and may be justified in feeling that they do not need to expend time and energy on this type of learning. Most people, however, probably fall somewhere between these two groups, and it is for them that sensitivity training is designed. Meanwhile, we can admit that anyone who is unalterably convinced that he or mankind in general is inherently too cruel or too weak to benefit from group interaction should not risk participating in a sensitivity training program, and probably should not be in a position of responsibility over other people in the first place.

The charge that there has sometimes been a cultish over-enthusiasm for new training procedures, and a neglect of sound methods of selection and prediction, probably has some justification, in view of the rapid growth of the field. It may well be true also that this has attracted some unethical, fast-buck operators who have misused training procedures. But this is a criticism that needs to be supported by documentation and investigation rather than by mere anecdotal reporting.

In any event, sensitivity training leaders are not unaware of these problems. Steps now being taken to overcome them include:

1. Better screening of participants to eliminate (a) unusually vulnerable or hostile people, who may not be able to maintain control in a loosely structured setting; (b) people whose repressed impulsiveness and dependency are extremely strong and whose defenses are rigid or crumbling, and (c) people who desperately need external structure to support their inadequate inner controls.
2. Selection of groups to insure maximum effectiveness from the interactions among a variety of personalities.
3. Efforts to improve predictions of individual and group behavior on the basis of selection and group composition data. (A current study at UCLA is attempting to isolate, for prediction purposes, the variables associated with above-average participation and learning in a sensitivity training program. Studies are also needed to determine which types of prior experiences and personality development are correlated with disabling stress and lack of learning on the part of the participants.)
4. Clarification of standards for professional sensitivity trainers and development of staff training programs.
5. Study of the excessively stressful incidents that occur in laboratory training with a view to developing concepts and techniques that will prevent such incidents or aid in their early diagnosis and prompt alleviation.

One way to assess the validity of the criticisms leveled at sensitivity training is to ask the participants themselves how they feel about the experience. Recently, at the end of a program in which there had been a great deal of intense interaction, I followed this course. The 13 participants were asked to write their frank reactions, based on their own experience, to the following statements actually made by critics:[4]

1. These programs are dangerous; they do more harm than good.
2. This is irresponsible, short-cut psychotherapy; the individual's privacy is invaded, his psyche is ruthlessly exposed.

[4]The author has collected and paraphrased many other brief statements criticizing sensitivity training which he will be glad to pass on to anyone interested in conducting a similar attitude survey.

3. Social order and personal stability are based on the maintenance of propriety, realistic defenses, and some degrees of façade; these programs inappropriately try to strip all this away.
4. If people try to become more open and direct about their feelings toward each other in a group, the experience will degenerate into destructive criticism, hostility, and hurt feelings.

Nine members of the group felt that these statements had little or no validity. Incidentally, among them were several participants who had undergone some very stressful interactions. Following are some typical comments by these nine dissenters:

This program is the acceleration of confrontations to be dealt with in the external world and, indeed, becomes an effective measure of the success of the participants' realistic defenses. It is advantageous that persons with untenable and readily transparent façades meet and effectively deal with that reality when there is no job, marriage, or truly meaningful relationship at stake. It is, furthermore, my contention that such persons with these untenable façades or defenses are, for the most part, at least subconsciously aware of them and have placed themselves in this program as a partial testing mechanism.

With respect to the question about invading our privacy, I would assert that people let other people know just what they want them to know about themselves. In other words, our privacy is not invaded unless we want it to be. I related to the group only certain aspects of my life that I thought were proper for group discussion, but always kept the personal matters strictly to myself.

Groups such as this don't try to strip a façade away just to expose a "phony," but do so for the sake of helping people realize that it is important to be yourself and act yourself.

If the individual is not strong enough to drop some of his façade, yet retain his feelings toward himself and his surroundings, not only sensitivity training, but life itself, will be destructive of his personality and his being.

While no doubt there has been a certain amount of hostility, a certain amount of unfair criticism, and more than a few hurt feelings, there has been evoked in each one of us a "new way" of viewing other people in the light of each of our experiences in this class.

The remaining four participants felt that the statements did contain some partial truths, but that when the total experience was evaluated its benefits outweighed its negative aspects. Actually, two of these four felt that they personally had benefited from the experience; they were concerned, however, that some of the other participants may have felt exposed or hurt. Interestingly enough, the individuals to whom they referred were among the dissenting group and had made no such complaints.

The other two participants who felt that the statements had some validity did so in the light of certain upsetting encounters they had experienced in the course of the program. Both, however, then went on to describe how they had subsequently progressed to a basically positive attitude toward the program. The first of these two participants was rated by the group on a research measure as one of its least accepted and also one of its least active members. Here is his response to the questionnaire:

"The first statement, 'These programs are dangerous; they do more harm than good,' is virtually identical with a statement I made about the third week. As the group progressed, and I with it, I changed my view. I believe now that perhaps I sensed there was danger in the group for me, and was trying to put up a defense by dismissing the experience. Up until about three-fourths of the way through, I would have agreed whole-heartedly with all these statements. I had absolutely no use for this program at all, and because of some of my statements and my actions the rest of the group knew it. Now, in looking back, and evaluating the course and what I learned from it, and the experiences within the group, I don't believe the statements are valid.

Where There's Smoke . . .

"In the first place, no one is in danger unless there is something 'wrong,' that is, unless there is room for improvement in his behavioral pattern. Those of us who had the most to be 'attacked' about got the attacks. Yet, all of us got over our 'hurt' and appear to be better able to function in a group environment. None of us was carried off by men in white jackets. Any irresponsibility, or irresponsible or 'false' individual, is seen through by the group and handled according to the standards established (ignore, 'shoot 'em down,' talk it through).

"Certainly, 'social order and personal stability are based on the maintenance of propriety, realistic defenses, and some degrees of facade,' but isn't a key word here 'realistic'? The type of defenses that I utilized in the group (rigid, authoritarian behavior) and, say, Joe (intellectualization, living in someone else's world or mind through his always quoting someone else) were not realistic and hampered individual growth. In this respect this group experience was beneficial, by showing me how unrealistic and harmful my defenses were. There certainly was no evidence in our group of degeneracy into destructive criticism, hostility, and hurt feelings. There were evidences of hurt feelings . . . but these seemed to be worked out, and I, for one, carry away no grudge against anyone in this group."

The second participant described an upsetting incident in which he had unsuccessfully tangled with an aggressive and verbally facile member:

"In a few minutes he had made a fool out of me. After that I told myself that it was true, that I did not fit in, that I was here but had no right to be. Everything I had gained in the sessions so far went out the window. Thus, in the short run I was worse off than when I started. It reinforced every fear I had. But in the long run I feel that the experience was most beneficial. The harm that was done was far less than the good that came later. It was not until the last few sessions that I benefited. I will say that each and every one of the statements listed are true to some extent — and if you asked people in the group if they were true at the time the sparks were flying most would agree. But to get an honest picture, look back after the whole thing has been over for a while, and you'll have a completely different view. At least this is the way that I feel after going through the experience."

The Picture Changes

In short, two of the 13 participants reported experiences that had inclined them to agree for a while with some typical criticisms of sensitivity training. In both cases, however, as the program went on these individuals were able to understand the reasons for their earlier dissatisfaction and finally emerged from the training with a sense of personal gain.

Attitude surveys of this kind would seem to offer one means of clarifying the issues in sensitivity training without recourse to speculative controversy. To serve any constructive purpose, however, representative samples of responses must be obtained from a variety of groups to insure that data are not selected merely to support some particular theoretical position. Furthermore, the lay public should be told what the critical issues in sensitivity training are and its support enlisted in a cooperative, nonpartisan effort to assess the validity of these charges. This kind of mutual involvement of trainers and participants in the appraisal of training experiences has long been a basic part of human relations training. It can appropriately be applied to appraising the criticisms of sensitivity training also.

Sense and Nonsense about Sensitivity Training

MAX BIRNBAUM

Max Birnbaum, "Sense and Nonsense about Sensitivity Training," *Saturday Review*, 52: 82–83+, November 15, 1969. © 1969 Saturday Review, Inc. Reprinted with permission of author and publisher.

During the 1960s, public education discovered the emotions. Cognitive learning and skill training, the traditional components of education, no longer satisfied the needs of a generation that had experienced the civil rights revolt, the widening generation gap, and the increasing confusion of teachers, administrators, and school board members about ends and means in education. The result was a growing interest in various approaches to affective learning that assigns to the emotional factor in education a role as important as — or, perhaps, more important than — the traditional substantive content and skills. Among these approaches the most enthusiastically embraced has been the so-called sensitivity training.

The term is used loosely to include a wide range of laboratory training approaches in human relations, group dynamics, organizational development (or, as I prefer, applied human relations training), as well as a number of verbal and non-verbal experiences that seek to increase awareness and release human potential. It is an unfortunate term because of its vagueness, but it appears that its very impreciseness and beguiling simplicity are the qualities that have helped it gain wide currency.

By whatever name it is known, however, human relations training is capable, if properly employed, of producing substantial educational change. It holds tremendous potential for improving education by dealing with its affective components, reducing the unnecessary friction between generations, and creating a revolution in instruction by helping teachers to learn how to use the classroom group for learning purposes.

The pity is that this promising innovation may be killed before its unique properties have a fair chance to demonstrate their worth. The opposition to its serious exploration is strong and is apt to grow. But it is not those who oppose sensitivity training because it smacks of therapy, which to a very small degree it does, nor even the members of the renascent John Birch Society, who would equate it with brainwashing, who pose the major challenge. Rather, the most serious threat to sensitivity training comes first from its enthusiastic but frequently unsophisticated school supporters, and second from a host of newly hatched trainers, long on enthusiasm or entrepreneurial expertise, but short on professional experience, skill, and wisdom.

What is needed today is a clearer sense of how sensitivity training developed, the varied forms it may take, and the results that can be anticipated in any given situation. Unfortunately, not all of the "experts" agree on the many issues raised by this kind of training, and there will be those who disagree strongly with many of the judgments presented here. But clearer definition of the issues, wider discussion, and more careful analysis of results should help schoolmen toward more effective use of training for fundamental improvement in the schools.

Contrary to the impression given by some recent popular writing on the subject, it was neither the author of *Joy* nor the devoted creators of Esalen who were responsible for the development of human relations training. Rather, it was Leland Bradford, then director of the Adult Education Division of the National Education Association, together with his old friends and collaborators Ronald Lippitt, now of the University of Michigan, and Kenneth Benne, now of the Boston University Human Relations Center, who were primarily responsible. Drawing on the work of the great social psychologist Kurt Lewin, they established the first training center more than two decades ago at Bethel, Maine, and founded the National Training Laboratories (NTL). And it was Bradford's tough and dogged fight against strong opposition within education that finally won sanction and support for human relations training, first from industry, then from the social and behavioral scientists, and finally from the education hierarchy itself. Now, as he is about to retire as director of NTL, Lee Bradford has the satisfaction of seeing human relations training widely embraced by the education world.

As the field developed, the T-group (Training group) became the heart of any laboratory or workshop that is devoted to the study of group dynamics or human relations. The traditional T-group consists of a small group of people — ideally ten to sixteen — who meet in a residential setting (the laboratory) for approximately two weeks. Although only one part of this educational experience (theory, interpretation, and skill development are also included), the T-group is, because of its intense emotional impact, by far the most significant aspect of any human relations lab. The objectives of the T-group are to help individual participants become aware of why both they and others behave as they do in groups — or, in the jargon of the professional, become aware of the underlying behavior dynamics of the group. This is accomplished, with the help of a trainer, by creating an atmosphere in which the motivations for typical human behavior, of which individuals are often unaware, are brought to the surface in an exaggerated form. Once they are made clear and explicit, they can be discussed and analyzed. Thus, the individual participant can observe both his own behavior and that of others in the group, discover sources of different kinds of behavior, and identify the effect they have upon the functioning of the group. The effort to stimulate exaggerated behavior in order to get at the motivation behind it more explicitly is an uncomfortable experience for many people, but the feeling is usually transitory. The emotional component of the experience makes it appear to verge on therapy, but there is a significant difference between therapy that is focused on the problems of emotionally disturbed people and training that aims at the improvement of human relations skills of normal people.

In the early years of the movement, the T-group emphasis was primarily on the sociology of groups rather than on their psychology — that is, on the roles and functions of leadership and membership, rather than on the individual personality and personal development. (Bradford, Benne, and Lippitt came from adult education, philosophy, and social psychology.) The trend toward a psychological emphasis appeared in the early 1950s when the movement began to attract a larger number of people trained in clinical psychology or psychiatry. And it was at that point the T-group emerged as a new social invention that bears some rough resemblance to a combination of seminar and therapy group, but it actually is neither.

Recognition of the power of the T-group, as well as its limitations, has led to wide experimentation with other applications. Laboratory sessions of varying length and widely differing objectives have been developed, ranging from a single day or weekend to two or three weeks, and having as their purpose varying kinds of individual and organizational change. Much of the confusion in the field stems from the lack of clearly defined purposes, and guidelines that indicate the kind of training session most effective in achieving a particular objective. Most specifically, confusion results from the failure to differentiate between those training experiences that are designed to improve an individual's capacity to work effectively as a manager or member of a group for educational or re-educational purposes, and those that are designed to stimulate the individual's personal growth and so are clearly in a domain that might be labeled para-therapy, in the sense that it is parallel to therapy, rather than therapy itself. Therefore, it is necessary to look at the varying kinds of training that are becoming popular today to see what purposes each is best designed to serve.

Organizational development is a general term that includes a variety of approaches that combine affective and intellectual components in the use of small groups as a medium for consultation, problem solving, and re-education of individuals in both public and private organizations. It developed primarily out of the earlier, sociologically oriented focus of the T-group that emphasized organizational change rather than personal development. My experience with school systems and other organizations with a process that I term applied human relations training probably falls within this definition. (See Thomas Cottle's "Strategy for Change" [*SR*, Sept. 20] for a description of one application of this process to the resolution of intergroup problems in a single school system.)

Encounter groups, confrontation sessions, and *marathon labs* are usually short term — most often twenty-four-hour or weekend — experiences where the emphasis is on the direct exposure of beliefs and feelings that usually are not put on public display by individuals. The term "encounter group" derives from the phrase "basic encounter group" that Carl Rogers, the noted exponent of non-directive counseling, coined to differentiate a new kind of experience from the traditional T-group. Trainers in these sessions usually encourage participants to explore in some depth their own feelings and motivations, as well as those of other group members. The objective is to stimulate an exchange that is inhibited by a minimum of reserve and defensiveness in order to achieve a maximum of openness and honesty. Marathons differ from encounter groups primarily in the unremitting intensity of the experience that seeks to achieve a significant break-through in normal defenses and so attain what many practitioners believe is a new level of open behavior. Confrontation sessions are usually contrived racial encounters in which militant blacks literally "confront" members of the white community (teachers, police, industrial management, etc.) with their angry reaction to white racism, discrimination, and prejudice. The theoretical basis for this type of experience is that the social conditions requiring this form of learning demand a maximum dose of aggression and hostility in order to convince the targets — the whites — of the seriousness of the personal situation. (Because most confrontation sessions of this kind are not part of a plan for organizational change, they usually end as paratherapeutic experiences rather than training.)

Non-verbal exercises have invaded the training field with a vengeance in recent years. The techniques employed are numerous and range from simple exercises with a minimum of body contact to physically intimate and emotionally revealing designs of the kind most often associated with Esalen and its derivatives. (It should be noted that the explorations of Esalen, on the West Coast, are making major contributions to the field of therapy, but it is less clear how the techniques developed there can contribute to education.) Non-verbal techniques derive their theoretical justification from theories of personality that stress the possibility of achieving greater honesty and authenticity through bodily expression that can become uninhibited more quickly than can verbal communication. Thus, participants can reach deeper levels of consciousness more quickly.

Each of these varied approaches to sensitivity training is designed to serve specific purposes. Undoubtedly each can be immensely beneficial to certain individuals — and provide little help, or have negative results, for others. What must be made clear is the purpose to be achieved, and the kind of training best designed to serve that purpose.

Clearly, organizational development — or applied human relations training — that is focused on organizational change, problems of human relations, and morale within an organization belong in the training area. These experiences may bring to participants great personal insights and lead to new ways of relating to family and friends, but these are *accidental* consequences of the experience that is directed toward increasing individual effectiveness as a member of the organization. Marathons, personal growth labs, encounter groups, and non-verbal exercises belong in the para-therapeutic area. These are frankly concerned primarily with individual growth and development, the achievement of authenticity, or "therapy for normals." In some cases, labs of this kind assume that there will be an organizational payoff from the experience, but others do not. The original T-group, from which all the forms of sensitivity training developed, can serve either purpose. It can provide the basis for a lab devoted primarily to personal growth, or one that rigorously relates all personal learning to an organizational context. But experience teaches that, unless a lab is consciously dedicated to the latter, the high degree of personal involvement inevitably pulls the focus toward individual growth.

When lab organizers are unable or unwilling to differentiate between various kinds of training, the results can be disastrous. There are many tales, some maliciously embellished, but many all too true, of school systems and communities where bad situations have been made worse by the unintelligent application of inappropriate forms of sensitivity training. Some examples of such misuse of training may help to clarify the point.

The T-group that aims at personal growth, for instance, is an experience that has tremendous validity for school people as long as it takes place in a setting away from home where the individual can be relatively anonymous — a summer laboratory or workshop, for example. But trouble comes when it is applied uncritically within a school system where the participants are co-workers. The result in this case is either impossible resistance, or, even worse, the revelation of intimate personal information that is so highly charged that it makes continuing work relationships very difficult, if not impossible.

Similarly, encounter groups or confrontation sessions between blacks and whites in the same school or community may lead to problems. In the past, such sessions have sometimes had useful shock value in revealing quickly the crucial problems that are polarizing the races today. Under skillful management, with careful control over degrees of resistance and levels of anxiety, and a systematic effort to relate the encounter experience to specific educational issues so that it can lead to follow-up plans for action and change, such training labs can be quite useful. Unfortunately, it appears that too often difficulty arises as a result of routine application of what are basically gimmicks to an involved and highly charged area.

In one large city school system an encounter group recently included teachers, most of whom were white, and students, most of whom were black, from the same school. The result was the opposite of what was sought — increased physical and verbal hostility of students to the teachers in the school. Carefully managed, however, the encounter between teachers and students, away from the school setting, has enormous possibilities for re-educating both teachers and students for a needed revolution in their relationships. But even at its most effective, the encounter session is a shocking and bruising experience. And because of the failure to follow through with concrete plans for specific action, it too often remains a memorable experience, but not one that produces change.

Non-verbal exercises also are susceptible to both effective and inappropriate use. In one recent case at a conference of foundation executives, a trainer was employed to lead the group in several non-verbal exercises designed to stimulate greater openness and trust — two attributes much to be desired in any conference. The result, however, was unexpected. The initially surprised and then outraged participants displayed an enormous amount of openness — all of it hostile — toward both the trainer and the conference sponsors. The simple exercises that may be effective in settings where people are clearly experimenting with behavior are often completely inappropriate in another context. Similarly, young school teachers, after an enthusiastic lab experience, return to the classroom to lead their students into such "games." No harm is done, but because some of these exercises involve body contact of a quasi-intimate nature, it is questionable whether students, especially teenagers, should be so encouraged. Under normal circumstances, teenagers do not need the sanction of the school to become so engaged.

There are, however, cases where non-verbal experiences are very much to the point. In police-community relations training sessions, simple physical contact exercises — a hand shake or, in special circumstances, a hug or touching another person's face — can be helpful. Where ghetto residents have never felt a policeman as a human being, such contact can be a wholesome revelation. For the white police, the personal experience that the black on the skin will not rub off has been equally salutary.

Two kinds of sensitivity training are particularly susceptible today to exploitation by the enthusiastic amateur or the enterprising entrepreneur: the area of non-verbal experience, and the confrontation session. Each requires a minimum of experience and knowledge to stimulate an initial response among participants, but in each case a maximum of expert knowledge and sophistication is required to extract a positive educational outcome. The most damning judgment that can be made about the non-verbal field is that a small bag of easily learned exercises, plus several $33\frac{1}{3}$ rpm records, makes anyone a trainer. As for confrontation sessions, it is not difficult to evoke profound guilt feelings among participants by employing the tactics of staged aggression, but it requires great skill and understanding to follow through to a positive learning experience.

Despite all the possible pitfalls, however, it is necessary today to recognize the affective aspect of the educational process, and to train both teachers and administrators for mastery of the area. Too many of today's teaching-learning problems — in the suburbs as well as the inner city — are in the emotional rather than the cognitive or the skill areas. Change is imperative. But changing individual behavior and organizational structure are extraordinarily difficult and thorny objectives. All too often new superintendents come along with prescriptions for innovation and reform that falter long before their efforts get off the ground. The longer one works in the field of planned change, the more difficult the task appears.

By chance, however, two unusually powerful forces for change in educational systems appeared during the 1960s. The first was the civil rights revolution, the second the extraordinary wave of student unrest that, according to a recent survey, has affected three-fourths of all secondary schools in the country. Although the civil rights movement has been fraught with bitter tension and physical violence, the student rebellion promises to be the more global in its effects on the schools. The former forces schools to examine racial attitudes, curriculum priorities, school culture, hiring and promotion policies, and other fundamental relationships in school administration. But the latter strikes directly at the heart of student-teacher and student-administrator relationships that have endured with only minor modifications since the turn of the century. These relationships, which determine who makes significant decisions within the schools, may in the long run prove the most troublesome, but also the most decisive stimulus for change. Schools, after all, have long been one of the most hierarchically organized institutions in our society — only the army and the quasi-military police are more authority-centered. To effect a significant change in the nature of the school and classroom authority, then, is a problem of the first magnitude involving both organizational and human change.

The devilish seductivity of human relations training stems from the fact that it can reduce individual resistance to change more effectively than any other known means. It promises the wishful decision-maker, therefore, that his desires for school reform can be fulfilled. This is the trap that awaits all school executives interested in using human relations training for planned change experiments.

The superintendent, then, who wants to set about planning for effective change in his school system, must be aware of the variety of training opportunities available for his staff members. He must also make a clear decision about the type of training he wants his staff to experience. If he decides that certain key personnel could benefit themselves — and the school system — by undergoing a personal growth experience that will help to decrease individual defensiveness and the tendency most humans share to ascribe value by status rather than by individual worth, then by all means he should send these individuals to labs away from home in the summer. It may be that both the schools and the participants' wives or husbands will benefit, and both may be legitimate objectives.

If, however, school personnel are to begin the long and complicated process of applying group procedures to organizational meetings, problem solving, or classroom learning, then laboratory training that focuses primarily on personal growth is likely to be minimally productive. Organizational development laboratories or applied human relations workshops focusing on intergroup or community-school problems may be more useful, because the emphasis is on problem solving. But human relations training labs differ not only in their overall emphasis, but often within the same laboratory trainers may run the gamut from exclusively personal growth-oriented sessions to the older concept of the T-group that is designed to help participants to function more effectively on the job.

School systems now infatuated with training will have to learn, as industry has, that not all sorts of training are functional for all personnel. They may also have to learn that under certain conditions a school system would be wasting money by investing in human relations training. When morale is poor — not because of organizational or human impediments to communication, but because decision-making is handled in an authoritarian fashion, or pay is poor and working conditions are worse — instead of training, the school system should opt for higher salaries or elimination of the authoritarian administrator. Similarly, if the middle echelon administrator — the principal — is fearful and unsure of his position, large-scale training for teachers, under the superintendent's sponsorship, can generate intolerable pressures upon him. For example, an effective human relations training program can result in increased enthusiasm among faculty, more demands for help in curriculum, introduction of new ways of class management, greater degree of experimentation, and demands for a larger voice in decision making. These demands can be fearfully unsettling for a principal who has always run a "tight ship" where everything was under his control. Unless he himself is ready for change, it would be wisest to forget training — or forget him.

The serious question remains, of course, of how a superintendent or school board can determine whether a trainer or training organization is capable and experienced. There is no bureau of standards or licensing agency for human relations trainers. NTL has some three or four levels of affiliation, but it is very cautious about claiming universal virtuosity for members of its network. As increasing numbers of psychologists become interested in the field, it is likely that school systems will be assured of securing individuals with reputable academic credentials, but these will provide no assurance of effectiveness in human relations training. Training, like teaching or therapy, is largely an art — based, to be sure, on a conceptual framework and multiple skills, but still a highly individual affair. Therefore, at this point in the development of the field, the school administrator's best bet is to check the length of the trainer's experience as well as his knowledge of schools and school systems, and to talk with his fellow superintendents who have already ventured into the field.

Whatever the difficulties, however, the promise that human relations training holds for fundamental improvement and reform in the schools cannot be denied. The need of school personnel for training in the affective area is great for several reasons. First, in an era of increasing tension

and alienation, both teachers and administrators must develop more fully
the qualities of empathy and human objectivity — the essential hallmarks
of the helping professions. Placed in a role where they are often the target
of juvenile hostility — directed at them either personally or as parental
substitutes — teachers more than most require a resilient personality
that can absorb aggression, and that can also remain open and sympathet-
ic to students and their problems without becoming personally involved
with adolescent hang-ups.

Second, training in the affective area can help to reduce attitudinal
blocks and group resistance to needed educational change. Normal resistance to significant change is no less for teachers than for other human
beings; the trouble lies in the fact that the institution of which they are a
part is the most beleaguered of any in society today. The need for change
to meet the multiple dissatisfactions and pressures that plague the schools
wants little documentation here. But if needed change is to be achieved,
the individuals involved will themselves have to be prepared to change.

We must remember, however, that attention to the emotions in the
learning process derives from an educational model, not a therapeutic
one. Despite the assumption by many people that attention to the emotional dimensions of learning demands a therapeutic model, teachers
cannot, and should not, be therapists.

Third, human relations training can make it easier for school personnel
to "hang loose" during these revolutionary changes in teacher-student
relationships so that both they and their students can survive. Moreover,
the experience school systems will acquire in integrating the emotions and
group process into classroom instruction will surely make for improvement in social intelligence that is so necessary for effectiveness in the
helping professions. This capacity for dealing effectively with other
humans individually or in groups that, for want of a more precise term,
is called social intelligence has largely been ignored, or taken for granted
as the schools have focused on stimulating and rewarding cognitive
learning. But as the abrasion of human existence increases in our
crowded world, it can no longer be ignored.

Finally, appropriate human relations training should begin to equip
teachers with a new teaching technology that is based on a learning group
of peers, in contrast to the traditional classroom with the teacher as an
authority figure and the students as a group of charges. The capacity to be
a group process teacher is undoubtedly the most difficult of all goals for
human relations training. But the ability to make a classroom into a
learning group where peers share in the teaching-learning transaction
holds the greatest promise for overcoming the all too familiar pattern —
in the suburbs as well as the inner city — of sullen and disaffected children mobilizing to impede the educational process. The objective of

making use of the emotional factor in teacher training, school reorganiza-
tion, and classroom learning is an extraordinarily difficult one, but the
revolution in education that this will achieve makes it imperative that
school systems begin now.

*Interpersonal Skills*_____

A REJECTION OF EMPATHY CONCEPT AND T-GROUP METHODOLOGY

ALLEN R. SOLEM

Allen R. Solem, "Interpersonal Skills — A Rejection of Empathy
Concept and T-Group Methodology," *Training and Development Journal*,
22: 2–9, July, 1968. Reproduced by special permission from the July,
1968, issue of the *Training and Development Journal*. Copyright 1968 by
the American Society for Training and Development Inc.

The function of any skill is to make possible the application of knowledge. For interpersonal skills, this means that a knowledge of behavior
principles is essential if one is to select the principles and skills appropriate to a given situation, and to have available the necessary methods and
skills for a variety of situations. Applications force one to deal with specific cases and it is at the point of application that the adequacy or inade-
quacy of knowledge, of proficiency in the performance of skills, or effectiveness of the behavior principles or methods used is revealed most
clearly. No knowledge of principles can substitute for practice nor can
any skill make use of knowledge that isn't there, and neither one can make
an unsound method or principle work effectively.

Problems in Acquisition and Performance of Skill

1. All skills require practice and in this respect interpersonal skills are
no exception; however, the interpersonal dimension creates certain prob-

lems. In music or golf the need for practice is taken for granted, its purpose is understood, errors are accepted and faulty performance hurts no one. In contrast, interpersonal skills are performed for keeps and errors can hurt. Thus, even when present skills are ineffective, there is reluctance to try the new, much less to risk the repeated failure which practice often demands.

2. Many skills involve merely an accommodative or manipulative relationship with an inanimate feature of the environment possessing known characteristics and consistencies. Interpersonal skills require one to deal with at least one other individual, and the unknowns are far greater, more complex and more variable.

3. That man is capable of and frequently demonstrates two qualitatively different kinds of behavior, one based on the logic of intellect and the other based on the logic of feeling,[1] adds a wholly new dimension requiring different concepts, skills, and sensitivities. Problem behavior based on feelings is often confusing and irritating and this complicates things even further.

4. Related to these difficulties is the elusive and frequently tenuous nature of feedback cues. The more highly-specialized sensory mechanisms tend to furnish immediate and sharply-defined feedback, such as a sour note or a missed ball. In interpersonal skills, the cues appear to be less clearly defined, less precise and more susceptible to distortion by the internal condition of either party as well as by the quality of the relationship between them. The recent finding of Maier,[2] that successful subjects in detecting deception in an interview situation were unable to verbalize free response cues in a meaningful way, highlights issues in both practice and performance, and suggests that sensitivity to others is not importantly, if at all an intellectual process.

5. A further complication arises from the frequently disturbing effects on performance of premature closure.[3] Most skill patterns have fairly well-defined beginnings and endings. Interpersonal skills do not always show similarly clear-cut definition. Recent interview studies of Webster[4] and Maier[2] suggest that the patterns of premature impression formation may be a manifestation of closure forces. Not only do these tend toward closure on the basis of sub marginal data but toward "manufacturing" cues, and filtering or distorting others so that closure can be attained. Once achieved, closure tends to alter or reject subsequent cues which are inconsistent with or disconfirming of the first impression.

Interpersonal Sensitivity

Many of the existing obstacles toward understanding the processes in the acquisition and performance of interpersonal skills appear to stem from theoretical confusion and conflicting viewpoints as to the nature of interpersonal sensitivity.

Our inference from the Maier data,[2] and others summarized in Smith[5] is that in man, sensitivity is basically not an intellectual process. Despite this, efforts persist to view interpersonal sensitivity in terms of the psychoanalytic concept of empathy and to encompass it within the concepts of conventional learning theory.

We believe, on the contrary, that the data argue for a process in which all of the available and more specialized sensory mechanisms are organized into focus on a family of cues. Alternatively, there may also exist a separate sensory mechanism, operating with the help of the other available and relevant mechanisms to detect an organizable set of cues. Either system would account for what has otherwise been called intuition, sizing-up, and the like. Risking the danger of disposing of a phenomenon by naming it, we prefer to call the process *axiesthesis*, or the sensing of the worth of another.

In either case, there is evidence to suggest that a lack of inter-personal sensitivity is not so much the absence of formal development as it is the presence of obstacles and deterrents. Thus tendencies toward evaluative judgments, as suggested by Rogers[6] and the existence of emotional blocks (Hayakawa,[7] Maier[8,9] Jenkins,[10] and Schachter,[19]), of attitudes and frustrations, and preoccupation with ideas or intellectual problems, seem to us illustrative of some of the main sources of competing stimuli, and hence deterrents to interpersonal acuity. We interpret these data, as well as others, notably from Chance and Meaders[12] as arguing for a state of psychological well-being under conditions of optimal arousal as the necessary and perhaps sufficient conditions for effective detection and perceptual organization of most interpersonal cues.

Stimulus deprivation studies of Bexton, Heron, and Scott[13] indicate that a lack of sufficient cues to form an organized whole may tend, with the help of closure forces, to induce the "manufacture" of an erroneous interpersonal impression. Conversely, excessive internal stimulation, particularly from an insoluble problem experience sufficient to induce a state of frustration, (Maier[9]) tends to distort some cues and block others, most particularly those central to the problem area. We believe, therefore, that improvement in sensitivity to others is not so much a matter of developing one's acuity through training as it is the circumvention or removal of obstacles.

Empathy and T-Groups

The conclusions we draw from our review of the investigations into sensitivity to others lead us to reject both the concept of empathy as a useful viewpoint and the assumptions and methodology of T-group training. The evidence that sensitivity to others is a biological process seems to us a compelling argument against the position that its origin lies in the psychoanalytic mechanism of identification, from which the concept of empathy is derived. In addition, there are the essentially negative findings in studies of empathy (Lundy,[14] Chance and Meaders,[12] and Mullin[15]). Further we examined and tried to resolve differing and sometimes conflicting definitions of empathy and its related terminology. As defined in Warren,[16] "a mental state in which one identifies with or feels himself in the same state of mind as another," seems first of all to posit a condition antithetical to our understanding as to the nature of sensitivity and, second, to be at best a somewhat delusional exercise.

Underlying T-group training are the two key assumptions that (1) sensitivity to others is developed by means of learning procedures, and (2) that self-understanding must precede one's understanding of others. As far as we know, neither assumption is supported by experimental evidence. The T-group method seems to us to yield a process for inducing group pressures, often experienced as devaluative of the individual. That such pressures are consensual and not expert does not lessen their force, and changes appear to reflect conformity with social pressures and not either development or freedom from interfering anxieties and frustrations.

Role Playing as a Training Method

It is fortunate for both research and training purposes that sensitivity manifests itself in role playing situations where the cues are to some degree artificially created and behavior is on what Lewin[17] has called a level of irreality. Although certain ingredients of reality are removed others remain and those that are preserved appear adequate for constructing standard situations which for many purposes are the equivalent of reality.

Role playing furnishes a number of essential training requirements. Of central importance for skill development is that training is brought to the action phase. A further asset is the opportunity to try new and different methods and skills without embarrassment or the risk of hurt feelings.

Of the many role-playing procedures, we will consider only the Multiple Role Playing Procedure which enables many persons simultaneously to experience new methods and processes and the Single Group Procedure which provides more advanced skill practice.

Skills for Routine Situations

Since skills are the application of knowledge, it follows that one's repertoire of interpersonal skills is limited only by knowledge of behavior principles and ingenuity in devising methods and techniques for using them. There exist marked individual differences in ability, and we suspect that most variations are accounted for by a number of factors, among the most important of which are differences in sensitivity to feelings and temporary lapses brought on by competing stimuli.

Skills for Problem Situations

The clearest differences are found in situations where intellectual effort and insight are needed and feelings obscure or distort reality. For both types of behavior, the appropriate skills are those which yield free expression, but in different ways and for opposite purposes. In dealing with feelings the aim is reduction of tension and conflict; for intellectual processes, its aim is the creation of differences in ideas. Skills for the release of feelings are highlighted in non-directive counseling and related methods, and for intellectual problem solving they cause free expression of ideas.

The Nature of Process

Determinations as to the nature and extent of the relative contributions of methods and skills to effective interpersonal process and outcome requires controlled experimentation. Methods, objectives, and values all are guides to performance. Methods, specifically, select skills and the effectiveness of a method depends on the degree to which it incorporates effective behavior principles and permits them to operate when activated by skills. If one views process as a product of the interaction of method and skill it becomes apparent that each contributes to process and outcome and that different situations require different combinations as well as differences in relative emphasis.

Contribution of Method

The contribution of method to process and outcome is illustrated in several experiments (Maier,[18] Maier and Maier,[19] Maier and Hoffman,[20] and Maier[21]). In a study of delegation (Solem[22]), using two very different group problems, half of the leaders were given a written instruction to present the problem and their preferred solution for discussion as to a solution and the remaining half of the leaders were given a written instruction to present the problem. One result was that the leader solution, though seldom accepted, tended to generate judgmental acceptance-rejection reactions and the problem tended to generate idea exploration with consequent quality gains. With skills constant, an orientation toward one method vs. the other influenced outcome.

An experimental situation in which achievement of a high-quality decision is hampered by considerations of feeling was used to compare two discussion methods (Maier and Maier[19]). One, the Free Discussion Method, is designed to give everyone his say; the other, the Developmental Discussion Method, is a way for structuring discussion toward a systematic exploration of the situation[23]. Despite some overlap, the skills for the most part are different. The results showed that when both intellectual and feeling factors are present, methods oriented toward discussion of feelings achieve increased acceptance with lesser quality and methods oriented toward intellectual analysis achieve increased quality but less acceptance.

Skills for Release of Feelings

Methods for the release of feelings aid performance by selection of skills and by contributing to process. Effectiveness of process depends also on which skills are selected and on degree of proficiency.

In one study (Solem, previously unpublished) the effect of intensive practice on the acquisition of skill in listening and in reflecting feelings was examined. Large groups of student subjects were given thirty seconds in which to respond in writing, as an expert counselor would orally, when each of a transcribed series of client comments was read aloud by a skilled actress. In all, there were 12 sequential client comments and, after each written response, feedback was provided by having the actual reflection of the counselor read aloud. Performance, as subsequently rated by three competent judges, indicated highly significant improvement over the 12 practice opportunities in the 40-minute period. However, even the later performances were generally quite rudimentary.

The contribution of skill to process is illustrated in an experiment involving a group problem of fairness (Maier and Hoffman[20]). Leaders all had some previous training in group decision method and were instructed to put the problem to the men. Following the conferences, group members appraised the foreman's performance in terms of whether the discussion was foreman-dominated, a true group decision or a mixed type. Of 98 groups, 24 were judged as foreman-dominated, 62 as group decision, and 12 as mixed. Measures of satisfaction showed that the foreman's conduct of the discussion, and not the nature of the solution itself, was the most important single factor, and this is a matter of leader skill.

Among the more difficult skills to acquire are those needed to accept and turn hostility toward one's person or values into an interview or conference asset. This is true even given the intellectual awareness that argument or defensiveness will mean an irreversible loss of control over process or outcome.

Evidence bearing on this is found in an experiment in which three levels of training (2, 10, and 13 weeks) were compared (Maier, Hoffman, and Lansky[24]). The problem was to deal with a peer who displayed an unreasonable attitude. Although training influences were highly significant between and across levels, the results indicated that only the more elementary skills had been acquired at the end of the 13-week period and that many skills remained untapped. Avoidance of defensiveness in both parties is one of the difficulties presented in this problem and this is a difficult and complex skill.

Skills for Expression of Ideas

A wide array of concepts and principles exist for increasing the intellectual effectiveness of others. All make use of interpersonal methods and skills for eliciting the expression of different ideas. Certain experiments highlight the issues involved. In one experiment, a production bottleneck was used for which many solutions are possible but only one is clearly superior and elegant (Maier[25]). This yielded an extremely wide range of difference in achieving the elegant solution, depending on the skill of the leader.

That skills yield a marked upturn in the quality of thinking beyond that contributed by an effective method is illustrated in an experiment (Maier and Hoffman[25]) using the Development Discussion Method referred to earlier. With increases in various skills there were marked increments in proportions of high quality decisions.

Skills for Complex and Optional Situations

Because the nature and function of skills for dealing with feelings are very different from those for improving intellectual processes, we have considered them more or less separately. However, problem situations frequently require application of both types of skills. Although solution acceptance, which is largely a matter of feelings, is considered by managers in one study (Maier and Hoffman[27]) to be an essential consideration in more than three-fourths of their job problems and overriding in more than two out of five, a third of their problems involve acceptance and quality considerations about equally. Despite the contributions of method toward achieving these two solution attributes, such problems confront a leader with a variety of skill demands and options. Thus, he may elect to rely on his own intellectual capacities and expertise and develop his own solution, in which case acceptance will depend on skills in persuasion. Alternatively, he may rely on methods for gaining acceptance and on interview or discussion skills for improving quality. A third possibility is possession of a skill repertoire inclusive enough to deal with problems of both feeling and intellect, and a fourth is a high level of proficiency, either in certain key representative skills, or across the board.

Some recent work bears on several of these issues. For example, several studies have established that disagreement in a group or between a leader and a member can lead to innovation, or to hard feelings. The most recent of these shows that which of these consequences will ensue is largely a matter of whether the leader judges the dissenter adversely as a troublemaker or as a potential asset and utilizes skills to capitalize on the situation. These contrasting leader perceptions frequently originate in value orientations toward judgmental versus asset value systems (Dembo, Leviton and Wright[28]). Even a skilled leader may be induced to judge a dissenter adversely; however, possession of knowledge underlying the skill should modify this tendency. Without skills for the constructive use of dissent, the leader has no choice.

Interviews

Interview problems often highlight interpersonal issues, in part because the one-to-one relationship is less diffuse than is true of larger group settings and in part because the pace and immediacy of the interchange imposes more acute pressures on the interviewer's resources of skill. In one study (Solem[29]), the interview problem is such that it can be conducted through the method of conventional performance appraisal or the method of Maier's Problem Solving Interview (Maier[30]). The first method necessitates a judgmental approach and the second abjures judgment in favor of exploration for improvement potentials. Interview process and outcome depended mainly on two factors and the relationship between them. One was the proportion of time the superior talked, the optimum being not more than 40 percent, with a sharp break at 60 percent toward deterioration of the interview. Of even greater influence was whether the predominant motivational method used was negative, in the sense that it reflected paternalistic values and skills, or positive, reflecting respect for the subordinates' views and leader values and skills of a helper. Further, the nature of the relationship between these two factors, particularly when both are adverse, was not merely summative but compounding in its effects. The fact that only one interview in eight, as judged from a series of process and outcome factors, was optimally conducted, suggests a widespread need among managers for new knowledge, methods, and interpersonal skills.

Techniques

Many situations call for the achievement of essential but relatively narrow and specialized objectives. For this purpose interpersonal techniques can be extremely useful. We have not discussed these or the relevant data in part because such techniques are numerous and in part because detailed discussion is in many cases available in the literature.

It goes without saying that techniques differ widely in the types and degree of skills required. Given the needed skills, perhaps the most important consideration is that their user understands their rationale so that they can be incorporated into a larger repertoire of methods and skills and not be viewed merely as isolated devices.

References

1. MAIER, N. R. F. "A Human Relations Program for Supervision," *Industrial and Labor Relations Review*, 1 (April, 1948), 443–464.
2. MAIER, N. R. E. "Sensitivity to Attempts at Deception in an Interview Situation," *Personnel Psychology*, 19 (Spring, 1966), 55–66.
3. ZEIGARNIK, B. "Uber das Behalten von Erledigten and Unerledigten Handlungen," *Psychologische Forschung*, 9 (1927), 1–85.
4. WEBSTER, E. C. *Decision Making in the Employment Interview*, Industrial Relations Center, McGill University, 1964.
5. SMITH, H. C. *Sensitivity to People*, New York: McGraw-Hill Book Co., 1966.
6. ROGERS, C. R. *Counseling and Psychotherapy*, Boston: Houghton-Mifflin, 1941.

7. HAYAKAWA. S. I. *Language in Action*, New York: Harcourt, Brace and Co., 1941.
8. MAIER, N. R. F. *Frustration*, New York: McGraw-Hill Book Co., 1949. Reissued by Arbor Press, University of Michigan, 1961.
9. MAIER, N. R. F. "Frustration Theory: Restatement and Extension," *Psychological Review*, 63 (November, 1956), 370–388.
10. JENKINS, R. C. "Nature of the Schizophrenic Process," *Archives of Neurology and Psychiatry*, 64 (August, 1950), 243–262.
11. SCHACHTER, S., B. WILLERMAN, L. FESTINGER, and R. HYMAN. "Emotional Disruption and Industrial Productivity," *Journal of Applied Psychology*, 45 (August, 1961), 201–213.
12. CHANCE, J. E., and W. MEADERS. "Needs and Interpersonal Perception," *Journal of Personality*, 28 (June, 1960), 200–210.
13. BEXTON, W. H., W. HERON, and T. H. SCOTT. "Effects of Decreased Variation in the Sensory Environment," *Canadian Journal of Psychology*, 8 (June, 1954), 70–76.
14. LUNDY, R. M. "Assimilative Projection and Accuracy of Prediction in Interpersonal Perceptions," *Journal of Abnormal Psychology*, 52 (January, 1956), 33–38.
15. MULLIN, J. "Reliability and Validity of a Projective Film Test of Empathy," Unpublished Master's Thesis, Michigan State Univ., 1962.
16. WARREN, H. C. *Dictionary of Psychology*, Boston: Houghton-Mifflin, 1934.
17. LEWIN, K. *Principles of Topological Psychology*, New York: McGraw-Hill Book Co., 1936.
18. MAIER, N. R. F. "An Experimental Test of the Effect of Training on Discussion Leadership," *Human Relations*, 6 (May, 1953), 161–173.
19. MAIER, N. R. F., and R. A. MAIER. "An Experimental Test of the Effects of Developmental vs. Free Discussions on the Quality of Group Decisions," *Journal of Applied Psychology*, 41 (October, 1957), 320–323.
20. MAIER, N. R. F., and L. R. HOFFMAN. "Group Decision in England and the United States," *Personnel Psychology*, 15 (Spring, 1962), 75–87.
21. MAIER, N. R. F. *Problem Solving Discussions and Conferences*, New York: McGraw-Hill Book Co., 1963.
22. SOLEM, A. R. "An Evaluation of Two Attitudinal Approaches to Delegation," *Journal of Applied Psychology*, 43 (February, 1958), 37–39.
23. MAIER, N. R. F. *Principles of Human Relations*, New York: John Wiley and Sons, 1952.
24. MAIER, N. R. F., and L. R. HOFFMAN, and L. M. LANSKY. "Human Relations Training as Manifested in an Interview Situation," *Personnel Psychology*, 13 (Spring, 1960), 11–30.
25. MAIER, N. R. F. "The Quality of Group Decisions as Influenced by the Discussion Leader," *Human Relations*, 3 (June, 1950), 155–174.
26. MAIER, N. R. F., and L. R. HOFFMAN. "Using Trained Developmental Discussion Leaders to Improve Further the Quality of Group Decisions," *Journal of Applied Psychology*, 44 (August, 1960), 247–251.
27. MAIER, N. R. F., and L. R. HOFFMAN. "Types of Problems Confronting Managers," *Personnel Psychology*, 17 (Autumn, 1964), 261–269.
28. DEMBO, TAMARA, G. L. LEVITON, and B. A. WRIGHT. Adjustment to Misfortune — A Problem of Social-psychological Rehabilitation," *Artificial Limbs*, 3 (Autumn, 1956), 4–62.
29. SOLEM, A. R. "Some Supervisor Problems in Appraisal Interviewing," *Personnel Administration*, 23 (September–October, 1960), 27–35.
30. MAIER, N. R. F. *The Appraisal Interview*, New York: John Wiley and Sons, 1958.

Marathon Group Dynamics:
I. Some Functions of the Professional
Group Facilitator

GEORGE R. BACH[1]

G. R. Bach, "Marathon Group Dynamics: I. Some Functions of the Professional Group Facilitator," *Psychological Reports*, 20: 995–999, 1967. Reprinted with permission of author and publisher.

Summary. — Because current public interest in Marathon Group participation is growing, there is an urgent need for providing legitimate psychologists, psychiatrists, sociologists, family and marriage counselors with training facilities where they can acquire the skills for conducting professional Marathon Groups. Some of the skills involved are outlined in this paper. The destructive effects of "Do it yourself" Marathons as evidenced in the problems encountered by "wild" Marathon Groups are described.

Our culture has become acutely "group-conscious." As the humanistically oriented sections of the American people, especially the younger generation, are searching for antidotes to societal alienation, they have become more receptive to and supportive of the various new forms of therapy-group life which have emerged on the psychological scene. Carl Rogers commented on the group-orientation in our culture during a recent interview (cf. Hoover, 1967): "It is a fascinating fact that with almost no support from universities, little recognition from academic people and no support from government grants, 'basic encounter groups' have become the most rapidly growing psychological trend in our culture."

The most dramatic and perhaps also the most "popular" representative of this trend is the intensive interaction, or "MARATHON GROUP," previously described by the writer (Bach, 1966). The Marathon Group encounter has been found — after the first three years of practice and research — to be the most direct, the most efficient, and the most

---

[1]Marshall Shumsky, Research Assistant, contributed field observations and other data on "wild" marathons.

economical antidote to alienation, meaninglessness, fragmentation, and other hazards of mental health in our time.

In the previous publication (Bach, 1966) the basic objectives and ground rules for the professional conduct of legitimate Marathon Groups were described. In brief summary, the Marathon Group is a social interaction laboratory in which participants can free themselves, at least for a 24-hr. stretch, from image-making and from manipulative game-playing and experience an improved quality of social contact for which the term *"authentic communion"* suggests itself.

Having experienced authentic communion with Marathon Group peers, the participants are encouraged to apply what they have learned to their daily lives and to attempt to improve the quality of their contact with significant others. This involves a change of interpersonal stance from manipulation to communion. This type of learning is in our opinion the most urgent social task for our alienated multitudes. Marathon Group participation provides an effective head-start in this learning.

In a Marathon Group, 12 to 16 participants interact continuously and uninterruptedly in a secluded setting. The sessions last for 24 hr. minimum and may be scheduled longer. The participants are usually not emotionally disturbed, psychiatrically "sick" persons who are desperately seeking therapeutic help. Rather, the Marathon experience appeals to healthy, growth-seeking individuals who sense in themselves and in others the need to have more authentic interactional experiences than regular living affords in our marketing-oriented and mechanized society.

This search for authentic contacts both by people in need of emotional rehabilitation as well as by more healthy "well-adjusted" people has made participation in Marathon Groups the "in" thing to do, and this trend has been recognized by various news media and been given a great deal of publicity (e.g., Hoover, 1967). This publicity makes it necessary to distinguish between "legitimate" (professionally conducted) Marathon Groups and so-called "wild" Marathon Groups.

Due to the current "group fad," many kinds of unprofessional, untrained group leaders are conducting weekend-long social talk sessions, sometimes with the aid of gimmicks, such as drugs or so-called psychodramatic techniques, and/or instant television feedback cameras. These self-styled Marathon Groups attempt to imitate legitimate Marathon Groups but without the leadership of group psychotherapists or other professionals who have the skill not only to facilitate candid communication among the members but also to make full therapeutic use of the resultant tensions that emerge during the group meetings (Bach, 1956).

Facilitative Services of Professional Group Leaders

To establish clearly the socially important distinction between professional and nonprofessional or "wild" marathons, it may be informative to list here some of the facilitative services that professional group psychotherapists do render during a Marathon Group session.

To begin with, prospective participants in professionally conducted Marathons are *screened and/or prepared* for the experience. The expectations of the participants are thoroughly aired and those with severely disturbed forebodings and dire anticipations of "group-shock" or trauma are invited to withdraw and encouraged to enter a therapeutic group which meets during regular office hours. Here such persons can work through their excessive group anxiety before participating in a Marathon.

At our Institute the pre-registrants are given the opportunity to participate in informative "Warm-up Groups" in which the basic rules are discussed and irrational expectations corrected before they become the instigating condition for disjunctive interaction experiences later.

The professional conductor facilitates the emergence and maintenance of a group atmosphere that is conducive to learning and sharing. This involves the proper timing and *focusing of feedbacks* and the channeling of interaction. Other leader functions are: (a) the full utilization of group influences to "bring out" individual members to the fullest; (b) the maximization and focusing of candid feedback reactions from the group to every individual in the group; (c) helping to decode the often unconscious motivational payoffs of self and other defeating interaction patterns; (d) recognition and solution of redundant interpersonal rituals and "set-up operations" (Bach, 1954), which are really intimacy-preventing "games" habitually played by psychologically sophisticated people (Berne, 1965); (e) *reinforcement of changes* through a "coaching" type of support in the tryouts and the practices of new ways of experiencing, of seeing and interacting; (f) maintenance of productively stimulating, yet manageable levels of *group tensions*, rather than either avoidance of tensions or letting them get out of hand; (g) demonstration to members of the differences between the effects of good and of "bad" (disjunctive) communications; (h) selective focus on here and now, apparently workable and soluble problems.

(i) *Helping people to share their acute feelings* and perceptions and ideas and judgments rather than letting them escape into reciting old records or inspecting old places in the "personal museum" of their past lives is also a meaningful function.

(j) The professional facilitator must use his expertise in providing safe channels for the full exploration and nondestructive expression of conflicts and aggression, that naturally emerge within a free-wheeling group and between particular members. This includes, for example, an opportunity for spouses to "fight it out."

(k) Providing members with a learn model in the person of the professional leader is accomplished by the leader's participation as an authentic person who makes his private world accessible to the group members on appropriate occasions.

(l) Helping the group to move on to new concerns and new phases of group life when there is a danger of the group's becoming exhausted with redundant concerns over growth-resistant game-playing members and, (m) helping the group make the most use of any of the many crises that should be allowed to emerge during a long Marathon session are also among the leader's responsibilities. Effective counteraction of the defensive avoidance strategies used by frightened members who resist the task of interacting intimately and authentically with one another is provided.

At the conclusion of every Marathon the professional leader conducts a *systematic survey* of everybody's reactions. He locates any individual for whom the Marathon participation was more destructively disturbing than constructively stimulating. The disturbed person is then further attended to and closely followed up as the leader's research must be continuous if he is to understand and influence the processes affected.

Last, but by no means least, professional group leaders must have the skills to facilitate the growth of the group's own *autonomy*, that is, to help the group become independent of him. He lets the group take over whenever it can do so productively. The professional is able to participate on several levels: as a person, as a learner, and also as a leader.

Some Problems Encountered by "Wild" Marathons

The above enumeration of professional group leaders' functions, while not complete, is sufficient for the recognition that considerable leadership skills are involved in the proper management of Marathon Groups.

Nonprofessional "wild" amateur Marathons, because they try to do without professional leadership, invariably run into a number of serious problems. One of these problems is the inability of "wild" Marathons to make creative use of the group tensions generated. For example, some "wild" sessions will be filled with explosions of excessive hostility, which then may panic the group so much that members fear, consciously or unconsciously, a loss of control. Some individual members may fear personally that they might "flip out." As a defense against these fears, "wild" groups tend either to break up prematurely or, more likely, to regress into a phony "*acceptance bath.*" This consists of a pseudo-peaceful, defensive, self-protective hand-holding "love-feast," or social chit-chat sessions in which authentic conflicts and aggressions are bypassed and avoided for fear of unmanageable "outbreaks."

However, not all nonprofessional Marathons are "wild." Many of them are *too mild*, *too defensive*, *too phony*, too much preoccupied with maudlin acceptance and pseudo-loving. And, there are at times outbursts of tearful sentimentality, popularly associated with gut level "exposures." The management of aggression tends to deteriorate into routinized "attack-strategies," a poor imitation of Synanon-Games (Yablonsky, 1965).

The problem is that nonprofessionals, while usually meaning well and wanting to be helpful, tend to oversimplify the complexity of the

Marathon Group dynamics by viewing its functions as a cathartic confessional, "a fishbowl," or an "exposure stage," or a "fight arena." They aim merely at the expression of "deep feelings," "love" and "hate," loneliness and hurts. They may probe into the past and enourage confessions of dark, presumably shameful secrets and guilt associated with stale, old "traumatic experiences."

In the professional Marathon, the reduction of shame and guilt through expression, followed by total acceptance, is only one relatively minor and fleeting aspect of the total learning experience, which centers more on experimenting with and actually trying out *new, improved ways* of openly dealing with the current conflicts that naturally emerge between self and others in the Marathon Group sessions.

Some participants in nonprofessional "wild" sessions have had emotionally damaging experiences, which are known to us from their later reports to their psychiatrists. Dr. Judd Marmor, Head of Psychiatry at Mt. Sinai Hospital in Los Angeles, when interviewed by Mrs. Eleanor Hoover (1967) about nonprofessionally conducted groups, reported: "All of us know of people, I personally know of at least two, who 'blew up' during or after one of these '*wild sessions*' and had to be hospitalized. ... These groups are as good as the people who conduct them."

In the legitimate Marathon Group, the atmosphere is carefully designed to maximize the exchange of authentically felt experience during the procedures. This includes the *full airing of conflict and aggression* between members, as well as the expression of affection and acceptance. The focus is on the experiences that acutely emerge within and among group participants during the long meetings. Candid confrontations, open sharing, and receptivity to feedbacks are called for night and day. Candid critique, honest aggression, even the opportunity to "fight it out," are all part of this process. Cuddling and Red Cross nursing are held to a minimum.

References

BACH, G. R. *Intensive Group Psychotherapy*. New York: Ronald, 1954.
BACH, G. R. "Pathological aspects of therapeutic groups," *Group Psychotherapy*, 9 (1956), 133–148.
BACH, G. R. "The Marathon Group: Intensive Practice of Intimate Interaction," *Psychological Reports*, 18 (June, 1966), 995–1005.
BERNE, E. *Games People Play*. Chicago: Grove Press, 1965.
HOOVER, E. "The Great Group Binge," *West Magazine, Los Angeles Times*, (January 8, 1967), 8–13.
YABLONSKY, L. *The Tunnel Back*. New York: Macmillan, 1965.

Accepted April 19, 1967.

Buyer Beware
Selected Bibliography

Periodicals

BLANCHARD, WILLIAM H. "Ecstasy without Agony is Baloney," *Psychology Today*, 3 (January, 1970), 8–10+.

CRAWSHAW, RALPH. "How Sensitive is Sensitivity Training?" *American Journal of Psychiatry*, 126 (December, 1969), 869–73.

FOLEY, ALBERT SIDNEY. "Group Dynamics: A Catholic View," *America*, 88 (March, 1953), 645–47.

FOREMAN, MILTON E. "T-Groups: Their Implications for Counselor Supervision and Preparation," *Counselor Education and Supervision*, 7 (Fall, 1967), 48–53.

GREENE, PAT RYAN. "Sensitivity Training: Fulfillment or Freakout?" *The Catholic World*, 211 (April, 1970), 18–21.

GUNDERSON, ROBERT GRAY. "This Group-Dynamics Furor," *School and Society*, 74 (August 18, 1951), 97–100.

"Hazards of T-Groups," *The Journal of the American Medical Association*, 210 (October 27, 1969), 719.

HOUSE, ROBERT J. "Leadership Training: Some Dysfunctional Consequences," *Administrative Science Quarterly*, 12 (March, 1968), 556–71.

JAFFE, STEVEN L., and DONALD J. SCHERL. "Acute Psychosis Precipitated by T-Group Experiences," *Archives of General Psychiatry*, 21 (October, 1969), 443–48.

KUEHN, JOHN L., and FRANCIS M. CRINELLA. "Sensitivity Training: Interpersonal 'Overkill' and Other Problems," *American Journal of Psychiatry*, 126 (December, 1969), 840–45.

LAKIN, MARTIN. "Some Ethical Issues in Sensitivity Training," *American Psychologist*, 24 (October, 1969), 923–29.

MACLEOD, JESSIE. "Sensitivity Training: What's That? Is it for a Local Church?" *International Journal of Religious Education*, 43 (December, 1966), 8–9.

MCCASLIN, NELLIE. "Critical Look at Group Dynamics," *School and Society*, 82 (November 26, 1955), 168–69.

QUAYTMAN, WILFRED. "Impressions of Esalen (Schutz) Phenomenon," *Journal of Contemporary Psychotherapy*, 2 (Summer, 1969), 57–64.

RAKSTIS, TED J. "Sensitivity Training: Fad, Fraud or New Frontier?" *Today's Health*, 48 (January, 1970), 20–25+.

ROSE, BRIAN. "T-Group?" *The Times Educational Supplement* [London], 2618 (July 23, 1965), 155.

SHOSTROM, EVERETT L. "Group Therapy: Let the Buyer Beware," *Psychology Today*, 2 (May, 1969), 36–40.

SIKES, WALTER W. "A Study of Some Effects of a Human Relations Training Laboratory," *Dissertation Abstracts*, 26 (August, 1965), 1200.

STEPHENSON, HARRIET. "Evaluating Human Relations Training," *Personnel Administration*, 29 (July–August, 1966), 34–39.

TAYLOR, K. F. "Some Doubts about Sensitivity Training," *Australian Psychologist*, 1 (March, 1967), 171–79.

Afterword

Encounter and Sensitivity Defined: Excerpts from J. L. Moreno*_____

"In the spring of 1914 Moreno published in Vienna the first of a series of poetic writings entitled *Einladung zu einer Begegnung* (*Invitation to an Encounter*), which is evidently the first literary definition of encounter, the concept which has become central in the existentialist movement. To describe the encounter, he portrays two persons exchanging eyes to comprehend and know each other: 'A meeting of two: eye to eye, face to face. And when you are near I will tear your eyes out and place them instead of mine, and you will tear my eyes out and place them instead of yours, then I will look at you with your eyes and you will look at me with mine.' "[1]

• • •

". . . Encounter, which derives from the French *rencontre*, is the nearest translation of *Begegnung*. The German *zwischenmenschlich* and the English 'interpersonal' or 'interactional' are anemic notions compared to the living concent of encounter. *Begegnung* conveys that two or more persons meet not only to face one another, but to live and experience one another — as actors, each in his own right. It is not only an emotional rapport, like the professional meeting of a physician or therapist and patient or, an intellectual rapport, like teacher and student, or a scientific rapport, like a participant observer with his subject. It is a meeting on the most intensive level of communication. The participants are not put there by any external authority; they are there because they want to be — representing the supreme authority of the self-chosen path. The persons are there in space; they may meet for the first time, with all their strengths

*These excerpts are taken from J. L. Moreno, "The Viennese Origins of the Encounter Movement, Paving the Way for Existentialism, Group Psychotherapy and Psychodrama," *Group Psychotherapy*, XXII (1969), 7–16. References to material also appearing in earlier publications by Moreno and cited in "The Viennese Origins . . ." are supplied in footnotes.
[1]The quotation is from Paul Johnson, *Psychology of Religion* (New York, 1959), pp. 42–43.

and weaknesses — human actors seething with spontaneity and zest. It is not *Einfühlung;* it is *Zweifühlung* — togetherness, sharing life. It is an intuitive reversal of roles, a realization of the self through the other; it is identity, the rare, unforgotten experience of total reciprocity. The encounter is extemporaneous, unstructured, unplanned, unrehearsed — it occurs on the spur of the moment. It is 'in the moment' and 'in the here,' 'in the now.' It can be thought of as the preamble, the universal frame of all forms of structured meeting, the common matrix of all the psychotherapies, from the total subordination of the patient (as in the hypnotic situation) to the superiority and autonomy of the protagonist (as in psychodrama).

"Summing up, *Begegnung* is the sum total of interaction, a meeting of two or more persons, not in the dead past or imagined future, but in the here and now, *hic et nunc*, in the fullness of time — the real, concrete and complete situation for experience; it involves physical and psychic contact. It is the convergence of emotional, social and cosmic factors which occur in all age groups, but particularly in adolescence (*Begegnung syndrome*); it is the experience of identity and total reciprocity; but above all, psychodrama is the essence of the encounter."[2]

• • •

Early formulations of the phenomenon of sensitivity and their consequences upon behavior have been published in my European writings.

"There are actors who are connected with one another by an invisible correspondence of feelings, who have a sort of heightened sensitivity for their mutual inner processes, one gesture is sufficient and often they do not look at one another, they communicate through a new sense as if by a 'medial understanding.' "[3]

"Some real process in one person's life situation is sensitive and corresponds to some real process in another person's life situation and there are numerous degrees, positive and negative, of these 'interpersonal sensitivities.' "[4]

"The relation between therapist and patient, whether in individual or group psychotherapy, requires telic sensitivity. Telic sensitivity is "trainable." It is tele which establishes natural "correspondence" between

---

[2]See J. L. Moreno, *Philosophy of the Third Psychiatric Revolution, with Special Emphasis on Group Psychotherapy and Psychodrama*, (eds.) Frieda Fromm-Reichmann and J. L. Moreno (New York, 1959).
[3]See J. L. Moreno, *The Theatre of Spontaneity* (New York, 1947), p. 68.
[4]"Statistics of Social Configurations," *Sociometry*, I (1937–38).

therapist and patient. It is an absence of this factor in professional therapeutic relations which is responsible for therapeutic failures; it must be
regained in order to make any technology work. Transference of the
patient may relate him to a person who is not there; transference of the
therapist may relate him to a patient who is not there. The result is that
patient and therapist talk past each other, instead of to each other.
Similarly, empathy and counterempathy do not add up to tele; they may
run parallel, and never mix, that is, never become a telic relationship."[5]

[5]*Ibid.*

Appendices

Appendix A
Sensory Approaches
Selected Bibliography

Some of the most publicized aspects of sensitivity training and encounter have been the use of physical contact and body movement. Individuals who had been taught to look but not touch, learn to express themselves and communicate with each other through touching, holding, and arm-wrestling. Techniques for facilitating such interactions have evolved from many sources, some of which are Wilhelm Reich's pioneering work on "character armor," Alexander Lowen's "bio-energetics," Charlotte Selver's "sensory awareness" and Albert Pesso's "psychomotor techniques." Other sources include dance therapy, music therapy, art therapy and various movement therapies.

The sensory area is broad and exciting, but still essentially undefined. As a result, we have been unable to find representative articles to serve as a general introduction to the field. Much of the relevant literature is too technical or therapeutically oriented for our purposes here. We do feel, however, that the reader interested in sensitivity training and group encounter deserves the opportunity to acquaint himself with some of the best work in this area. Therefore, we are including the following selected bibliography:

Books

FAST, JULIUS. *Body Language*. Philadelphia: J. B. Lippincott Co., 1970.

FRANK, LAWRENCE K. *Explorations in Communication*, eds. Edmund Carpenter and Marshall McLuhan. Boston: Beacon Press, 1960.

GUNTHER, BERNARD. *Love View*. New York: Collier Books, 1969.

———. *Sense Relaxation Below Your Mind*. New York: The Macmillan Co., 1968.

GUSTAITIS, RASA. *Turning On without Drugs*. New York: The Macmillan Co., 1969.

HOWARD, JANE. *Please Touch: A Guided Tour of the Human Potential Movement*. New York: McGraw-Hill, Inc., 1970.

LOWEN, ALEXANDER. *The Betrayal of the Body*. New York: The Macmillan Co., 1968.

———. *Love and Orgasm*. New York: The Macmillan Co., 1965.

———. *Pleasure: A Creative Approach to Life*. New York: Coward-McCann Inc., 1970.

PERLS, FREDERICK. *Ego, Hunger and Aggression: The Beginning of Gestalt Therapy*. New York: Random House, Inc., 1969.

———. *Gestalt Therapy Verbatim*. Lafayette, California: Real People Press, 1969.

———, RALPH F. HEFFERLINE, and PAUL GOODMAN. *Gestalt Therapy*. New York: Delta Books, 1965.

PESSO, ALBERT. *Movement in Psychotherapy: Psychomotor Techniques and Training*. New York: New York University Press, 1969.

SCHILDER, PAUL. *The Image and Appearance of the Human Body*. New York: International Universities Press, 1950.

SCHUTZ, WILLIAM C. *Joy: Expanding Human Awareness*. New York: Grove Press, Inc., 1967.

SELVER, CHARLOTTE in conjunction with Charles V. W. Brooks, *Explorations in Human Potentialities*, ed. Herbert A. Otto. Springfield, Illinois: Charles C Thomas, Publishers, 1966.

Periodicals

ATCHESON, RICHARD. "Big Sur: Coming to My Senses," *Holiday*, 43 (March, 1968), 18–24.

BORTON, TERRY. "Reach, Touch, and Teach," *Saturday Review*, LII (January 18, 1969), 56–70.

DEROCHE, EDWARD F. "A Study of the Effectiveness of Selected Creative Exercises on Creative Thinking and the Mastery of a Unit in Elementary Science," *Dissertation Abstracts*, 27 (June, 1967), 4162A–63A.

DUNNETTE, MARVIN D. "People Feeling: Joy, More Joy and the 'Slough of Despond,' " *The Journal of Applied Behavioral Science*, 5 (January-March, 1969), 25–44.

"Esalen: Three-Day Session at Hotel Diplomat," *The New Yorker*, XLVI (May 2, 1970), 27–28.

GALPER, JEFRY. "Nonverbal Communication Exercises in Groups," *Social Work*, 15 (April, 1970), 71–78.

GROSS, AMY. " 'Getting Together': Human Potential Movement," *Mademoiselle*, 71 (May, 1970), 154–55.

"The Group: Joy on Thursday," *Newsweek*, LXXIII (May 12, 1969), 104–6D.

GUNTHER, MAX. "Secrets of Working with a Group," *Popular Science*, 176 (March, 1960), 109–12.

LITWAK, LEO E. "Joy is the Prize: A Trip to Esalen Institute," *The New York Times Magazine*, CXVII (December 31, 1967), 8–9+.

OTTO, HERBERT A. "Depth Unfoldment Experience: A Method for Creating Interpersonal Closeness," *Adult Education*, 17 (Winter, 1967), 78–84.

PERLS, FREDERICK S. "Workshop vs. Individual Therapy," *Journal of the Long Island Consultation Center*, 5 (Fall, 1967), 13–17.

ROLF, IDA P. "Structural Integration," *Systematics*, 1 (June, 1963), 66–83.

Appendix B
A Selected General Encounter Bibliography

BLANK, LEONARD, MONROE G. GOTTSEGEN, and GLORIA B. GOTTSEGEN (eds.). *Encounter: Confrontations in Self and Interpersonal Awareness*. New York: The Macmillan Company, 1971.

BURTON, ARTHUR (ed.). *Encounter: The Theory and Practice of Encounter Groups*. San Francisco: Jossey–Bass, Inc., 1968.

EGAN, GERARD. *Encounter: Group Processes for Interpersonal Growth*. Belmont, California: Brooks-Cole Publishing Co., 1970.

GOTTSCHALK, LOUIS A. *Comprehensive Group Psychotherapy*, eds. Harold I. Kaplan and Benjamin J. Sadock. Baltimore: Williams & Wilkins Company, 1970.

MALAMUD, DANIEL, and SOLOMON MACHOVER. *Toward Self-Understanding: Group Technique in Self Confrontation*. Springfield, Illinois: Charles C. Thomas, 1965.

O'Banion, TERRY, and APRIL O'CONNELL. *The Shared Journey: An Introduction to Encounter*. Englewood Cliffs, New Jersey: Prentice-Hall, Inc., 1970.

OTTO, HERBERT A. *Explorations in Human Potentialities*. Springfield, Illinois: Charles C Thomas, 1966.

———. *Group Methods to Actualize Human Potential: A Handbook*. Beverly Hills: The Holistic Press, 1970.

————. *Guide to Developing Your Potential*. New York: Charles Scribner's Sons, 1967.

———— and JOHN MANN (eds.). *Ways of Growth: Approaches to Expanding Awareness*. New York: Grossman Publishers, Inc., 1968.

Appendix C
Notes on the Contributors

George R. Bach, Ph.D.

Dr. Bach is founder and Director of the Institute for Group Psychotherapy, Beverly Hills, California. He formerly taught at several universities throughout the United States. Dr. Bach is an editor of three scientific journals and has written extensively on group psychotherapy. He is author of *Intensive Group Psychotherapy* (New York, 1954) and senior author of *The Intimate Enemy* (New York, 1969).

Paul Bindrim, M.A.

Mr. Bindrim is a licensed clinical psychologist in private practice in Hollywood, California. He has taught at Finch and El Camino Colleges. He originated and led the first nude marathon in 1967 and since then has conducted nude marathon sessions throughout the United States. His work has been reported in *Time* and *Life*. He has made presentations at major universities and professional conventions. His publications include articles in *Psychotherapy*, *Psychology Today*, and a chapter on cultivating peak experiences in *Ways of Growth* (New York, 1968). The Canadian Broadcasting Corporation has produced a documentary on his work.

Max Birnbaum

Mr. Birnbaum is Director of the Boston University Human Relations Laboratory (operational headquarters, New York City). He is Associate Professor of Human Relations and Associate Professor of Sociology, Boston University. He is a Fellow of the National Training Laboratories, and has been involved in T-group training and organizational development for the past two decades.

Howard A. Blatner, M.D.

Dr. Blatner is a psychiatrist in the United States Air Force. He was formerly a Fellow in Child Psychiatry at Cedar-Sinai Medical Center, Thalians Clinic, Los Angeles. His studies in psychodrama were at Stanford University and the Moreno Institute at Beacon, New York. Dr. Blatner is the author of *Psychodrama, Role-Playing and Action Methods: Theory and Practice* (Thetford, England, 1970).

Daniel Casriel, M.D.

Dr. Casriel is the founder and former Medical Superintendent of Daytop Village, a therapeutic community for narcotics addicts. He is in practice in New York City where he has founded A.R.E.B.A. (Accelerated Re-education of Emotions, Behavior and Attitudes), a therapeutic community. Dr. Casriel is past president of the American Society of Psychoanalytic Physicians, and Visiting Associate Professor of Psychiatry at Temple Medical School.

John E. Drotning, Ph.D.

Dr. Drotning is Professor of Industrial Relations, University of Wisconsin. He was formerly on the faculty of the State University of New York at Buffalo and Purdue University. He is a member of the National Labor and Education Panel of the American Arbitration Association, and a panel member for the Public Employees Relation Board of New York State. Dr. Drotning is a consultant to the American Behavioral Science Training Labs in Detroit and has published widely in the field of labor and management relations.

William F. Glueck, Ph.D.

Dr. Glueck is Associate Professor of Management and Faculty Research Associate in Research Center, School of Business and Public Administration and Faculty Research Associate, Space Services Research Center, University of Missouri–Columbia. He has taught organization, employee relations and business policy at Missouri, University of Texas, University of Aston in Birmingham (United Kingdom) and Michigan State University where he received his Ph.D. He is the author of five books and over forty-five articles and spent five years in industry prior to his academic career.

Louis A. Gottschalk, M.D.

Dr. Gottschalk is Professor and Chairman, Department of Psychiatry and Human Behavior, College of Medicine, University of California at Irvine. He is a member of the Clinical Psychopharmacology Review Committee of the California State Department of Mental Hygiene. He is on the editorial boards of *Psychosomatic Medicine, Psychiatry, Science,* and *Psychopharmacology and Behavior.* Formerly he was Training and Supervising Analyst, Chicago Institute for Psychoanalysis, Associate Professor and Research Professor of Psychiatry and Coordinator of Research in the Department of Psychiatry, College of Medicine, University of Cincinnati.

Thomas C. Greening, Ph.D.

Dr. Greening studied in Vienna as a Fulbright Scholar, and returned to the University of Michigan to complete his Ph.D. in clinical psychology. He is now a partner in Psychological Service Associates, Chairman of the Board of the Topanga Center for Human Development, Editor of the *Journal of Humanistic Psychology,* and an Associate of the National Training Laboratories Institute.

Spencer Klaw

Mr. Klaw is a freelance writer. He was born in New York City, educated at Harvard, and has worked on the editorial staffs of *The New Yorker, The New York Herald Tribune,* and *Fortune.* His works have appeared in many of the nation's major magazines, including *Harper's, Playboy, The Reporter, The Saturday Evening Post* and *Esquire.* Mr. Klaw is the author of a book entitled *The New Brahmins: Scientific Life in America* (New York, 1968).

Elizabeth E. Mintz, Ph.D.

Dr. Mintz is in private practice of group and individual psychotherapy in New York City. She is on the faculty of the National Psychological Association for Psychoanalysis and Supervisor in group therapy, New York Clinic for Mental Health. Dr. Mintz has demonstrated encounter games, marathons and sensitivity training before numerous professional groups. She is the author of numerous articles, and an acknowledged pioneer of the marathon group. Dr. Mintz's book, *Marathon Groups: Reality and Symbol,* is to be published in 1971.

J. L. Moreno, M.D.

Dr. Moreno is President of the Moreno Academy and Director of the Moreno Institute. He is the creator of Psychodrama and Sociometry. Dr. Moreno is the recipient of many awards and honors, including the Golden Doctor Diploma of the University of Vienna and Professor and Doctor *Honoris Causia,* University of Barcelona. He is the editor of *Group Psychotherapy and Psychodrama.*

Carl R. Rogers, Ph.D.

Dr. Rogers is noted as the founder of client-centered therapy and his impact on therapeutic practice and work with groups has been considerable. He is presently a Resident Fellow at the Center for Studies of the

Person, La Jolla, California. He is the author of many articles and a number of books including: *Client Centered Therapy* (Boston, 1951) and *Freedom to Learn: A View of What Education Might Become* (Columbus, Ohio, 1969). He has taught at Ohio State University, the University of Chicago, the University of Wisconsin, as well as shorter teaching stints at institutions ranging from Harvard on the East Coast to Occidental on the West. He has served as President of the American Association for Applied Psychologists, the American Psychological Association, the American Academy of Psychotherapists, and other professional groups.

Gilbert A. Schloss, Ph.D.

Dr. Schloss conducts workshops in writing and poetry therapy at the Institute for Sociotherapy, New York City. He is Executive Director, Association for Poetry Therapy and Assistant Editor of *Literature and Psychology*. He is on the faculty of Mills College of Education, New York City. Dr. Schloss received his Ph.D. in English at the University of Wisconsin. Currently, he is completing a D.S.Sc. in Psychology at the New School for Social Research, New York City.

Ellen Siroka, M.A.

Mrs. Siroka is Co-Director of the Institute for Sociotherapy, New York City and a Director of Psychodrama at the Moreno Institute, New York City. Mrs. Siroka is a Diplomate in Group Psychotherapy and Psychodrama of the Moreno Academy. She has conducted many workshops in group methods for individual professionals, community organizations and agencies. Mrs. Siroka was formerly on the faculty of Iona College, New Rochelle, New York.

Robert W. Siroka, Ph.D.

Dr. Siroka is Co-Director of the Institute for Sociotherapy, New York City, and Director of Training and Evaluation for the Easter Seal Society for Crippled Children and Adults of New Jersey. Dr. Siroka, a Diplomate in Group Psychotherapy and Psychodrama of the Moreno Academy, is on the staff of the Moreno Institute, New York City, where he conducts demonstrations of psychodrama. Dr. Siroka was formerly Associate Professor of Special Education, Jersey City State College and Visiting Associate Professor of Education at New York University.

Allen R. Solem, Ph.D.

Dr. Solem is a Professor in the Department of Management, School of Business Administration at the University of Minnesota. He directed the behavioral sciences program in the College of Business Administration, University of Rochester, and undergraduate and graduate training in the industrial psychology program, University of Maryland. He was formerly Visiting Associate Professor of Psychology, University of Michigan. He is co-author, with Norman and Ayesha Maier, of *Supervisory and*

Executive Development (New York, 1958). Dr. Solem serves as a consultant for industrial firms and government agencies.

Eugene Walder, Ph.D.

Dr. Walder is in private practice in New York City and Westport, Connecticut. He holds a certificate of specialization in psychotherapy and psychoanalysis from the New York City Program for Post-doctoral Study and Research in Psychology. He was a principal investigator for a New York State Department of Mental Hygiene grant: "The Effectiveness of a Group Screening Procedure in a Voluntary Outpatient Clinic for the Treatment of Adult Offenders." He has taught at Columbia University Teachers College, the City University of New York, and has been a staff psychologist at Hofstra College and a psychologist in the Roslyn, N.Y. public schools.